HARD LANDINGS

HARD LANDINGS

CHASING A DREAM IN CANADA'S CHANGING
ARCTIC

BONNIE MCGHIE

Self-published by the author in Chilliwack, British Columbia

HardLandings.ca; bonnie@hardlandings.ca

Layout and design: Crystal Hunt, TechnoMagical Creatives LLP

Cover photo: The author with her husband, George Clarke, and Arctic Wings' first Cessna 180. All photos are from the author's personal collection unless otherwise credited.

Map rendering (page xii) and apartment diagram (page 46) by Jeffrey Pernitsky.

Project management: Lin Perceval

Editing: Naomi Pauls, Paper Trail Publishing

The quote from Prime Minister Diefenbaker in chapter 2 comes from "John Diefenbaker, a New National Policy, 1957," Great Canadian Speeches, para. 3, https://greatcanadianspeeches.ca/2020/08/16/john-diefenbaker-a-new-national-policy-1957/.

Publisher's Cataloguing-in-Publication data
Title: Hard landings : chasing a dream in Canada's changing Arctic / Bonnie McGhie.
Names: McGhie, Bonnie, author.
Identifiers: ISBN 978-1-7387950-0-0 (paperback) | ISBN 978-1-7387950-1-7 (e-book)
Subjects: McGhie, Bonnie. | LCSH Bush flying—Canada, Northern—History. | Women in aeronautics—Canada—History. | Bush pilots—Arctic regions. | Air pilots—Canada, Northern. | Air pilots—Arctic regions. | Bush pilots—Canada.
Classification: LCC TL523 M34 2023 | DDC 629.13092—dc23

Please note this is a work of non-fiction. No names have been changed, no characters invented, no events fabricated. However, human memories are complicated. This book portrays the truth as the author remembers it.

To my children, David, Lesley, and Duncan,
who were my precious companions for this Arctic journey

To my husband and friend, Gordon McGhie, who shared with me
the important task of guiding my children to adulthood, and who
always encouraged me to pursue opportunities and adventures with
meaning for me

And to Lin Perceval, whose belief in me and the value of my story
made this book possible

CONTENTS

AUTHOR'S NOTE

CAPTURING MY MEMORIES of living in the Arctic in the early 1960s—more than sixty years ago—can sometimes challenge my recollections. However, more importantly, that passage of time is underscored by the major changes that have taken place. I cannot ignore these changes, so I owe my readers some background.

Most notably, the 1950s and '60s brought increased political and government interest in the North. Government and religious leaders increasingly focused on trying to change northern people's societies, culture, and language to align with those of the South. Today the people of the North assert their cultural identity and sovereignty, yet as I think of the past and the people I knew, it is important to be aware of the reality of that time if we are to value and recognize the way things are now. The western Arctic of the 1960s would become a big part of my life, and there was no way to ignore how fraught with colonialism and racist policy-making the government was. At some level, my story needs to reflect that reality and avoid sanitizing history, yet the colonial language and labelling of the past I knew then is likely to be offensive today, particularly to those who are part of this story.

In years past, the federal government waffled between treating all Indigenous people alike and then differently. During one period Inuit were not seen as Canadian citizens while First Nations people were. Then they were lumped together and both seen as "Indians" under the *Indian Act*. Later they were separated again within the act, and then Inuit were removed once again. Inuit were given the right to vote in 1950, but First Nations people were not allowed to vote until 1960. Mostly, the government resisted assuming responsibility for the care and control of Inuit, encouraging them to live off the land in traditional ways and otherwise ignoring them. However, starting in the early 1950s, the federal government began to assume more responsibility for the education and health care of Inuit. It wanted these traditionally nomadic people to live in settlements where government could more easily keep track of them, improve their health, and ensure their children were being educated. When Arctic Wings first began its flying services, and for a while longer, the cultural, social, and personal value systems of most northern people, along with aspects of their traditional ways, remained, particularly in Tuktoyaktuk. Changes had begun, but the early '60s was a time when Indigenous people still experienced a sense of autonomy.

When I lived in the North, Indigenous people in their conversations with me freely spoke of themselves as Indian, Eskimo, or Métis, while referring to me as white. I have no recollection of people exhibiting any discomfort with these terms then—terms which had been in use for hundreds of years. They were a generally accepted part of how we communicated with each other. These labels would start to change in the 1970s, and of course change has progressed significantly since then, with the growth of self-determination and the North's people claiming the right to name themselves. The term "Eskimo" was replaced by Inuit or Inuvialuit (in the western Arctic), meaning "real people"; the northern Dene became known as Gwich'in. In the 1960s, I never heard the now common labels "First Nations" or "Indigenous People."

In this book, "Inuit" refers to the people living in the High Arctic and earlier labelled Eskimo. I acknowledge that their lifestyles, culture, housing, and dress differed in many ways, reflecting distances along with varying land and resources. "First Nations" refers to a number of different tribes or nations, but primarily the Dene. This term also includes the southern Cree, some of whom had moved north along the Mackenzie River. I also use the term "Gwich'in," referring specifically to the northern Dene. My use of "northern people" or "local people" does not imply any similarity between different cultural identities, but rather refers globally to the original people of the North.

Besides the names of northern people, place names in the North have also changed over the past sixty years. I will use the place names in the Mackenzie Delta that I was familiar with in the '60s. Some changes to the place names coincided with the division of the Northwest Territories into two territories in 1999, and other names continue to change.

Another major difference between my time in the North and our world today was the use of imperial versus metric measurements. Again, in keeping with the times I'm writing about, I use feet, pounds, and gallons as measures. To help those unfamiliar with these old-fashioned dimensions, I've included metric conversions.

It's astounding to think of the radical changes that came to the western Canadian Arctic over the past hundred years. Life in the western Arctic of today seems totally unrecognizable compared to what my life was like there in the 1960s, and I realize that knowledge of my experiences, as a white woman living in this time, in this place, and with these special people, might be lost if I didn't share my story. So my narrative starts with our plans to make the dream of our northern business a reality.

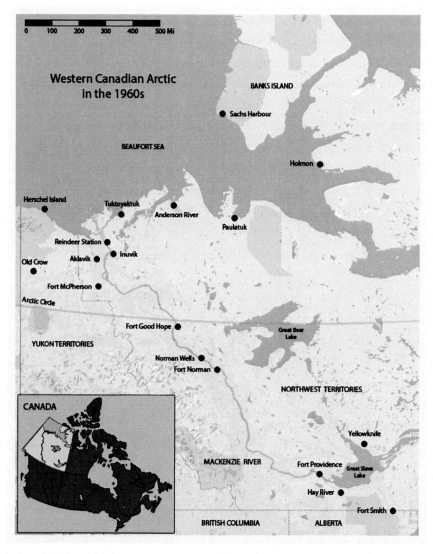

Arctic Wings, based out of Inuvik and Aklavik, accepted charters in much of the immense Mackenzie Delta.

1

ARCTIC WINGS

The day my young son David and I first landed in Inuvik, Northwest Territories, in early June 1960, undeniably qualified as a milestone event. We were joining George, my ambitious pilot husband, catching up with the dream we shared for a northern charter air service, Arctic Wings, and at the same time embarking on the next phase of our married life. The day was made even more memorable because one of our company's two essential planes had caught fire that same morning, putting it permanently on the scrap heap. Later I would wonder at the coincidence. Should I have interpreted this disaster, the loss of our single-engine Fairchild 24, as a warning sign of the challenges that lay ahead for our business, our lives in the North, and even, indeed, for our marriage?

At the airport, there was very little to see beyond a long runway, a small terminal, and a few other buildings, all surrounded by short trees and bush. A narrow gravel road led into Inuvik. My first observation was surprise at how straight the gravel roads were and how the side roads all appeared to meet our road at ninety-degree angles as we entered Inuvik. It seemed as if a symmetrical grid of roads had been laid on the landscape without any concern for natural anomalies like streams or ground variations.

Taken from an approaching plane in 1960, this photo shows Inuvik as a small, isolated island in a huge sea of wilderness. © *NWT Archives / Emily Stillwell / N-2005-006-0154-0*

The houses and buildings I first saw marched along in straight lines too, made more eye-catching because they were painted a variety of bright colours. The huge federal school, built to accommodate 800 students, appeared even more dominating because it was flanked by a large Catholic residential hostel on one side and an Anglican residential hostel on the other, all creating the impression that education was a major reason for Inuvik's existence.

This new northern townsite, two degrees above the Arctic Circle, was bordered to the west by the East Channel of the mighty Mackenzie River. Trees, brush, and small lakes created borders for the town's other three sides. Inuvik appeared to be an isolated little world unto itself. There were clusters of government facilities and buildings but no apparent business area; there were also areas with roads but no buildings. The brighter, bigger buildings tailed off to scrubby trees and, among the trees, less uniform-looking houses, although the roads still appeared unnaturally straight.

An aerial view of Inuvik illustrates the priority placed on education, with the 800-student federal Sir Alexander Mackenzie School in the centre, flanked by the 250-student residence Grollier Hall (Catholic) on the left and Stringer Hall (Anglican) on the right. © *NWT Archives / NWT Department of Information / G-1979-023:1664*

As we bounced along the gravel road in our company's truck, I suddenly fell quiet, thinking of what our past five years' efforts had created and what it meant to me to finally be in Inuvik. To be here and to now be part of Arctic Wings' future was an emotional tug that left me fighting tears. My pride in what we had accomplished making this business a reality couldn't be diminished by the news of the loss of our first plane. There surely would be difficulties, but the plane was insured and could be replaced.

A little background on our new company and its operations may help explain my sense of awe and near tears. Arctic Wings had started its flying service a year earlier, in 1959, when we had earned enough money to buy the company's first airplane. This was the Fairchild 24 single-engine plane, which provided Al, George's step-father, with the means of launching our charter services from Aklavik, about 30 miles (50 kilometres) southwest of Inuvik. After the Fairchild came to a fiery end the same day David and I arrived in Inuvik, it would soon be replaced by another single-engine plane, a Howard DGA-15. George flew the company's Cessna 180 from our Inuvik location while Al would fly from Aklavik with the Howard. Later we would add another Cessna 180, following another accident and the loss of the Howard. The final aircraft for Arctic Wings would be a Cessna 185, replacing the older Cessna 180s. Our earlier dream of Arctic Wings operating a rotary-wing aircraft would never happen. It was a dream too early to be needed or even to be prof-itable. Arctic Wings would continue to operate its bush flying services with fixed-wing aircraft until the company was sold in 1967 to a subsidiary of Pacific Western Airlines (PWA). Arctic Wings oper-ated for less than ten years, but during that time so much happened to the company, to us, and in the western Arctic.

We accepted charters in much of the immense Mackenzie Delta, west to Old Crow and Herschel Island in Yukon Territory, more than 170 miles (275 kilometres) distant, as well as north over the Beaufort Sea to Sachs Harbour and east to Paulatuk. Our regular, bread-and-butter trips were those between the nearer settlements of Inuvik, Aklavik, Reindeer Station, Fort McPherson, Arctic Red River, Fort Good Hope, and north to Tuktoyaktuk. As an aside, people who lived in Tuktoyaktuk usually referred to it simply as "Tuk."

Our passengers used our services for a variety of reasons. These included counting caribou and polar bears and supplying prospec-tors, miners, and oil exploration camps as well as Canadian Wildlife Service and other research camps. Charters served government administration, medical and legal purposes, emergency flights, church people, film crews, and the occasional tourists and fishermen. However, the majority of our flights were to transport local people to and from settlements, or to their fishing, hunting, seal hunting, and trapping camps as well as to resupply camps and take out furs, meat, and fish. Flights crossed back and forth over the tree-line and the Arctic Circle. They passed through mountains, over tundra plains or the Barren Lands, over pingos (ice-cored hills) in the Tuk area, over both the frozen and open Beaufort Sea, along sinuous rivers and over lake after lake, all breathtaking in the beauty distinctive to this part of the Arctic. During my time in the North, the only way to appreciate the vast scope of the western Arctic was by air in a small plane, like a Cessna 180, flying at an altitude of about five hundred feet (150 metres), in an environment that could not be experienced or even found anywhere else.

The mighty Mackenzie—Deh Cho, "Big River," to the Gwich'in —was central to navigation for all bush pilots. Flying in the vast Mackenzie Delta and the High Arctic in the 1960s was a major navigational challenge, lacking much in the way of help from radar beacons or other electronic navigational aids used in southern Canada. Interpreting map references was no easy task, in a place where tundra, lakes, mountains, scrubby trees, and bush displayed little notable variations during the summer and became a whole world of white in the winter. A common saying back then was "There are old bush pilots and there are bold bush pilots, but there aren't any old, bold bush pilots." Any flying mistakes were costly and seldom resulted in second chances.

Navigated by Alexander Mackenzie in 1789, the less than straight, indeed very winding Mackenzie River system wandered all over the delta landscape for about 2,635 miles (4,420 kilometres) from its headwaters near Fort Providence to the Beaufort Sea. It twisted and turned so much that it caused boat and barge trips to be many times longer than the direct flying distance between the same two points. The Mackenzie, with all its tributaries, is the thirteenth-longest river in world, and the watershed area of the

Mackenzie makes up 20 percent of all Canadian territory. To the people of the western Arctic, it was the central focus of life and transportation. To bush pilots, it was the greatest single and most consistent visual navigational aid. Whenever possible, keeping the river in sight or on the horizon was comforting and made flying in a land with few distinguishable aids, markers, or electronic navigational supports so much safer.

Local maintenance services for our aircraft were somewhat limited in Inuvik, so when engine overhauls or more sophisticated inspections and maintenance were required, we had no choice but to fly the planes to Edmonton. The Department of Transport required an inspection of the airframe and engine at regulated intervals, carried out by a licensed maintenance shop. We usually flew to Edmonton a couple of times a year and roughly followed the Mackenzie River to Fort Providence or Hay River, then turned southwest into Alberta. Sometimes we chose to make stops or side trips, depending on the purpose of the journey.

Where we could fly was dependent on the availability and location of aviation gas—gas that usually needed to be hand pumped into the planes from stockpiles of forty-five-gallon drums left at various strategic locations. We recorded our use of gas taken from Esso stockpiles and then paid the Esso oil distributor. Alternatively, we used stockpiles we had created ourselves when we had extra space on flights, or from barge deliveries in the summer. When lakes, rivers, and the Beaufort Sea were not frozen over, our planes were fitted with floats or pontoons for water landings, while in the winter, we landed on ice or snow using skis. Rushing through these details doesn't begin to tell the full story of how much creativity and tenacity were needed to operate a flying service in the Arctic. Nor do these logistics capture the immense courage and skills essential to being a successful bush pilot.

George was continually tested by the weather and by having to find remote locations, land on uncertain surfaces, keep equipment running (particularly in extreme conditions), and generally cope with the unpredictable. Environmental hazards included winds off the Beaufort Sea, shifting pack ice, and freezing rain that coated plane wings, weighing them down to reduce lift and affect airplane handling. Bush pilots also contended with snow whiteouts that obscured everything, and the extreme cold that stopped the ability of the plane or the pilot to fly. As mentioned, knowing where you were or where you were going always required skill and care. One example of an uncertain surface was Aklavik's muddy and rutted landing strip at spring breakup. George needed to keep power up when landing as the mud grabbed hold of the wheels and could potentially stop the plane so quickly that the nose would dip or send the plane looping off the strip. In the bitter cold, metal plane parts, oil, and gasoline didn't always act as expected. Along with all the more usual issues, the unpredictability of flying in the North required constant vigilance in situations such as landing or taking off in a massive bird nesting area. And if a pilot landed on a mud strip and then failed to check the pitot tube, which measured fluid flow velocity, for mud before taking off, they could discover they had no or faulty airspeed readings.

THE FIRE ABOARD THE FAIRCHILD HAD OCCURRED AS GEORGE'S stepfather, Al, was taxiing to take off. A backfire spark had caused the plane's canvas cover to burst into flames. Fortunately, Al and his passengers were able to jump out and avoid any injury. However, this disaster resulted in an urgent need to find another suitable aircraft. To solve this problem as quickly as possible, Al booked a seat for himself to Edmonton, leaving on the same Pacific Western Airlines plane I had arrived on. In Edmonton, Al very quickly identified a replacement: a Howard DGA-15 aircraft that was readily available and could be flown to Aklavik, to be put to work within a couple of weeks. This speedy turnaround was essential because long summer flying hours meant that Arctic Wings' two planes were already heavily booked. The Howard was another canvas-covered single-engine plane, but it was bigger and had a larger freight and passenger capacity than the Cessna 180, our remaining plane. A canvas-covered plane had the advantage of being lighter, creating a greater payload possibility than a similarly powered plane with a metal-covered frame. Its disadvantages were both the fire risk and possible tears to the canvas cover; both issues needed preventative care and careful attention.

Regardless of the shocking news and what it might mean for Arctic Wings, we were together and I was excited that, after five years' preparing and the delay my unexpected pregnancy had created, George and I were finally united again and could begin to live our dream together. However, my practical side showed through and after we had shared Arctic Wings news, one of my first questions dealt with a place for us to live. George explained he had temporarily sublet a government house for us, until the official residents arrived in Inuvik. Our temporary home—we would have it for just two months—was one of a cluster of identical row houses connected to the government's utilidor system. This system, a feature entirely foreign to this southerner, consisted of a square aluminum tunnel, about three feet by three feet, supported on pilings and about three feet (one metre) above-ground. This tunnel snaked around all the government housing and buildings, starting from a central power plant that delivered super-heated water for home heating, along with regular potable water. Its other feature was to return sewage and wastewater to the plant for disposal. This system served all official buildings, including government houses, offices, and warehouses, the station of the Royal Canadian Mounted Police (RCMP), the naval communication centre, the Catholic and Anglican residential hostels (Grollier Hall and Stringer Hall), the federal day school, and the hospital.

Starting in the 1960s, an essential feature of new Arctic construction was the utilidor, an aboveground insulated conduit used to deliver services such as heat and water, and to return sewage for disposal. The system primarily served government housing and facilities. © *NWT Archives / Ben Hall / N-2013-015-0190*

Government houses were mostly a series of attached units comparable to the usual small three-bedroom homes found in the South, except they were sitting on pilings to ensure the ground remained frozen under them. Although everything was built on dirt and gravel, around the government houses the area was new and clean. I soon learned that our new hangar and future apartment within it, currently under construction, was down at the river—too far away to be connected to the utilidor system. So I quickly grasped the harsh reality: running water, central heating, and flush toilets would be a luxury I would enjoy for only the few short months until the new residents came to claim their house.

Aside from government structures, most other buildings in the town were not connected to the utilidor, with the result that non-government houses, along with most independent businesses and buildings, lacked the convenience of either water or sewage services. Instead, for water, residents had to rely on melting ice in the winter, and on visiting centrally located water taps or getting water delivered in the summer. They used oil or wood stoves for heating and cooking and dealt with the never-ending labour of managing chemical toilets. Non-government people had to haul their non-government garbage to the dump themselves. In addition, residents of these homes and businesses had to remove all wastewater and sewage to dumping sites, although grey water (used washing and bathing water) was often spilled on the ground near the houses. This area of town was not maintained by the government and therefore did not look quite so clean and tidy. These very different ways of sourcing water and managing waste disposal clearly and visibly differentiated the status of the town's residents.

Once we left our government sublet and moved to a home with no access to the utilidor system, I would soon learn how water had to be carefully managed, protected, and used. All water used in these houses in winter came from ice hauled from nearby freshwater lakes and melted in large drums (45 gallons / 205 litres) inside the houses. In contrast, during the summer, water was hauled by bucket into the house or delivered by a privately operated water truck and pumped into the house's storage drums. For a few homes or businesses, water was pumped into large oil storage tanks set up and used exclusively for water storage and only during the summer. Without running water, I spent large amounts of time and energy to make sure it was available, never wasting a drop and disposing of it appropriately. Even in this land of countless water sources, potable water was a precious resource.

2

SIGNING UP FOR THE DREAM

The Arctic dream which captured my young imagination and sense of adventure held great promise. Its most notable feature was that it didn't come with a prescription for how I should live or what my role should be. Instead, it promised freedom from the usual and the predictable. As I began my life in the North, the certainty of youth had encouraged me to believe I could mould my world to fit my beliefs, expectations, and wishes. But my sense of certainty and my self-confidence were to be challenged and irrevocably altered during the short five years my family and I lived in the western Canadian Arctic. My beliefs and youthful arrogance would be changed by the land, its people, and the realities of living in that place and at that time. As I view the North today, I realize that regardless of my early sense of my own importance, I left not even a faint footprint in the places I travelled through during those five years, but their influence on me was priceless.

As I was growing up in Southern California during and after the Second World War, I had struggled with people's view of what I should do and who I should be. I knew with certainty that I wanted to learn, to explore, to follow adventures wherever they might take me. All the while I was being reminded that since I was a girl, all I needed to focus on was finding "Prince Charming," marrying him, and being entirely fulfilled by tending to him and the children we would have together. I was frustrated that my life should be so narrowly defined and with such limited expectations. As well, I had been warned about being a tomboy and appearing intelligent, in case I scared my "prince" away. Surprisingly, when I spoke of wanting to go to university, I found that idea was supported—not as a place to build a career but as a good place to find that up-and-coming "prince." Everywhere I turned, even at university, as I spoke of seeking a career, I received a figurative "pat on the head" and was told a career would be only a temporary concern until I married.

When I had taken all the courses I could in the college system and prepared to enter my third year at a university, I needed to work full time to earn the money to complete my last two years. In play, as a child, I had learned some of the skills of film editing when my best friend and I accompanied his film editor father to Warner Bros. Studios. There we gathered discarded film bits from the cutting room floor and spliced them together to make our own stories. Based on the skills I had learned (despite being female), in 1954, I had an opportunity to travel to Juneau, Alaska, on a contract to establish a film library for the Alaska Department of Health. I left classes temporarily to pursue what I hoped would be an exciting adventure. At the same time, I would earn money to help me continue my studies.

An adventure the trip certainly was: the result was finding a dream that had not even been in my mind as I headed to Alaska. In Juneau, I met an exceptionally bright and ambitious—oh yes, and handsome—young Canadian "planning to be a bush pilot," George Clarke, who was living temporarily in Whitehorse, Yukon Territory, with his mother and stepfather.

With George, my Prince Charming, in Juneau, Alaska, before we were married, and as we were sharing plans for our future in the North.

George's stepfather, Al Boles, was a bush pilot, and together, the two men told me of their evolving dream to start their own charter air service in the High Arctic: in Aklavik and the proposed new town of Inuvik in the western Northwest Territories.

George was of well beyond average intelligence, ambitious, and fully focused on his plans for the future. He seemed to believe I was capable of being an equally talented, intelligent, and worthy partner when he decided to share his dreams and plans, persuading me to embrace them and share life with him. I finally felt I had some direction and purpose and I had found my "prince." His exceptional drive and his willingness to take on challenging ideas with enthusiasm and creativity attracted me, even though we had quite different backgrounds. I came to this partnership seeking to be an equal contributor and to have opportunities to use my skills, as well as what I had learned from a difficult childhood. Initially, I was drawn by George's focus and ambitions; only later did I come to understand that he was a complex character whose above-average talents became more of a liability than I first expected.

My younger years lacked much in family security. When my father died, I was three and my brother was six. We faced family disintegration, with the result that we became wards of the state and lived in a residential home/school for more than seven years, until I was nearly eleven years old. I was too young and too powerless to change my circumstances, so I could only dream of a future when things would be kinder and gentler. Returning home after these years brought different problems and disappointments, but also freedom from much supervision or many restrictions, enabling me to explore new relationships, new ideas, and new experiences. I learned that some dreams were within my control, when those dreams were fuelled by commitment and hard work.

In particular, I came to understand that freedom was most easily bought when I had my own money. So I worked. In a rural area in Glendale, California, living at my grandparents' home, neighbours needed help with their horses: I fed and exercised them as well as cleaned stalls and tack. I helped with gardening, cleaned swimming pools, and signed up for every available job. Once I was older and had a driver's licence, I was employed part time as a second driver in a camera car/truck on movie locations. This led to a job with the movie actor Wild Bill Elliott, riding his cutting horses and doing public performances with him to advertise his movies. Bill paid me, while the studio also paid for the PR work. All these efforts gave me what I needed—the ability to pay my own way was a path to making my own choices. I paid my school fees and bought my own cars. At university I was a general studies student, with a keen focus on understanding why people did what they did. My psychology and sociology courses helped answer some of my never-ending questions about people and how I was going find my way in a world where there seemed little acceptance of a girl with different dreams. While this sounds like a very difficult start in life, and it was, it also offered valuable opportunities to learn independent thinking, problem-solving, and steely self-reliance—characteristics that would serve me well as I committed to our Arctic adventure.

George had trained as a pilot in the Air Force Reserve while he attended the University of British Columbia, and he was now waiting for his transfer to the Canadian Navy. There he was committed to full-time service, focusing on rotary-wing or helicopter training and building the flying hours needed to qualify for commercial insurance endorsements essential for a professional pilot. During his time in the navy, George was recognized for his exceptional flying talent and instincts, easily achieving success in everything he did. The navy wanted him to build a career with the service, but his plans hadn't changed, and he was certain the navy would not feature in his chosen future.

This story visits our shared dream, a dream that started with five years of planning and preparing in our navy time, and then encompassed another five years of creating our unique reality in the Arctic.

After we married in Southern California, we travelled to Royal Canadian Naval Air Station Shearwater in Nova Scotia, where we planned that our navy time would be an opportunity for both of us to work and save money so we could buy aircraft for our proposed charter air service, Arctic Wings. While living in Nova Scotia, I worked a series of jobs, including maintaining and distributing film for the National Film Board and teaching physical education and swimming at the navy base's K–12 school. My work life was interrupted briefly for the birth of our son, David.

During our time in Nova Scotia, I was eager to read everything I could about the history of the western Arctic, noting the past changes that would influence its future directions. I was excited to know about this place we were going to call home and what it might be like to be a part of life there. I learned that for most of Canadian history, the Arctic had been ignored and was left untouched other than during periodic exploration epics like the searches for a Northwest Passage, searches in the Richardson Mountains for the motherlode of the Klondike gold, and the long and ongoing history of the fur trade. Changes to northern life in the western Canadian Arctic were to be more rapid than in the eastern Arctic for various reasons, and especially due to the transportation potential of the mighty Mackenzie River. In contrast, the lack of natural south-to-north waterways in the east would remain a critical factor in its much slower development long into the future.

The Yukon gold rush beginning in the 1880s was supported by travel on the Klondike and Yukon rivers, as well as the construction of a narrow-gauge railway from the Pacific Ocean port at Skagway, Alaska, to Whitehorse in the Yukon. Access was created for people and supplies, opening this part of the North to southerners and supporting its development. The Mackenzie River began close to the Alberta border and was joined by subsidiary rivers on its journey north to the Arctic Ocean. The wide-ranging water access in the Mackenzie Delta was a contributor to exploration, trade, the religious ministries, government intervention, and business development. Additional developmental differences between the western and eastern Arctic would be recognized in 1999 when the Northwest Territories was divided into two separate territories, with the West retaining the name of Northwest Territories and the East named Nunavut.

Development in the Mackenzie Delta was accelerated by the establishment of the Northern Transportation Company in the mid-1930s, with regular barge and boat transport of equipment and supplies along the Mackenzie River as far north as the Beaufort Sea/Arctic Ocean and then on east to the settlement of Tuktoyaktuk. The river was the only method of shipping supplies to the far northern regions, which lacked rail or road access and had very limited places for larger airplanes to land.

Another driver of change was the decision during World War II to extract oil from the massive deposits found at Norman Wells. A small refinery was built, and an attempt was made to develop a delivery system with a pipeline and a winter road to Whitehorse called the Canol Project. Problems with the development and maintenance of the pipeline, limitations of the winter road, and the costs for both caused the project to be quietly abandoned before the war ended. Important to the future of the North, limited oil would continue to be refined at Norman Wells, for local use and for distribution by barge along the Mackenzie River. The production of gas and heating oil within the North was a major facilitator for future development.

Prime Minister Diefenbaker proposed "Roads to Resources" and "New Directions for the North" in the 1950s. Famously he said, during a 1957 speech, "The North, with all its vast resources of hidden wealth, the wonder and the challenge of the North must become our national consciousness." His plans involved building all-weather roads, pipelines, and other means to explore and extract the North's untapped resources, including oil, and he had other plans that would truly impact the lives of the North's people. His minority government was defeated in February 1963, and the "Roads" part of proposed changes quietly ended, although the other plans, like required education, would continue. Roads would not become a focus for the government again for another twenty years.

More forerunners of the rapid change to come by the second half of the century and beyond were the Canadian government's 1950 declaration that all Canadian children must become literate. As a result, in 1955, the government took over responsibility for educating the North's children from religious organizations, although for practical reasons, these religious groups continued to operate hostels where schoolchildren resided. In 1950, only four residential schools and nine elementary day schools served the entire eastern and western Northwest Territories. The government mandated that all school-age children living outside the nine settlements with elementary schools were to be sent to live in residential hostels and attend school there. The RCMP was assigned the task of enforcing this requirement.

In 1954, because of the United States' concern over Russia and the Cold War, a system of radar stations called the Distant Early Warning Line (DEW Line) was proposed and funded by the U.S. government to be built in the Canadian Arctic. At the time, Canada had its own sovereignty concerns over its claims on islands and waterways in the Arctic region, so the DEW Line was considered a win for both countries. In 1955, construction began, and the line became fully operational in 1961. This construction introduced many Inuit to the temporary opportunity to be wage earners, but without any prospect for ongoing jobs.

To support the mandated creation of the "New North," an entirely new town, Inuvik, was built between 1957 and 1960. Partly it came to be because the regional centre of Aklavik was prone to erosion and flooding. When complete, Inuvik featured an airport capable of handling all commercial and military aircraft, a modern hospital, as well as better access for boats and barges on the deeper part of the Mackenzie River. As mentioned before, the residential hostels and large federal school were built to house and educate children of the western Arctic. Once again, northerners had a chance to learn new skills and to be wage earners during Inuvik's construction, but again without future employment opportunities.

The construction of Inuvik, with its new airport, provided more extensive year-round access to this remote area. The building of the huge educational and student residential facilities combined with the mandated federal policy that all children must attend school created yet another major shift in northern lifestyles. I wanted to understand what all this would mean to the North's future and to life there. As I read and learned more, I also tried to picture how these significant developments would affect Arctic Wings, our lives, and David's education.

3

HOMELESS IN A WORLD OF COLD

At the start of 1960, with our navy life completed, George, David, and I left Nova Scotia to begin our lives in the Northwest Territories. Arriving in Vancouver, British Columbia, prior to travelling north, I became aware of an unplanned second pregnancy and the development of related kidney problems that would delay David's and my trip north for a few months. David and I flew to California to stay with friends until my health improved. Meanwhile, George flew to Edmonton, where he bought a Cessna 180—a fixed-wing aircraft, not the planned helicopter—and then flew it north to begin his introduction to "bush flying."

The Cessna 180 looked like a small, sleek plane, but it was a true workhorse in the North, with a payload of 1,000 to 1,200 pounds (450 kilograms). For each flight, the combined weight of the pilot, any passengers, freight, and fuel was carefully calculated to ensure a safe load. For anyone wanting a reliable and useful plane for bush flying, the Cessna 180 was a popular option at a reasonable cost.

With George and our Cessna 180, a truly reliable workhorse in the Arctic. Our other planes included over time a second 180, a single-engine Fairchild 24, a Howard DGA-15, and finally a Cessna 185.

My health and the issues with my pregnancy improved so David and I could finally head north to join George. California was shrouded in darkness as a very excited three-year-old David and I set out for the western Arctic at the beginning of June. Our journey, starting in Los Angeles, required us to change planes in both Seattle and Edmonton, while the last leg involved landings in Fort Smith, Yellowknife, and Norman Wells, before we finally reached Inuvik. On the map, Inuvik looked very far north, and that seemed to be confirmed by the eight or more hours' travel time from Edmonton. When we gained altitude after our takeoff from Edmonton in the Douglas DC-4 prop plane on this last leg of our trip, hour after hour went by with nothing to see but huge expanses of treed lands, lakes, and rivers. There were no roads, railway tracks, or signs of people, except as we approached the few towns where we landed to drop off people and freight. Commercial considerations extended the distance we flew by about 350 miles (560 km), which considerably extended the time required for the flight. A non-stop trip from Edmonton to Inuvik would involve 1,225 miles (1,971 km), but our stops at Fort Smith, Yellowknife, and Normal Wells to deal with passengers and freight turned our journey into almost 1,600 miles (2,575 km).

Our trip was unexpectedly a social event as, at each stop between Edmonton and Inuvik, when the doors were left open, thousands of mosquitoes invaded the plane. Each time the door closed, and we were airborne, people got out of their seats and teamed up for the job of killing mosquitoes. Much laughter and conversation ensued as people shared this task for the common good. As we flew on, it was night by my watch and would be dark in Los Angeles, yet the sun was still high in the sky as we approached our final landing in Inuvik. We seemed to have flown under the arc of the sun, making it bright and warm as we descended the stairs from the plane. The length of the day, or hours of daylight, would peak later in June, approaching the summer solstice, when the sun never set. After June, sunlight hours would begin to grow ever shorter, as the summer and fall passed into winter, when the sun wouldn't rise at all. Natural light then would be a couple of hours of twilight in each twenty-four-hour period. After the December winter solstice, the process would reverse, and daylight hours would begin to steadily increase once again.

George met us when we landed and loaded us into a very old, tired-looking company pickup truck for the trip into town. He was keen to share stories of his amazing flying experiences, but first he told me about the loss of the plane that morning. He again told me that his decision to buy the Cessna rather than a helicopter was the right one and that operating a fixed-wing aircraft was much more economical. The decision became even more important now with the loss of the other plane and the scheduled work needing to be done. Despite his unused rotary-wing training, we both agreed that the time we had spent in Nova Scotia was time well spent. George had logged enough flying hours for him to get the necessary insurance, and we had earned the money needed to buy our first aircraft. He went on to say there was lots of work for Arctic Wings, we were doing well financially, and the future looked promising.

Prior to my arrival, work on the hangar building, including the apartment for us at the back, had been progressing very slowly. Because almost twenty-four-hour daylight allowed for long flying hours every day for both pilots, George had little time left over to supervise construction. Priority went to flying as many hours as possible when our services were in such high demand. Arctic Wings needed to get so much done before freeze-up. At that point, flying would mostly end, except to settlements with landing strips, until the ice had thickened enough so planes could land with skis on frozen lakes and rivers. Plus, daylight flying hours after freeze-up would be severely limited by winter's growing darkness and visual flight rules that defined the amount of daylight needed to fly.

With the loss of the Fairchild, George alone was left to manage Arctic Wings' heavy workload, with only one plane available to do the work of two. As we waited for Al to return with the second plane, construction on the hangar came to a complete halt. It soon became apparent that the apartment was not going to be ready for us to move into before the residents of our sublet house arrived to claim their home. I was stunned to realize that the most dramatic fallout from the accident was that very soon the three of us would be homeless. The seriousness of our situation was made clear when I saw the number of local people living in tents, as they waited for more permanent homes to be built.

Hurriedly, George began the search for an alternative place for us to live until the hangar apartment would be ready. Just as we were wondering whether a tent was our only choice, George learned of a small empty Quonset hut that had served as a cookhouse for one of the private construction companies during Inuvik's major construction period. He was given permission to use the hut for as long as we needed it. A year earlier, when the work had finished and the crews returned south, the hut had been abandoned and its doors locked. Before that, all of the construction company's spare supplies, equipment, and bedding had been gathered up and dumped in this one building, leaving a huge dirty mess. The hut had been slated for future demolition, although that was not a high priority. Its construction was the standard for its original use—corrugated metal —definitely not designed for use as a house or for residents' comfort in the North's hostile winter climate, but it would be a roof over our heads.

George took me to see what was to be our next home, this former cookhouse, the Quonset hut. As I stepped into the dark windowless building, I was shocked into silence. My immediate awareness was of a pervading sense of cold, dampness, and a strange unidentifiable smell. Turning on the lights revealed plates on counters and tables, all covered with what I assumed had once been food. Now they all had intriguing unidentifiable growth. When I looked into the cooking pots left on the cold oil stove, I could not identify their contents. Dirty dishes lay scattered everywhere, and grimy whiteish grease covered most surfaces. Opening the two unplugged fridges produced yet another shock. Both contained various types of leftover food in different stages of growing something. A honey bucket had been left full in the toilet closet, and the bucket's contents had turned mostly to a dark thick sludge. The hut floor consisted of dirt with wooden planks on top. I could not think what to say as I looked around, except to tell David not to touch anything. George's only comment was that nothing else was available in town and I would have to find a way to make the space work until the hangar apartment was finished.

I knew George was too busy flying to have much time to help, so I *would* have to find a way, on my own, to make this hut habitable. I needed a plan, but more importantly, I needed to believe I could conquer such an overwhelming task. This would surely take all the confidence and good humour I could muster. As I stood there, dumbstruck, looking at the challenge confronting me, I considered where and how to start. The old saying of "taking a single step at a time" came to mind, creating some faith that I could find a way to transform this dark, dank, and dirty place into a home.

The morning after my shock at seeing the Quonset hut, David and I, wearing our oldest washable clothes, walked there again to face the reality of what lay ahead for me. Fortunately, some tools, cleaning equipment, and supplies were among the piles that had been left in the building. My first task was to establish heat to begin to combat the cold and dampness, so I took the pots off the oil stove and worked up my courage to light it. I went outside to the oil tank and thumped on it to see if there was heating oil. Luckily there was, so I had no excuse not to try to light the stove. Oil stoves had never been part of my experience before. I stood David near the door, ready to run out if I did something wrong. I turned on the oil, took a paper, lit it, and suddenly I had a flame and could adjust the burner. As the stove heated, I was able to burn off much of the stuck-on stuff and surface grease, although because of the awful initial smell and smoke, I needed to leave the door open. This served as an invitation to hundreds of mosquitoes to join us in the hut.

I then started lifting a few planks from the floor in front of the stove, sweeping them off and the dirt floor underneath until it was down to the cleanest looking dirt. I turned the planks over, swept that side, and laid them back down. Now at least I could start working from a cleaner—if tiny—island amid the chaos. My next goal was to create a safe and clean area where David could play while I worked. Letting him run loose in such dirty and unsafe conditions simply wasn't an option. I pushed a couple of the cots together, and with a broom I beat the dust out of what seemed to be the cleanest mattresses. I then put the mattresses crosswise on top of the metal cot frames to make a play area.

Once David was settled, I started to plan what had to happen to get the hut ready in time to move from the house. It would be difficult to clean without running water, and by late summer, the overnight temperature would also become an issue. The two most immediate priorities were the need for a clean water supply and a clean chemical toilet. To order water from the private delivery truck serving non-utilidor homes required containers—clean containers —so I returned to our rented house and filled buckets of fresh water that I carried back so I could bleach out the hut's old water barrels. Luckily, rust was not an issue, but bending over to clean the barrels while being five months pregnant was. As I tried to avoid my baby bump and at the same time reach the bottom of the barrel, I started to laugh at my predicament. Once I could stop laughing, I figured out a solution. To avoid too much bending, I wound some rags around a broom. With the barrel scrubbing issue solved, I ordered water for my now clean barrels.

Then I needed to do something about the chemical toilet and the garbage that surrounded me. Enough time had passed since the hut had been used that, although there was an odd unidentifiable smell, it wasn't a bad smell. Yet I knew I needed help to get rid of the old chemical toilet, all the spoiled food, and the other trash. I could use the company truck to haul garbage to the dump, but I would not be able to lift and move awkward heavy things on my own.

Although we are very early in this Arctic story, a brief discussion of toilets and the significant effort required to manage them seems timely. Throughout our northern life we would deal with chemical toilets, colloquially referred to as "honey buckets," along with their liners, otherwise known as "honey bags." Since flush toilets featured so seldom in my northern homes, managing a toilet designed for the frozen North cost me significant time and labour—a huge amount of work that few "outsiders" could possibly understand, living in a world of simple flushing.

The long months of below-zero temperatures made using an outhouse in the High Arctic totally unworkable. The need to bundle up enough to cover your entire body to go outside each time and then baring one's bottom and sitting on the frozen seat, in the extreme cold, was one reason an outhouse was impractical. However, two much greater issues made this unworkable. First was the great difficulty of chipping away the permafrost to create a big enough hole in the ground to contain the waste. The second, and equally valid inhibiting factor, was the complete lack of drainage, even in the summer, since the permafrost never melted, nor would the waste contents thaw. The northern answer was to use a chemical toilet inside the house. The toilet unit was a galvanized metal frame with a standard toilet seat. Inside was a separate five-gallon (23 litre) catch bucket—the honey bucket—usually lined with a clear plastic bag—the honey bag. The deodorant chemical Mistovan was added to hide the smell or, more realistically, to replace the smell of the contents. Disposing of full honey bags was a time-consuming but essential and frequent chore.

Early August was already giving me a taste of what was to come, when days and nights would get much colder. Initially, due to safety concerns, I didn't feel I could leave the oil stove burning when we weren't there, so it took about an hour each morning to warm the place and heat water. However, my approach changed after the first few days, when each morning I was greeted by invasive cold and damp. After that I left the stove running on low at night, making it possible to have hot water and start to work as soon as I arrived. I borrowed the company truck and hired a local man to help me lift, load, and haul garbage to the dump. Pregnancy was limiting what I could do safely, so I needed to be careful. Now that I had help, we were able to move the old chemical toilet outside. Then I thoroughly cleaned the toilet room, bought a new toilet from Semmler's trading post, and we set it up. We loaded the truck and made endless trips to the dump, disposing of the old toilet, all the spoiled and opened containers of food, and everything that could not be repaired or cleaned. Once that was done, things began to look more positive.

Now that I had another set of hands, we used more cots to expand David's living space. We tied mattresses over cots and covered the whole area with newly washed blankets. Now David had about six by seven feet of covered mattress space, a clean area where he either played with his toys or slept, while I cleaned and organized what would be our new home. Once we moved into the hut, he would basically live and sleep in this padded area. Because blankets, pillows, bedding, and linens had been left in the hut, I took what I needed back to the house and washed load after load. We moved four more cots, side by side, closer to the stove and added crossed layers of mattresses where George and I would sleep. My hired man cleaned off the rest of the planks and scraped the dirt floor, while I started scrubbing the stove, counter, and fridges.

I created a section in the building to store all unneeded items that were too good to consign to the dump. This mountain of extra tables, chairs, cots, and mattresses as well as excess dishes and pots was then hidden under blankets—out of sight, out of mind. I was warned that nothing should touch the interior metal walls, to prevent anything freezing to the walls as the air grew colder. I sorted out what I wanted to use and took everything to the house to scrub, feeling blessed for my temporary, unlimited supply of hot running water.

After a few weeks of intense work, I got both the hut and the house well cleaned, all our clothes and bedding washed, and David and me bathed, just in time to vacate the government house and move into our far-from-beautiful living place. Reluctantly, on the last day, I closed the door on the house, with its wonderful heat, running water, and flush toilets, and returned to our new windowless, reasonably clean, but very ugly home. The rightful occupants of our temporary home, Vern and Dell Hawley, with their children, arrived in

Inuvik and moved into their house; then they came to visit us in our hut. When Dell saw where we had moved, she immediately realized how difficult it was going to be for me to keep it and us clean. She was insistent that I come to their place to bathe myself and David and wash clothes whenever I wanted. This was the beginning of a special friendship that would continue for most of my time in the North. Vern and Dell's children were generous younger teens who were warm and kind to David. If they were home when I visited Dell, David was welcome to spend time with them and enjoy being his usual curious, talkative, and active self. Vern was a research biologist who'd brought his family to the North when he accepted a Canadian Wildlife Service contract to study muskrats in the Mackenzie Delta.

My never-ending learnings since arriving in Inuvik extended to appreciating the wonders of the northern people's clothing. Parkas, mukluks, and duffel socks would be essential as the temperature fell, so important to keeping warm in a place where forty below was not unusual. George had bought a parka, mitts, and mukluks for himself when he had first arrived, so he arranged for me to meet with a Gwich'in woman, someone with great sewing talents, who would make beautiful and practical custom parkas, mitts, mukluks, and duffel socks for David and me. As we faced living in the Quonset hut and being outside, we would have the clothing needed for the increasing cold.

Our parkas had muskrat hides sewn together to fit like a coat, with the soft fur turned inside to trap our body heat. The skin side of the fur was covered with heavy cotton twill, with lots of brightly coloured decorative tape sewn around the wrists, around the bottom edge, and up each side of the front zipper on my parka. David's parka, like his father's, just slipped over his head, with no front opening zipper. Men and boys, who spent more time outside, stayed warmer when air couldn't get in through the zipper closure. My zipper was more a white person's convenience. I later learned the Inuit women's parkas called Mother Hubbards did not have zippers.

Wolverine fur trim sewn around the hood prevented frost from building up around our face from our breath when the hood was up. Our duffel inner boots were made from heavy blanket material and made a cushioned padding for the feet. The outside covers (mukluks) that fit over the duffels were made of canvas uppers decorated with yarn ties and embroidery and had caribou soles. Later we would buy dressy caribou mukluks that had wool tops with exquisite beading and embroidery. Mukluks and duffels were designed to let the foot move without restriction, thus trapping the heat produced. Our mitts were made from duffel material and had an attached braided yarn harness so they could easily come off but were hanging right there to immediately slip on again. This became our standard apparel throughout the winter, for the rest of our northern life. Our footwear changed to gumboots in the summer, when conditions were warmer, melting the first few inches of the permafrost and turning the ground muddy underfoot.

The talented woman who sewed our clothing was an unexpected but welcome source of new learning. She, along with her family, gave me a growing understanding of the northern Dene society and culture. This knowledge could not come from a book, as they shared with me how they had lived in the past and how they were feeling about the changes they were facing now. I was overtaken by sadness as I listened and thought of how I would feel about being so powerless to protect what was important to me and my family.

WHENEVER I NEEDED TO—AND SOMETIMES EVEN BEFORE I REALLY needed to—I would load David and my wash on a toboggan and set off for Dell's house. I popped a load in the washer, took a bath with David, and then sat, talked, and drank coffee with Dell in her warm, convenient, and clean home. Often we did baking so I could take some back for our family. Later I would load a clean David, along with the clean laundry and our baking, onto the toboggan and return to the hut. It was reassuring to have a trusted friend, and Dell was a person with broad interests, who read a lot and had lived a busy outdoor life in Montana before coming north. She gave me the sense I was not struggling on my own in this new world. George tended to shut down my conversations unless they were about him or Arctic Wings. He wasn't happy listening to anything he could loosely interpret as a complaint, even when I used humour and tried to laugh about it. At times, when he felt I might complain, he would refuse to listen, reminding me of my need to be a "good sport." So I truly appreciated having someone like Dell to talk to. With her, I could feel free to bitch about my struggles, and she joined me as I laughed at myself, at my mistakes, and at the many challenges I now faced.

George had been very busy up to the time of freeze-up and whenever he came home, it was to eat, wash, change his clothes, and sleep. I was aware I had to solve all our living issues by myself, because he was focused on the flying he needed to get done and later on trying to get the apartment at the hangar completed. I helped with the workload by monitoring and passing messages on the radio aircraft channel, doing accounting and bill paying, and booking flights, all from the Quonset hut. The hut was central to much of the non-utilidor part of town, so David and I soon began to meet people who came to the hut on Arctic Wings business or on our short walks in town, giving me more opportunity to learn about the place I now called home.

Establishing a home in the North without government support was truly a physical and emotional challenge when access to so much that was believed necessary to southern Canadians was not available to us. I was learning to plan ahead and to sort between true need and desire. I had to let go of expectations from my past life outside, seeking compromises and different ways of keeping a family cared for and making a home. When George had space for us on one of his flights to Aklavik, David and I made a quick trip with him to choose furniture for our apartment from the government's used-furniture sale there. The government houses in Aklavik had all been well furnished, yet none of the used furniture was to be transported to Inuvik for use in the new houses there. Hence a wide range of furniture and household equipment was for sale in the Aklavik warehouse. A crib was one of our needs, along with a table and chairs, beds, a dresser, sofa and chair, oil stove and fridge. The cost for everything we needed was small, and we were able to quickly get our purchases onto a barge and shipped to Inuvik. I was beginning to believe our family would have a home soon.

Another immediate concern was to sort through our things that had arrived by barge from Hay River. Before we came north, we had been advised of the need to ship many months of food supplies by barge during the summer because buying food from the trading posts in Inuvik would be very expensive over the winter. I really had no idea what I should buy, nor did I recognize the amount and variety of food we would want to eat in ten months, so I guessed. Our food and some of the personal items I didn't want to leave behind were put on pallets in Hay River, wrapped in tarps, and eventually loaded onto a barge for the trip down the Mackenzie. Now, before the weather grew colder, I needed to sort through everything, finding the supplies that should not freeze. George had arranged with Father Ruyant to store these items in the Catholics' heated warehouse until we moved into our apartment. Those things not harmed by freezing temperatures were to be stored in a locked shed in the partially completed part of the hangar. Sorting and repacking kept David and me busy for a number of days. In time it would become clear just how much I had been guessing in my estimates of what we would need until the barges came again the following summer.

As the days grew colder, our immediate task was to complete the apartment and have an alternative to living in the Quonset hut. As the hours of daylight became shorter, George had longer periods of time when he could supervise work at the hangar. Al also did more flying to help lighten George's load, so George's priority switched to completing the small apartment upstairs at the back of the building and then finishing the hangar itself sometime later. Moving into our new home could not come soon enough for me, as the Quonset hut was very cold during the increasing hours of darkness. The hut was getting harder to keep warm, beyond the immediate area near the stove, even during daylight hours. Thin layers of frost built up on the inside of the metal door and walls during the night. The frost tended to melt some during the day, at first, making flat surfaces and bedding feel damp. But as October approached, nothing melted any more, and then we were living in a house made mostly of frost, making me think of what it must be like to live in an igloo. David and I spent a lot of time close to the stove during the day, and we were early into our beds after dinner. I often snuggled into his bed and hugged his wonderfully warm little body to read to him or read to myself, after he fell asleep. However, cuddling a sleeping David was like holding on to a kicking heating pad, and I would retreat to begin to warm up our bed before George arrived.

Then the time came when it was no longer possible to keep the temperature of the Quonset hut above freezing during any time of day. It no longer felt damp; it was just very cold. Another issue, now urgent, was the impending arrival of my baby and the fact that the only hospital in the western Arctic was in Aklavik. As my late-November due date approached and the possibility of going into labour increased, both of us were forced to consider the risks we faced living in one community with the only hospital in another. When I went into labour, it would mean an urgent need to fly to Aklavik, about half an hour away, at a time when we faced less than two hours of twilight flying time in each twenty-four hours, as long as it didn't snow. It was now so cold that George would also need to sit for at least a half-hour in an engine tent with a blow pot to heat the engine oil so it would be warm enough to circulate when the plane's engine was started. George solved this worrying situation by arranging for David and me to stay with the Burnett family in Aklavik until the baby was born.

The thought of living in a real and warm house again sounded such a relief. George said he would hire extra help to ensure the apartment would be finished by the time we returned after the baby was born. I couldn't see how I could bring a newborn infant back to the Quonset hut. Bob Burnett, a government employee working in northern communications, was waiting to move his family to Inuvik as soon as all the communications systems were up and running there. Then he and his large family would have the luxury of a bigger new house on the utilidor system. Luckily for us he still needed more time in Aklavik, to complete the shutdown and dismantling of the communications centre there. Thankful for this opportunity and the willingness of the Burnetts to have us, I packed up a few clothes for David and me, and we flew to Aklavik in our Cessna.

4

NEW HOME, NEW BABY

A safe place to give birth was obviously my essential reason for being in Aklavik. Other than that, staying there was not my preference, particularly since it meant a complete loss of my personal privacy and the need to adjust to others' plans and schedules. However, I welcomed the Burnetts' generosity and the opportunity to learn about a special place that was so often the focus of people's conversations. I found that the settlement did not have the same services and conveniences as Inuvik, but the government houses were warm, well maintained, and had water delivery, waste disposal, and garbage collection.

The Burnett household was a joyful, disorganized, and noisy large family with four active young children. Bob and Bev were a very generous couple who, surprisingly, did not seem to mind David and me staying with them, even though their small house was crowded before we arrived. David was happy because the children had loads of toys and a home that mostly centred around their activities. It was great to see David actively enjoying time with children his own age. He had been so isolated in the hut and spent so many hours without playmates.

To give the Burnett household a bit of space and privacy, each day David and I bundled up and went walking around the settlement. This gave me a chance to meet people and learn about Aklavik and life there. When I asked about the origins of the name, I was told it meant "barren ground grizzly bear place," but no one seemed to know why it was called that or remember hearing of a time when Aklavik was overrun with bears. On our walks, we also visited George's mother Alice and met some of her and Al's widely diverse group of friends. As we investigated the trading post and shops and chatted with people we met, I gained a much better understanding of why Aklavik had been the hub in the western High Arctic for so many years.

This view of Aklavik from the air shows both its winter and summer river accessibility. At spring breakup, the potential for flooding was always an issue. © NWT Archives / Robert C. Knights / N-1993-002-0571

During our "walkabouts," my interest and questions were met with good humour and friendliness: people spoke with pride as they told me the many ways Aklavik was special. In the weeks while

I waited for the baby's arrival, I would learn more of Aklavik's history and talk to people about why they were unwilling to follow government urgings and move to the new and more "modern" Inuvik.

Before Inuvik was built, Aklavik had been the federal administration and RCMP centre for the western Arctic. The town had both Catholic and Anglican missions, and during the last few decades the missions each operated a small hospital and a residential school. A small federal day school also offered learning opportunities for local children. This list of facilities could create the impression that Aklavik had a large population, warranting two hospitals and three schools, but that was not the case. In the past, there had been some competition between the missions and the services that each offered. Aklavik was a dynamic gathering place where people came to trade furs, to buy supplies, and to be with others for a while before routinely returning to their hunting, trapping, or fishing camps.

Each of the small mission hospitals had one or two trained nurses or nuns, who trained local women to be aides. They relied on the services of a periodic visiting doctor for additional medical care. Tuberculosis (TB) and widespread flu epidemics in the 1950s resulted in the federal government eventually hiring a community doctor, who then served patients in both hospitals. By the '60s, TB patients were mostly sent to Edmonton and members of the wider population were being vaccinated against TB. With the building of Inuvik, the Catholic hospital had closed in 1958 and the Anglican-affiliated All Saints Hospital would close at the end of 1960, leaving Aklavik with no hospital. The Anglican and Catholic mission schools had already closed, and students and staff had moved to Inuvik's one large federal school, which included both Catholic and Anglican sections. In addition, two separate large hostels in Inuvik, one operated by the Anglican Church, the other Catholic, housed children from across the western Arctic. The small federal day school was the exception to all the other closures in that it remained open, awaiting Aklavik's ultimate fate.

Aklavik had been a major centre for trapping muskrat, and many hunting, trapping, and fishing camps were close to the settlement. Local people had been able to live in camps in the area, within easy travelling distance to churches, hospitals, and trading posts. First Nations people, Inuit, Métis, and whites had lived side by side, developing a sense of community that made Aklavik a place where people worked, traded, bought supplies, and shared religious and social events. In my brief time there, I saw a community with a reason to be and with a shared history that people were proud of.

Inuvik offered so little in comparison, having no innate purpose for northern people and being, as it were, a mandated settlement. By 1962, the government would completely move its services and personnel to Inuvik, but many people would decide to stay in Aklavik, regardless of government pressure to leave. In the future, people would defy attempts to shut down the settlement completely, and it exists to this day. Indigenous people could no longer decide if or when their children would go to school, but they could decide whether or not they were going to leave their home territory. I sometimes wondered if their refusal to leave Aklavik was partially an assertion of some free choice.

As mentioned, Aklavik's All Saints Hospital was scheduled to close at the end of December, when everyone would move to Inuvik and its new government hospital, but that wasn't happening soon enough for this baby's arrival. I had not been to see a doctor since I had come north because the only doctor in the western Arctic at that time was Norman Schweda. He would continue to work at the small Anglican hospital for the next few weeks, until he would move to the new hospital in Inuvik. As soon as I flew to Aklavik, I went to see Norman, as I called him one-on-one, a Czechoslovakian immigrant working in the North to qualify for his Canadian physician's licence. It was difficult for the government to find doctors willing to practise in the Arctic, and those who came usually stayed only a year or two. These were either young doctors who had just finished their training or foreign-trained doctors such as Norman.

The Aklavik hospital had served the community and the western Arctic for many, many years. It served tubercular patients as well as patients from various epidemics—such as flu, measles, mumps, and chicken pox—that swept through settlements. These diseases decimated northern families, especially the children who had been born since the last epidemic of that particular disease.

Late in 1960 my daughter, Lesley, was one of the last two babies born in Aklavik's All Saints Hospital. It would close fifteen days following her birth. © *NWT Archives / Archibald Fleming / N-1979-050-1326*

The hospital dealt with weather-related injuries and illness, especially respiratory illnesses, along with accidental shootings, near drownings, burns, and all sorts of other accidents that occurred where lifestyles were less protected and safe. Patients also came to the hospital when alcohol substitutes acted as poisons. More frequently now, some women came to give birth. Nurses from the few settlements with nursing stations, as well as travelling public health nurses, assessed pregnant women to identify high-risk births, so these women could be sent to Aklavik to give birth in a hospital setting.

I BECAME CONCERNED AS DECEMBER BEGAN AND STILL NO BABY HAD arrived. I went into labour a couple of times and walked to the hospital, only to have the labour stop. The due date seemed certain from my original visit to and care by a doctor in Vancouver. However, Norman told me everything seemed fine with both the baby and with me, so it was a matter of waiting. As time went on, the doctor too became concerned about the delay in the baby's arrival. It was my second birth and the baby seemed on the small side. His concern was about a narrow birth canal and some difficulties with David's birth, when for a while a Caesarean section delivery had been considered. Norman talked to Pacific Western Airlines to see if they would fly me to Edmonton. Since it was so late in my pregnancy, they would only take me if he accompanied me on the flight. Yet because he was the only doctor in this part of the North, he could only leave for a true emergency. Norman's concern was, if Caesarean surgery became necessary, he did not have an anaesthetist to assist him. However, in reality we could do nothing except wait to see what happened and if I would deliver without incident. The doctor assured me that in an emergency, one of his nurses could assist him. He just thought it would have been better for me to be in Edmonton, if that had been possible.

Now that flying hours were further limited, I was glad to be staying in the noisy and busy Burnett household. I had confidence in Norman, and he continued to monitor the baby as we waited. The baby seemed fine, with a strong heartbeat. Finally, on December 14, I went into labour once more and this time the labour progressed.

Norman knew that David had been repositioned with forceps during delivery, so he decided to adjust this baby's position manually ahead of birth. He then put a binder on my stomach to maintain the baby's position in the birth canal.

Reluctantly, our daughter was finally born about one in the morning on December 15. She was tiny, with a wee nose that was a bit pushed to one side and with a bruise above her nose on her forehead. I frequently gave in to the urge to gently press her nose towards the centre of her face. She looked like she had been in a battle, but she was beautiful, very vocal, and healthy. Norman explained that she was a bit bruised because of the binding to keep her in place, but he assured me the bruising and discolouration would all go away within a few weeks. Judging by her fingernails and abundant hair, he felt she was up to two weeks or more overdue. He felt she hadn't come at the expected time because her head was not staying locked in position in the pelvis. He also felt she was naturally small, and she might have decided to wait until she was ready. Norman believed that by my taking vitamins and calcium combined with eating a healthy diet, as well as avoiding alcohol, I had made her a healthy, strong baby. Even in those days, Norman believed that when mothers drank alcohol and smoked cigarettes, they compromised the health and size of their babies.

George said he would try to be there when the baby was born this time, as he had missed David's birth during our navy days. But getting to Aklavik would be difficult: the twilight flying hours were now very short, as we were getting close to the late-December solstice and almost twenty-four-hour darkness. Under visual flight rules, our planes could only fly in "daylight," a definition that was stretched a bit to mean, on clear days, those few semi-daylight or twilight hours unique to our part of the Arctic. When this baby was finally born, George could not fly until midday, so he missed her birth too.

Once again, as when David was born, I was amazed as I gazed at our baby daughter. I was in awe over the life process and the birth of this precious little person who was beginning her life with us. She seemed so tiny and fine boned. I was quite astonished that I had a girl as, for some unknown reason, I had assumed the baby would be another boy, and I had not given any thought to a name for a girl.

The hospital was small and old enough that a narrow closet with a long table was considered adequate to serve as its nursery. The table had a lineup of a few wicker laundry baskets that served as each newborn's first bed. My baby and one other were the only infants in the nursery as the staff prepared to close the hospital. Much of the hospital had already been closed; only a few patients were waiting to be transferred to the new hospital when it opened.

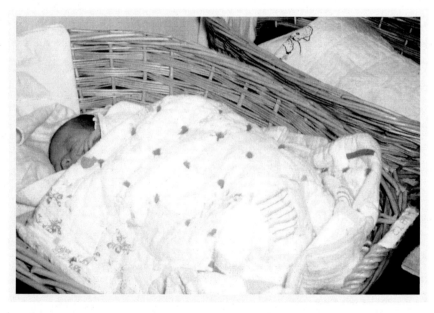

Wicker laundry baskets served as first beds for both Lesley and the infant beside her. Finding this photo in the NWT Archives sixty years after Lesley's birth was an unexpected surprise. © *NWT Archives / Emily Stillwell / N-2005-006-0130-3*

That evening, when my first hospital dinner arrived, I was pleased to find arctic hare on the menu. As I started to eat, a nurse, passing by my room, came in, looked at my dinner, and whisked it out from under my nose, much to my astonishment and disappointment. As she was making off with my dinner, she said I had been given the Indigenous meal by mistake. She stopped long enough to tell me that, as a white patient, I should have been served the same meal as the one the nurses were eating. She returned with a pork chop that looked and tasted freezer burnt, accompanied by an unadorned potato and canned peas. I'm sure the chop had been stored in varying freezing temperatures for at least six months. I looked at it, tasted it, and definitely wanted my hare back. I asked if, the next time hare was being served to others, I could have it since I particularly liked rabbit. Other than that one time, I was sentenced to eat the invariably unappealing white diet while I was in the hospital. So freshly baked bannock, reindeer stew, and whitefish were served to other patients, but not to me. Regardless of the food, the hospital was a warm and friendly place, and the staff gave lots of loving care and attention to both baby and me.

After five days, my hospital stay was over, and with our still nameless baby girl in my arms, I walked from the cozy, brightly lit hospital into the shocking wind and cold and semi-darkness. The cold was so encompassing that it seemed to suck the breath from you, tightening your chest. Our nearby plane, warming up on the snow-packed strip, was waiting to take us back to Inuvik. David had been reluctantly extracted from his life with the Burnetts. Once in the plane, he gave me a hug and peered through all the blankets at his new baby sister. George, David, the baby, and I settled into our Cessna 180 for the flight to Inuvik and our next adventure—living at the back of the hangar. I was excited and relieved to be going home. The word "home" was so special to me now. No longer did I need to worry about finding my family homeless again. We had a home; the hangar with its built-in apartment belonged to us.

Following the short flight, we landed on the windblown, frozen river just outside the still-to-be-finished hangar. Once again, we emerged into the numbing cold and walked off the river, then along the side of the hangar building to the back. Climbing the exterior stairs to the apartment brought us to the outside landing with its three doors. Once we entered the storm door to the enclosed porch, the one ahead gave access to an uninsulated storage area where we would keep frozen food and paper goods. It was also, during the short summer, where we hung winter clothing and kept boots. The third doorway, immediately on the right, was the entrance to the apartment. Next to this door was the apartment's only window.

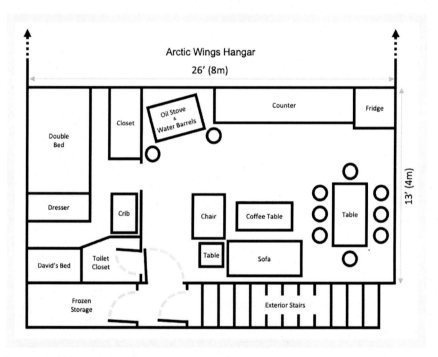

The floor plan of our hangar apartment, which measured all of 340 square feet. This very small living space also had to serve as a waiting room for Arctic Wings' passengers. *Sketch by Jeffrey Perknitsky*

I had seen drawings of the interior and had an opportunity to design how the space would be used, but until I walked through the door, I had no idea how seriously I had overestimated the size of our apartment. Our total living space was 13 feet wide and about 26 feet long (4 by 8 metres), or about 340 square feet (31.5 square metres). This space was divided into three rooms: the largest served as our kitchen, eating, and living areas; we all shared the one bedroom; and the third room was the small toilet closet (3 by 4 feet), just over a metre square, the only room with a door. For ease of comparison, a small single-wide manufactured home nowadays would amount to about 400 square feet (37 square metres). The unfinished hangar space was below the apartment floor and the apartment's back wall was within the hangar structure. This left an open, vaulted ceiling in the rest of the hangar. Truly important was the fact that all of the apartment's walls, its painted plywood floor, and its ceiling were well insulated, so our family was assured of easily warmed living quarters.

As I walked through the door into the living/kitchen area, I saw a counter and shelves, a small fridge, and an oil stove (our only source of heat) along with water barrels (where the ice melted). There was a table and half a dozen chairs, buried under boxes of the canned food we had been storing in the Catholic church's heated warehouse since its arrival by barge during the summer. George had also moved all the used furniture we had bought earlier at the government sale in Aklavik from the hangar, including the chesterfield and chair placed under the window. Immediately inside the door to the left was the door to the toilet closet. Its location would prove to be very convenient for emptying the honey bucket, a frequent chore as our space was endlessly busy with waiting passengers. Fortunately, since we lived out of town on the river at the end of the road, with nothing but bush beyond the hangar, I would be able to dump my honey bucket nearby, on the ice down at the river.

The bedroom seemed even smaller than it had looked on paper, measuring about 13 by 8 feet—just about 100 square feet (just over 9 square metres). This space contained one double bed, one child's cot, one baby's crib, a closet, and a four-foot-long dresser that served as a headboard for our bed as well as a privacy screen. The space was really tight but seemed to be quite functional. If David wanted to leave his cot and the bedroom, he walked between his cot on one side and the front of the dresser on the other, then did a ninety-degree turn, passing the baby's crib to reach the doorway. If we wanted to fully open the bottom drawers of the dresser or take things from under David's cot, we had to sit or lie down on the cot. The small closet, along with space under the bed, cot, and crib, served as storage for personal items as well as extra canned food. This small room would be our only private family space during daylight or flying hours.

Starting when she was about eight months old, our wee girl would stand up in her crib and try to bop David on the head, with her soft toys, as he walked alongside her crib. He was not happy with this "assault," so he ducked and tried to stay out of her reach. He learned to check to see if she was awake and standing in her crib. If so, he would drop to his knees and crawl by the crib to avoid being bopped and she would jump up and down, rattling her railing in frustration and complaining when she couldn't reach him. If I heard David giggling, I knew he had avoided providing her with one of her favourite forms of entertainment.

Once he had set up the stove and had heat and water, and while David and I were still in Aklavik, George had moved out of the Quonset hut and into the new apartment. But even having a much-improved and warmer space had not inspired him to clean up dishes, hang up clothes, make beds, or unpack the many stacks of boxes scattered everywhere, so we walked through the door into complete chaos—warmth, but chaotic warmth. Adding a northern touch to the mess was a freshly killed caribou hindquarter, bleeding, on the counter, with its hair coat and one hoof still attached. In keeping with tradition, this was a generous gift from a local Inuit family, to welcome our new baby.

As we stood there, I was utterly overwhelmed. David no longer understood what was happening, sat down on the chesterfield, and started to cry. He didn't comprehend why he had been uprooted from Aklavik and his friends, and now he was in a strange place, surrounded by total confusion. The baby was hungry, so she started to cry too. Overcome, my response was to move things off the chesterfield, sit down, gather David to me, hug him and the baby, and join them in crying. George became angry and frustrated and stomped out, making it clear he felt very unappreciated for all his hard work in getting the apartment finished in time for our return.

After crying myself out, I covered the now sleeping and exhausted David with a coat, breastfed the baby and put her in her crib, and began to make sense of the chaos that surrounded me. The first job was to boil water and wash dishes. Next came preparing a meal, starting with getting the hide off the caribou leg and cutting the meat into small enough pieces to put it in the freezer box in the storeroom. I then found a pot and put some meat on the stove to make stew, adding dried onions and spices, and, later, boiled some dry pasta. I searched boxes for some of the most immediate necessities, so I could make up beds and begin to plan how to use the available space. George made time to help me unpack boxes, putting up hooks and generally finding ways to adapt the place to fit our needs.

Making sense of our new world consumed almost all my time over the next two days. My never-ending priority was to gain the maximum benefit from every bit of space. Dell arrived for a visit to see the new baby and after having tea, she helped me find still more sensible and creative solutions for the potential use of every available inch of space I had.

Christmas arrived a mere four days after we had returned to Inuvik and moved into our new home. On Christmas Eve day, while George and the baby were asleep, I hiked, along with a very bundled up David, in the thirty-five-below temperatures into the dark and snow-covered bush to cut down a Christmas tree. In such frigid temperatures, and of course with added wind chill, we weren't fussy in our selection. The first little fir we chose, I tried to chop with an axe. It was too cold for the sap to be running so when I hit the slim trunk, the tree began to drop needles. We abandoned that one and the next one we chose, I cut down very gingerly with a small saw. I carefully carried it back to the apartment and brought it inside to warm up and get the sap running before we attempted to do anything else with it. Our tree was only about two feet tall, but it was a Christmas tree. I tied some ribbons on it, and David and I found a place to hang up that important stocking. Now we were ready for Christmas and to welcome Santa Claus during the night, as he left the presents I had wrapped while waiting for the baby's arrival in Aklavik.

For our first Christmas in the North, we feasted on caribou stew with macaroni and fancy butter buns, a gift from the Burnetts when we had left Aklavik, plus fruitcake and cookies Dell had brought on her visit. The four of us celebrated in the warmth and privacy of our first real home since arriving in the North. There were small gifts, but the best gift, for me, was a healthy little baby girl, although she was still lacking a name. For his part, David still had his doubts about how well she measured up as a gift. Another gift of Christmas was the few days of much-needed privacy to enjoy the newest member of our family and her brother. On Boxing Day, we planned to visit Dell, Vern, and family, where we were to enjoy leftover turkey and have the first opportunity to show off our daughter to Dell's family. But first I took a practical moment to face up to one of the major challenges of having a tiny baby in the Arctic: keeping her in clean diapers. For the first time, in what would become a regular routine, I gathered up soiled diapers I had soaked to launder in Dell's wondrous washer and dryer while we visited.

After Christmas, an RCMP officer came to our hangar apartment to record our daughter's birth. We had delayed registering her birth because we couldn't decide or agree on a name. The officer told us that we had only thirty days from the day she was born to decide, and he asked when we would be ready to name her. George right away announced we would name her Lesley. I thought he might have talked it over with me first, but I didn't have any real objections to the name, nor did I have an alternative in mind. I then suggested we add Anne to Lesley and finally she had a name. Her birth was duly registered along with the mandated identification disc number. The federal government had started assigning "disc numbers" (*ujamiit* or *ujamik*) to adults, in lieu of surnames, and then to children and babies born in the North beginning in 1941, a practice that continued until the 1970s.

Many Inuit used only one name or even if they used a second name, several other people also used these same names. Besides being similar, many names were difficult for southerners to pronounce and there was also inconsistency with phonetic spelling. The RCMP had the responsibility for registering all births, and parents were often pressured to use at least one anglicized name for their newborn, although the child might be known by another name in the family and the community. As well, a family with several living children might give a child to another couple who had lost children or had none. Problems with identifying children and their parentage or caregivers would become an even greater issue when Inuit families became eligible for family allowances. To the government, cultural practices and inconsistencies with names qualified as a massive bureaucratic nightmare, so all children born during these thirty years were given an identifying or disc number on their birth certificates. Those born before this were given physical discs with their numbers engraved as the primary means of identification and tracking their genetic heritage. In order not to appear to be singling out a racial group, any child born in the Arctic within this time period would have a disc number assigned and included on their birth certificate.

A few days later, Dell came to help me with more ideas on how to organize our living space and brought me some material I might use for curtains. We made the necessary measurements so, when I went to her place on a laundry run, we could sew curtains for the window, for the doorway into our bedroom, and for the shelves under and above the counter. Use of standard room or cupboard doors wasn't possible since heating of the house was centred at the oil cookstove, and warm air needed to circulate without interference. We had planned that our home would also serve as the winter waiting area for our passengers until the hangar could be finished. I would have passengers in and out of the apartment during flying hours, making it difficult to maintain any sense of family privacy: this made establishing a visual barrier to our bedroom, without interfering with the circulation of warm air, particularly important.

Equally critical was the need to hide the extent of our food supplies. Northern people did not usually have either the money or the heated space essential for stockpiling canned goods and other supplies when the barges were running in summer. I quickly learned that when the waiting passengers noticed extra food I had not stored away, I would be asked to share some of it. We had limited money and I couldn't risk giving our food away, so extra food had to be stored out of sight. More coveted items were assigned to bedroom storage: under the beds or on the closet floor, where they were more truly hidden.

Eventually I learned to appreciate just how generous most northern people were and also understood their assumption that if I had more than a few days of food on hand, I had enough to share with others who did not. However, I never lost the awareness that I had to keep my own family fed. If I had stew cooking and passengers came in to wait, it was quite common to be asked to share some. Still, I needed to watch the pot and be sure I kept enough to feed my family. Later, when we lived in Tuk, if I visited an Inuit home, I was expected to ask to be fed if I was hungry. I learned to mostly avoid giving away our dinner by making sure I served coffee or tea and baked cookies, cupcakes, or cinnamon buns. Since I had to bake all our bread, I usually tried to time baking during the dark non-flying hours. Otherwise, I watched my cooling loaves—representing many hours of hard work—going out my door with the passengers.

Lesley Anne was a very beautiful and even-tempered baby. She had the fine features of my mother and lots of darkish hair, even as an infant. Her hair would lighten, but she continued to have attractive features, including striking grey-green eyes. Living with Lesley was easy except for her sleeping habits. She didn't seem to need as much sleep as David. At the same time, she was good-humoured and would play happily in her crib while he slept. She liked everybody, which was good because of the large number of people in and out of our place all day long. David enjoyed playing with children waiting for flights, but he had become a bit quiet and shy with adults. Lesley, however, was eager to relate to anyone who wanted to hold or talk to her.

George and I asked Reverend Holman, a minister at the Anglican hostel, to baptize Lesley in the chapel at Stringer Hall. Duncan Shaw, a friend in Vancouver, became her godfather and Wilma Hagglund, from Ottawa, became her godmother. Neither of them could be at the baptism in person, but they were there in spirit and in commitment. It was a moving service, the chapel filled entirely with children except for the Hawleys and ourselves. Reverend Holman talked to the children about why babies were baptized and what godparents did, and the children's choir sang for Lesley. It was such a special moment, made even more special when groups of children wanted to come up, admire and touch Lesley, and talk to David. Seeing their young faces was a forceful reminder to me that most of the children, living in the residence, were separated from their own families and from their younger sisters and brothers. They obviously missed having babies and little children as part of their lives, making this gathering extra meaningful for everyone involved.

Living down on the river, we had few visitors other than our passengers. One exception was Mona Thrasher, whom I had met through the Catholic priests when we were living in the Quonset hut. Mona was a young Inuk about eighteen and mostly deaf, although she was able to lip-read quite well. She had a speech impairment and was difficult to understand, but she seemed to have no difficulty communicating with David. Whenever she visited, she also enjoyed holding and caring for Lesley. She was always a big help when she was around. I could take a moment to head out to the ice to dump a honey bucket or go find someone in the hangar below without having to bundle up the children or worry about leaving them alone even for the few moments I might be away. If I needed a short-term babysitter, I was always confident leaving Lesley with Mona, providing David was there too, to serve as her ears.

Mona was a talented self-taught artist. She would become well known for her paintings of the fourteen stations of the cross in Our Lady of Victory Church, commonly known as the Igloo Church. Mona and David would spend hours drawing together, so I made sure to have crayons, pencils, and paper available when she visited. David didn't share her talent, but Mona was unbelievably patient with him, and she was able to teach him the rudiments of making things he drew look more realistic. With her help, his stick people and animals steadily began to take on some more recognizable shapes. As a result of her tutoring, he spent many hours creating pictures, and his artwork was considered very advanced for a four-year-old.

Mona Thrasher, an Inuk teen who babysat for me, became a celebrated Canadian artist. One of Mona's most notable achievements was painting the stations of the cross at Our Lady of Victory Church in Inuvik, also called the Igloo Church. © *NWT Archives / NWT Department of Information / G-1979-023:0197*

5

CREATIVE FOOD GATHERING

I nspired, or perhaps driven, by our tiny hangar apartment and its riverside location, I found that the isolation and winter darkness offered unique opportunities for both a change of scene and keeping fit. I came to appreciate the joys of solitary snowshoeing, heading out for short trips most evenings during the many hours of darkness when I had fewer demands on my time.

I looked forward to these moments of peace and privacy and the chance to reflect on the awesome beauty of the aurora borealis. Standing on the river ice, it seemed like I was seeing a ballet as the stationary and distant stars joined me as I watched the dancing colours of light that dominated the sky down to the horizon. In the quiet, the spectacular colours and variety of each night's light show fascinated me and helped me feel grounded. I can't remember ever thinking one night's display was a replay of another. I felt so alive during this time of serenity, surrounded by such breathtaking beauty, when the crunch of my snowshoes was the only sound I heard.

On other nights, I walked down the stairs and into falling or blowing snow. As I stepped into my snowshoes, I knew I wouldn't wander far on this night, but venturing outside was a challenge I couldn't explain. Once out on the ice, the snow closed over me and everything that wasn't snow disappeared. I could no longer make out the shape of the hangar, the shoreline and even the sky. An aloneness surrounded me, including an amazing sensory depletion that at first seemed peaceful. Yet feeling so alone would become stressful, a bit frightening, and created a need to turn back and follow my tracks in the snow until the hangar took shape and I could use my mitted hand to guide me up the stairs again.

During the dark days of winter, I let few demands or even bad weather interfere with this time on my own. I never wandered too far from the hangars, so I didn't really worry much about harm from any wildlife. I was in more danger if I inadvertently wandered into a temporary dog chain line, set up on the river by a visitor to town, so I made sure to listen for that particular hazard.

No other children lived near us down on the river and David was not yet old enough to attend school, so one of his favourite expeditions was to walk down to our closest neighbours in the PWA hangar and visit with the crew there. One day at the hangar, he was told about a lone wolf that had been seen out on the nearby river ice. David loved to listen to his record of the story and music of Peter and the Wolf. However, after the crew's story of their wolf sighting, David could be seen at a full run whenever he was on his way to or from their hangar. Noticeably, he kept a keen eye for movement on the river ice as he ran as fast as his four-year-old legs could carry him. Listening to the recorded story about the travels of Peter and the Wolf gave the local wolf story a whole new meaning.

Weekly I visited Dell, and bathed all of us and did my washing at her house. I would bundle up David and Lesley, pile bags of laundry on the toboggan, and hike for about a mile and a half (2.4 kilometres) on a trail up the hill and then through town to her house. One day on the way up the hill, unnoticed, Lesley rolled off the toboggan. When I got to the top of the trail and out of the woods, she was gone.

I left David with the toboggan and frantically ran back down the hill. There she lay in her insulated bag, in the snow, still sleeping. I was so scared and so upset with myself for being careless. After that, I strapped her to the toboggan and checked regularly to make sure I didn't lose her again.

In the spring and thanks to my friend Dell, I was introduced to a distinctly Arctic event. About once a month, a group of women, mostly government wives, would plan a large get-together. At a different home on each occasion, these social events initially involved a welcome coffee and chat. However, these gatherings had a much more focused purpose. Each person came with a list of food or general supplies they had available to trade. As a result, comparing lists and identifying the possible—and especially the best—trading options was the chief purpose of these gatherings.

During the summer, when the Mackenzie River was ice free, huge amounts of supplies were barged north from the railhead at Hay River to all northern settlements. After freeze-up, if something had not already arrived by barge, you either had to order it by very expensive air freight or you learned to do without. The government provided each of their northern employees with supply packages meant to last each family until the barges could come again—at least ten months away. These supplies were an official component of each employee's salary. Obviously, packages were standardized, while individuals and families had greatly varied tastes. Trading parties offered an opportunity for women to trade their excess foods and paper products as well as personal and cleaning products, exchanging them for family favourites or items in short supply.

Each government house had a storage room or pantry to accommodate much of a year's worth of canned foods and general supplies. Frozen food allotments were stored in individual lockers, which were part of a huge central government freezer. In addition, moderately heated and non-heated storage lockers were particularly useful to preserve the more perishable items that required cool space, such as apples, oranges, potatoes, onions, cabbage, and eggs, and paper and bulkier items where freezing didn't matter. However, once Christmas was over, few perishable and frozen items were considered viable for trading.

The most cost-efficient northern supplies came in either a can or a package, and the government gave these items purchasing priority. Frozen foods or foods needing to be kept cool were much more expensive, both to ship and to store. A government employee's northern supply packages featured an extraordinary variety of quality canned products. These canned goods included butter, shortening, whole milk powder, powdered eggs, bacon, chicken, ham, tuna, salmon, lobster, crab, clams, sardines, corned beef, stews, meatballs, wieners, beans, and chili, along with soups, vegetables, fruits, and fruit juices. In addition, packaged goods contained various grains, cereals, and dessert and baking products. Even though this sounds like a lot of food, certain items were in short supply, with resulting predictably high trading demand. These items included canned stews, chicken, ham, Spam, tuna, fruit juices, meatballs, chili, baked beans, spaghetti sauce, chocolate chips, baking chocolate, walnuts, coconut, dried fruit, Kool-Aid, pudding and Jell-O mixes, cake and frosting mixes, powdered sugar, cocoa, and marshmallows.

Dell had introduced me to other government wives, who were delighted to invite me to their food trading sessions. I had no spare canned or packaged food to trade, but Dell let them know I had easy access to local meat and fish as well as the means to bring trade items to Inuvik from camps and other settlements. I could get arctic hare, ptarmigan, moose, caribou, reindeer, dried fish, dried caribou, and, depending on ice-fishing conditions, fresh fish. These meats and fish were particularly appreciated in the spring, prior to the arrival of the first barges, when last summer's frozen meats began to taste odd or food boredom had set in. I also knew talented local women sewers who could supply mukluks, duffel socks, beaded moccasins, mitts, and other craft items. I acted as a contact point for anyone who wanted to make their own arrangements with these talented sewers to supply special clothing items.

I didn't expect to trade for the items in high demand, but I could trade well for what I really needed. The surplus items most commonly available for barter included canned staples and baking supplies, dried beans and pasta, oatmeal, peanut butter, some less popular flavours of jam as well as coffee, tea, a wide range of canned vegetables and seafood, and many different spices. I could also get yeast, honey, some nuts, raisins, and especially much-needed toilet paper. The government packages contained a surplus of these items for some families, so they were still available. My small heated storage space restricted my trading options, so Dell kept some things for me in her storage area. She continued to be such a special friend —a friend who was willing to trade just with me for some of the scarcer items, so my family could enjoy them too.

It amazed me just how tired government families were of luxury items such as canned lobster and crab, and I happily traded to get these treats for my family. The food that government families had tired of or had in surplus was what both Indigenous families and our family needed. For two spring seasons, I was able to act as conduit between the groups, although by our second spring, we needed less food ourselves since we had brought in more supplies during the second summer. However, I did trade for some luxury items that we hadn't splurged to buy in bulk during the summer. I also continued to trade for some Dene women friends. During our first summer in the North, we hadn't really understood the extent of supplies we should buy, so trading with the government wives was vital in helping us through our first year, until the river was ice free again.

At "Slim" and Agnes Semmler's trading post, I bought small amounts of candies, which I knew were popular additions to the traded staples. These I added to the traded items, particularly for women friends out in camps. In return I ordered northern clothing as well as fish, hare, dried fish, dried caribou, and ptarmigan, along with various craft items. Having our own air transport gave me the critical advantage to achieve successful trades, since having supplies and other necessities in the right place, when needed, was always a northern challenge. Usually, no money changed hands during these activities, except for the more expensive sewing and craft items. My "commission" was the opportunity to trade for the food, cleaning, and personal items my family needed. At the same time, I had the satisfaction of knowing I helped local women meet their families' food needs too. The other option, for our family as well as for the Indigenous women I traded with, was to buy our food and supplies at the Hudson's Bay post or Semmler's trading post. The food they had for sale had come by barge from Hay River and then been stored for many months in heated and unheated storage. These businesses needed to make a profit, so their products became very expensive to buy, and by springtime, food choices were very limited.

The government employees, with access to central food lockers, could store frozen food at constant temperatures so they mostly escaped the difficulties of freezer burn. Unfortunately, freezer burn was an endless challenge for me, since my freezer box on the porch was subjected to such wide-ranging temperatures. There was no risk of the food thawing, but at forty below, the problem was freeze-drying or burning the edges of frozen meat. I had so much to learn about using the very cold rather than fighting it. Although fresh caribou or reindeer meat was easy to get, it came to me in very large pieces. I first had to manage to saw through the bones and then cut the meat into the steaks and roasts I was more familiar with from the South. I was told of the wonders of the *ulu* (traditional "woman's knife") in cutting big pieces of meat into more manageable sizes. I tried to learn to use it, but even with coaching from some female passengers, I never became good at wielding this half moon-shaped knife with its caribou bone handle. My clumsy efforts were a great source of entertainment for my coaches.

I learned that a hunk of meat was just a hunk of meat to most local women and in Inuit culture, no one part of the animal seemed more favoured. This gave me the opportunity to specify the sections of meat I could most easily deal with and make look like the cuts of meat I remembered from "outside." Unfortunately, I couldn't grind any meat, but I used a jigsaw to cut through bone. I wrapped the cut and trimmed pieces of meat in waxed paper, then brown paper, and labelled them, all to simulate familiar-looking packages of meat bought in the South.

Hanging fresh meat to drain fluids and tenderize it, as was done in the South, was not feasible in the Arctic. During most of the year, living spaces were kept warm enough for people to be comfortable, while outside temperatures were well below freezing. Neither temperature was suitable for hanging meat. Whether the caribou or reindeer meat was fresh or frozen, when thawed, it needed some care and time resting in the fridge on a rack, so fluids could drain off. Otherwise, fried or broiled meat tended to boil in its own fluids. Most Inuit women stewed meat in a pot on top of the stove. I expect the meat fluids that were usually drained off in southern meat plants just added to the rich flavours these women created in their stews.

Meat from caribou, reindeer, or moose killed in the summertime was eaten right away or cut into strips and preserved as dry meat. In the summer, meat and fish could be frozen underground in ice houses chipped out of the permafrost, wherever these were available. When I moved to Tuk, I would see another good example of the sense of community and caring for others when people's joint efforts created a large ice house in the settlement for all the community to use. Food preservation became easier in the winter, when meat was cut into pot-size chunks and frozen in outside boxes or on house roofs. Using roofs or closed boxes for storage solved the issue of roaming dogs either eating or soiling someone's valuable meat supply.

Lichen-eating animals, like caribou or reindeer, had generally tender meat with a delicate flavour. This contrasted noticeably with the strong wild taste of similar animals farther south. Of all the similar meats available, moose had the strongest flavour and was the least tender. But all of these meats were quite lean, and very good when handled and prepared properly.

When I was trading with government women, I was expected to make sure fish were gutted and heads removed before freezing. Hare and birds needed to come to me gutted and without feet, fur, or feathers, again before freezing. As I had to be able to cut the meat into recognizable and usable pieces for trading, I usually bought meat from the reindeer herders before it was frozen. This sometimes created a need for George to make a side trip to Reindeer Station, some 25 miles (40 kilometres) to the northwest, where a herd from Alaska had been established in 1935. Here he could pick up meat when animals were being slaughtered.

Refrigerators required power, which wasn't widely available in settlements and was non-existent in camps, so more creative methods of preserving food were required. A good option was the underground freezer carved into the permafrost. Making one took a lot of time and effort, but once done, it was used summer after summer. With the almost twenty-four-hour sunlight in the summer, meat, whale, and fish were routinely cut into strips and dried on racks. Reindeer, caribou, hare, or other stews were cooked and kept hot all day long, and people ate whenever they were hungry. Usually, a fresh stew was started each morning and any questionable leftovers from the previous day were fed to the dogs.

Another plus to my meat trading was being able to do my meat cutting and wrapping at home. The trimmings from my meat cutting, along with the bones, went into stew or meat stock that I could freeze. All the planning and work of meat handling was well worth my time and effort, given the quality of canned food and other essential supplies I received in trade and then had available to trade with Indigenous women. I appreciated that while I worked on meat preparation, I could also manage waiting passengers, care for the children, and make daily supplies of tea, coffee, and baked goods. On top of all that, I answered the phone, booked flights, kept the company books, took and relayed messages, and monitored aircraft radio calls.

Besides the chance to trade, the monthly coffee parties provided a wonderful opportunity to get to know some of the government wives. At the same time, David had a chance to play with other children his age and enjoy sharing their toys. It wasn't always easy to meet people in the winter, when many, particularly in the utilidor community, stayed inside or only ventured out to have coffee with their immediate neighbours. Inuvik did not yet have a community hall or many planned community activities to draw government people outside their homes or beyond the utilidor service area. Some exceptions were sports and religious activities at the churches or children's activities at the federal school, the Anglican hostel, or the Catholic hostel. Town-wide entertainment and socializing didn't happen much yet, given the lack of a theatre or similar gathering places. House parties were where most of the government people socialized, and those were usually limited to people on the utilidor. The utilidor system with its running water and flush toilets created an exclusive community similar to our navy, "officer only" experience, isolating those residents from the rest of the community. Unlike during our navy time, *we* were outsiders now.

AS THE SEASONS CHANGED AGAIN, RESULTING IN FEWER HOURS OF darkness each day, the utter quiet of our frozen world began to shift. It was a subtle sound to begin with, and I would learn that this sound represented the first hints of the coming summer and the end of the long, cold, dark winter. Spring sunlight increased daily, along with greater warmth in the air. Hints of seasonal change became more obvious. Living as we did right next to the river, our surroundings were particularly quiet over the winter except for the coming and going of aircraft, but each day now, the low whisper of the ice grew louder, and soon it became a voice that couldn't be ignored. The sound surrounded us every hour and announced with increasing certainty that summer would soon be here.

The solid river ice began to melt from both the bottom and the top, forming long vertical ice crystals shaped like candles. As the ice continued to candle, we were surrounded by sounds unlike anything I had ever heard before, as changes to the ice caused it to complain, moan, and groan. It seemed like the river was giving birth to summer, and it was happening with a great deal of sound, reluctance, and effort.

In the early stages of candling, the ice surface remained strong. The river currents tended to melt the bottom of the ice and the surface melted in the sunlight and warm air, but the ice was still strong enough to bear the weight of planes landing and taking off. However, getting to the planes created some problems, since the shallower water on the shoreline was where the ice melted first. To those with experience, the voices from the ice were a good indicator of its strength and integrity: translating the ice's grinding and snapping sounds was a vitally useful skill. George needed to take off from and land on the ice surface for as long as possible. Only a limited number of settlements had dirt or mud strips where we could land with wheels as we waited for open water and could change over to floats.

During the candling and melting process, both Arctic Wings pilots landed on the river, where they would drop off and pick up passengers. When the ice showed signs of breaking up or beginning to move with the current, it immediately became necessary to move the planes to the airport. As the surface of the ice began to melt, it was time to put away our mukluks, and gumboots became our regular footwear for the next three months.

Each spring, candled ice washed ashore to melt after most of the ice moved down the Mackenzie River to the Beaufort Sea. © *NWT Archives / NWT Department of Education, Culture and Employment / G-2004-004:1633*

The early sounds of melting ice alerted George to the need to focus and plan for the many activities that had to be completed before the ice was unsafe and he would have to operate from the airport. Fortunately, longer daylight created longer flying hours, so when there was much needing to get done, there was light in which to do it. People wanted to move into settlements or have camps supplied before flying was shut down to so many places as we waited for the river ice to clear. Most lakes thawed more slowly, which created added downtime as we waited for clear water.

As the ice melted along the shoreline of the Mackenzie River prior to breakup, flights involved a canoe ride to and from shore. © *NWT Archives / Emily Stillwell / N-2005-006-0009-0*

When the river ice had the necessary time for natural candling to occur, before water pressure forced it to move downriver, ice jams caused very little inconvenience. If the ice candling was mostly complete before the pressure grew, then the columns of ice bumped into each other, shattered, and were pulverized, creating a continuously moving ice mush. When ice candling was incomplete, and the ice was forced to move too soon, the pressure broke the ice into large chunks that jammed against each other and backed up the river water until it flooded over the riverbanks and into nearby settlements. Early ice movement could be caused by southern weather warming too quickly. It could also happen if there was more than the usual amount of spring rain in the southern watershed and the ice didn't have enough time to candle naturally in the North.

Along with the arrival of late spring and the impending river breakup, informal but traditional annual celebrations occurred in most settlements along the Mackenzie River. Annual betting pools became the centre of attention in settlements as people tried to predict when the ice would first start to move at Fort Providence; then when it would move at each settlement; or when it would finally clear the river mouth at the Beaufort Sea. Once the river mouth cleared, barges and boats gained access to the entire Mackenzie River and summer had arrived in the North once again.

Flying during breakup was uncertain and stress filled. The ice began to move shortly after this plane took off. Once the ice began to move, planes switched to wheels and all takeoffs and landings moved to the settlements with mud strips or to Inuvik's airport. © *NWT Archives / Emily Stillwell / N-2005-006-033-0*

I HAD ALWAYS LIVED AN ACTIVE LIFE, AND ALTHOUGH I'D BEEN pregnant when I arrived in the North, I was fit. When I returned from the hospital, I had so much physical work to do each day—including hauling five-gallon honey and grey-water buckets down the stairs to dump on the river ice and hauling big blocks of ice up the stairs to melt in our water barrels—that I had soon recovered from Lesley's birth and was physically strong. Life was very busy, and Arctic Wings continued to grow and do well.

A very varied group of passengers used my living space as they waited for flights, and our conversations gave me a special chance to learn about the lifestyles, social structures, and cultures of the northern First Nations people and Inuit. I learned of the confusion they lived with; the pressures they were feeling over the need to educate their children; and their sense that their children were losing respect for them, their ways, their language, and the food they ate as well as what it meant to live off the land. We talked about the lack of work now that construction was mostly finished in Inuvik. The high cost of food at the trading posts was another constant topic of discussion. These local people taught me about the benefits and problems of living in settlements and what they missed by not going out to their trapping, hunting, and fishing camps. The issues created by the cost of getting alcohol and its abuse became increasingly common subjects. Also, I was frequently asked to share information about my life outside, and to explain why whites acted and thought so differently than they did.

These discussions made me realize that I had come north with the idea that northern peoples needed to change and learn to be more like their predominantly white neighbours in southern Canada. I had thought, through education and learning job skills, that Inuit and First Nations people would readily adapt their lifestyles to white ways, thus giving them a chance to live happy, healthy, and fulfilled lives. I soon became aware that my beliefs were narrow in understanding and arrogant. Assuming one lifestyle was better than another failed to consider the differences in people's environments and in people's history between northern and southern Canada. I became confused as I got to know more people, spent time talking about their lives, and especially when I came to understand why their ways had worked successfully for generations.

Yes, I saw the need for everybody to speak at least one of the official languages of Canada; I saw the need for children to be literate; I saw the need for people to have accessible health care. But I came to the conclusion that the lifestyle I knew was not necessarily well suited to being imposed on the Arctic's people. I began to wonder if the price to be paid, for accepting southern ways, would be the total destruction of old, resilient, and viable cultures. The arrogance of the government's black-and-white approach to Indigenous peoples and their cultures—with no room for compromise—left me questioning, but unfortunately finding no answers. I wondered if it would help if northern people had a greater understanding of the government's policies and goals. I also wondered why the government was insisting that only their ways were best. Unfortunately, and perhaps predictably, government officials were expecting blind acceptance of their mandates.

In my conversations with our passengers, waiting for flights, I realized how concerned many of them were about what was happening to their lives. I also saw how few of them had any idea why change was deemed to be so necessary and, in particular, why it was happening so quickly. It occurred to me that no one seemed to be exploring a possibility of melding cultures, rather than the changes being exclusively imposed only the one way: destroying one culture to impose the other. Why wasn't the government looking for small steps, towards mutually agreed on goals, where some control remained with the northern, local people? It seemed the future was destined to leave local people with little freedom of choice about the direction of their lives, since so much was being decided without their involvement. I kept returning to that one question: Why was there such a hurry to instantly change the North to be like the South? What was the imperative?

Time would help me understand that the driving force was really resource exploration, development, and extraction, even though this imperative was framed as meeting people's need for education, health care, and employment skills, and giving the North's people the opportunity to live like southern Canadians. When I talked with government representatives, who also waited as passengers, I heard how important it was to teach the North's people how to live good and successful lives and help them adopt the ways of other Canadians. These representatives were confident that their mandated changes and the government assuming control of people's lives would result in broader humanitarian outcomes.

6

POLITICS VISITS THE ARCTIC

The summer of 1961 brought a new experience when the then prime minister John Diefenbaker and his wife, Olive, with a large group of businessmen, press people, and other dignitaries, visited the western Arctic July 18 to 22, to officially open Inuvik. After the visiting party finished their walkabout, they came down to the riverside hangars to talk to those of us in the aviation business. John Turner, a young Montreal lawyer, was in the group. John and George knew each other from their time attending the University of British Columbia. George invited John to have coffee at our hangar, where they enjoyed sharing stories and catching up with each other's lives. John then invited us to join him for dinner and to listen to the prime minister's speech. The two men were anxious to spend more time together at dinner, to share more memories. (John would be elected to the House of Commons in 1962 and go on to serve as Canada's justice minister and seventeenth prime minister.)

That evening, as I listened to Diefenbaker's speech, he focused on his agenda of "Roads to Resources," presenting it as a realistic answer to all of the North's issues. He seemed excited about his ideas and confident that he had the best solutions. His comments were the first time I so clearly heard of the government's focus on resource development and extraction as the driver for change. I realized then how lacking, in real knowledge, the prime minister was about significant issues facing people in the North and what the cost of change meant for them. (He was the first prime minister to visit the North.) I also thought he didn't seem to comprehend or perhaps even consider the realities of the physical world in our part of the Arctic. For instance, he wasn't taking into account the failed attempts at road-building in the past, or possibly he was minimizing them because they didn't fit his agenda.

The Mackenzie Delta (top) at the beginning of breakup, when ice on the lakes and rivers melted and the land became muddy, limiting travel to boats or planes. In 1960, road-building was decades in the future. © *NWT Archives / NWT Department of Information / G-1979-023:2405*

Much of what he spoke about had little real relevance or any meaningful connection to those of us who lived in the North. We had been told the purpose of his trip was to make announcements about the future of the North, but somehow his speech just left me wondering why he believed "Roads" was the way to solve all our issues. The historical failures and extraordinary costs experienced during the Canol Project, from 1942 to 1944, were widely known. That project had attempted to build roads and pipelines in the Mackenzie Delta while ignoring issues such as permafrost and a lack of drainage in the summer. Well beyond plans for roads, Diefenbaker's "New Directions in the North" had already created a host of social and cultural challenges. Many in the visiting party were media people, and I began to recognize that the trip was primarily a great photo opportunity for all the politicians and businesspeople travelling with the group. I wondered if we were just being used for that purpose. However, the visit was a welcome break in the routine of our lives. And it provided a chance to think and to talk to people of things other than everyday concerns.

A real plus for us personally was George and John's opportunity to reconnect while we spent time with him at dinner. Our private conversations during the meal were fun and full of laughter, as John and George traded university and other stories. Our other companion was Claude Jodoin, president of the Canada Labour Congress. At dinner, we had time to ask many questions about life in the rest of Canada and in return, I think the two of them left with a better understanding of some of the issues in our part of the North. John was a wonderfully warm person and Claude was bright, funny, and entertaining. I asked Claude what workers he thought he might want to unionize in the North. We had a great laugh, as he tried to answer my question and wandered off into various unrealistic, hypothetical situations. It was a memorable evening for me, far beyond the dynamics of the official visit and the prime minister's speech. Following our brief time together, John would keep in touch with us through Christmas cards and notes from him and his wife Geills each year. However, predictably, the politicians left and were soon forgotten.

Trips by Arctic Wings to remote hunting and trapping areas in winter often meant just taking the hunters and their dogs, but summer trips to fishing camps often included whole families. These camps then needed to be resupplied throughout the season. We loaded furs, meat, and fish on our plane for the return trip. Periodically, when there was a small load to go out to a fish camp, the kids and I would go along on the flight, much as we might have done in a car when living in the South. When we arrived, we were expected to stop long enough for tea and a visit. I usually took candy treats for the family we were visiting. I was impressed by how tidy and organized the camps were and the skills the women used to keep their tents clean and warm, even when they seemed to have so very little to work with. I truly appreciated the creativity of the northern women in making nature a partner in their efforts to create a comfortable home for their families in what I considered such a hostile environment. Where possible, tents had fresh-cut tree boughs to keep people up off the cold ground. It seemed things all had a place and everything in the camp was practical and had a purpose.

When we visited fish camps, I usually made sure to remind David not to play under the racks of drying fish. At one camp we visited, however, the children were playing hide and seek, and David decided to hide under a rack of drying arctic char. The unfortunate result was that he came home with oily orange spots all over his clothes. Both the colour and the oil residue were difficult to get out, requiring a few trips through the wash. I urged him not to repeat that adventure on future fish camp visits.

Fish—vital food for both people and sled dogs—needed to be preserved for winter. One method was freezing, and another was drying it on racks in the long days of sunlight. © *NWT Archives / Robert C. Knights / N-1993-002-0045*

During my first winter, I learned of snow's surprising cleaning potential. Parkas could be rubbed with clean snow both on the fur side and the covers, mitts were scrubbed, buckets and other containers were rubbed clean, and anything that was still muddy from summer use was now rubbed clean with snow. So many things that might have been cleaned with soap and water elsewhere were efficiently cleaned with snow crystals. The natural world of the North had so much to teach me.

Using nature was essential to life in the Arctic. Snow crystals could be used to clean clothing, containers, and anything muddy. In this case, it's time to clean summer's tracked-in dirt from a rug. © *NWT Archives / Robert C. Knights / N-1993-002-0130*

Occasionally, we were able to take the longer trip east to the Anderson River. This happened when we had a delivery for Tom Barry, a Canadian Wildlife Service biologist, at his bird camp. David and I both enjoyed visiting Tom, who had extraordinary knowledge about seabirds and their habits. He spent the summer months on his own at the Anderson River camp, and I wondered if he ever got lonely. He had a radio and was in contact with others, but still it seemed a very solitary life. David particularly liked Tom because Tom took his questions seriously and didn't try to put him off. David would follow him around and ask questions as quickly as he could, hardly waiting to hear the complete answer before he came up with yet another question.

At his camp, we enjoyed going out into the nesting areas with Tom. We chased seagulls off their nests so we could collect some fresh eggs to take home. Tom would leave marked eggs in a number of nests, and each day he either harvested the freshly laid egg to eat or he would mark it too. The eggs tasted amazingly good and not as fishy as I had expected. By the springtime, the previous summer's delivery of chicken eggs was pretty questionable. Each egg needed to be broken separately into a cup, inspected, and smelled before it was used. By then, chicken eggs could only be used in baking: few people were brave enough to fry or boil them. The seagull eggs were small and a bit different in appearance, but they made great scrambled eggs. More important than the eggs was our increasing understanding of Tom's world of birds.

With an annoyed seagull chick at the Anderson River nesting grounds, where Tom Barry, a Canadian Wildlife Service biologist, had a research camp.

Early in the 1960s, most white people who lived in Inuvik either worked for the government, were families of government employees, worked for companies hired by the government, or were part of a religious group or order. Whites involved in private business were limited mostly to the trading posts and transportation-related employment. Although the businesspeople were often competitors, we all shared common problems not faced by government people. As a result, a small group of white people not affiliated with the government or with any specific religion turned to each other for support. Slim and Agnes Semmler operated a trading post in competition with the Hudson's Bay Company and were happy to be part of our informal group. However, the Hudson's Bay manager chose not to join us. The Bay people seemed to have a strong network between posts across the North, or possibly the company's policy was to maintain some distance from any competitors. At any rate, the Hudson's Bay people and some other businesspeople more closely associated with the government were not part of our small social group.

The transportation members of our group included Mike Zubko, who operated Aklavik Flying Service in competition with us. He had moved his company to Inuvik from Aklavik. Dave and Mary Jones had the Esso fuel franchise and sold us gas and oil. PWA had either a Beaver or an Otter aircraft on site with their crew, as well as office agents and maintenance people supporting the scheduled Edmonton flights, and these people teamed up with our group. Our many challenges gave us so much in common that it was natural to help each other, when and if we could. Although Al and George did the basic maintenance work–on their planes, when more sophisticated work required a licensed mechanic's signature, they hired a qualified mechanic from the Inuvik PWA crew.

When it became apparent that people were not going to abandon Aklavik, Al decided to continue to live and maintain Arctic Wings' services there. Plenty of housing was available. Since most government people had moved to Inuvik, the government was selling off all their buildings and houses in Aklavik. George and Al bid for houses and got them. Ours was a small three-bedroom house, in great shape, but it was in the wrong place. Most government houses in Aklavik were well built and on pilings to keep the permafrost from melting underneath them. Moving our house involved building a big sled underneath it and cutting away the pilings. At that point it could be skidded across the river ice during the winter or loaded on a barge and floated to Inuvik in the summer. Having a real house with separate bedrooms and privacy sounded like an extraordinarily good idea, but the house was destined to sit on the river's edge in Aklavik for the next year, waiting to be moved.

We would continue to live, for the next eighteen months, in our 340 square feet of hangar living space. Its advantage was warmth, and being new, it was also easily kept clean. However, privacy would continue to be a problem, because of the number of passengers who spent time in my living room waiting for their flights. My honey bucket, the only available nearby toilet, needed emptying often.

My innocence and my trust in George were jolted during my second summer in the North. I heard from some of our waiting passengers the very distressing story that George had been involved with a young Dene woman during the time I was in California. I was told that she had a child that everyone believed to be his. When I asked him, George told me that the relationship didn't mean anything. He was lonely when we had been apart for so long, and he was sure the child was not his. He said it was a mistake he had made, he was sorry, and it would never happen again. I was utterly shocked. I was so naïve that it had never occurred to me he would not be faithful. I didn't know what to do about it except to be hurt, unhappy, and confused. From then on, my trust in him would be challenged, along with some of my confidence in myself as a woman.

As I tried to come to terms with what George had told me and with the blow to my self-confidence, I began to see George in a different and much less naïve way than previously. We had shared and sacrificed so much to make our dream happen. I just couldn't understand why he would choose to behave in a way that he must have known would hurt me greatly. Trying to accept that it really had happened, I didn't know what to do. I had believed our marriage was a partnership. I now recognized that our lives always had to go George's way. I saw that he had assumed the decision-making for both of us, and I mostly heard about decisions after they had already been made. I was also becoming aware that George seemed to go out of his way to alienate some people, which in turn limited our opportunities to be included in activities and events. I became increasingly conscious that his great intelligence, along with his arrogance, resulted in his lack of patience as well as his habit of putting others down. Had George changed or had I just failed to recognize some of these things before? Most difficult was my sense that I loved him. But seeing him as I did now left me feeling powerless to regain the sense of being secure in our relationship. As I struggled with these personal changes, I questioned myself—my sexuality, my expectations, and my role. Only later would I realize how self-centred George was as an intimate partner.

Everything around me now seemed different, and even with wall-to-wall passengers underfoot much of the day, I often felt isolated in the hangar, with few opportunities to get away from my disillusionment or the business, except when I washed clothes and visited with Dell. Caught up in being loyal to George, I kept my relationship issues to myself. However, in the summer, I made some time for fun, playing pickup softball games with Dell and other women on the community's dirt field, which was either dusty or muddy, depending on the weather. An added challenge, along with the condition of the field, was swarms of mosquitoes. It was hard to concentrate on catching a ball when you were swinging your hands in front of your face, trying to ward off the hundreds of insects. But it was great fun to laugh at our mistakes and celebrate our successes. In the winter, I went snowshoeing alone, in the dark, when George was home and the children were asleep. Getting outside gave me an opportunity to clear my head, and the activity distracted me from my demanding and uncertain life.

As time passed, the reality of my busy life fortunately left little time to dwell on unhappiness, uncertainties, and things I could not change. Occasionally I went ptarmigan hunting across the river in the local bush with the PWA crew. I had learned to handle and shoot guns as a child but had never had any real interest in hunting. However, it was fun to be outside and sharing time and laughter with other people. I much preferred to get my ptarmigan from Indigenous friends—gutless, headless, featherless, and ready for the pot. Ptarmigan was called "the chicken of the North," and although it was not quite chicken, its taste and texture were really good. However, my favourite northern meat remained arctic hare. It had a distinctive flavour, somewhat like a nutty-flavored rabbit, but again, I preferred to have it provided skinned, cleaned, without a head, and ready to cook.

After the busy and successful second summer season for Arctic Wings, George flew our Cessna 180 (and Al flew the other plane) to Edmonton for maintenance and inspection at freeze-up. This down-time for Arctic Wings gave me a chance to unpack and store the year's supplies of food that had arrived by barge, get ice cut and stored for the winter's water, and prepare for the other winter challenges to come. My responsibilities included scheduling most of the government charters before extreme cold and darkness would surround us again.

We spent our second northern Christmas with Vern and Dell. The government families had frozen turkeys, sent on the summer barges, along with other festive goodies flown in from outside, and the Hawleys wanted to share with us. Dell was a great cook and I tried to make my grandmother's German biscuits and shortbread— I'd say with moderate success. The Hawleys' home was warm, happy, big, clean, full of colour and good smells and, of course, a load of diapers went into the washer.

We appreciated this brief access to a flush toilet as well as hot running water. Washing dishes after dinner was almost a treat. Lesley had begun to walk at about eleven months, and the added space of the house and encouragement from others gave her an opportunity to practise her new skill with great enthusiasm. It was so special to spend Christmas Day sharing good food and laughter with friends.

Lesley celebrating Christmas 1961 in a party dress, a gift from outside, and her usual mukluks.

BY THE END OF 1961, IT BECAME APPARENT THAT FEWER INDIGENOUS people were choosing to live off the land in hunting and trapping camps; rather, many families had now elected to live permanently in settlements. The reasons for these choices were many and had varying impact on their family needs and lifestyles. These changes decreased people's need to travel to hunting and trapping camps, and thus led to less work maintaining and feeding large teams of sled dogs. People continued to fish for the family's food during the summer and to dry fish for food for the winter, but the need for fish as dog food was greatly reduced.

With less demand for fish, many families now limited or even eliminated travel to their more distant traditional fishing sites; this left them with fewer ways to ensure their family food supply, but for some it was mostly feasible to catch enough fish for the table closer to the settlements. As a result, children lost opportunities to learn traditional ways while living on the land at these fish camps. As well, in the early days of Inuvik, hunting birds and hare for family food was also possible close to the townsite. If a family could afford it, slaughtered reindeer were brought in from Reindeer Station. But again, this created increasingly less interest in travelling to the traditional hunting sites in search of caribou. These changes in people's lifestyles, however, had little effect on Arctic Wings' business because there was so much other work for our aircraft.

First Nations people mostly fed fish to their dogs, but on the coast, dogs owned by Inuit families were also fed seal and whale meat that was frozen, dried, or could be stored and fermented in forty-five-gallon drums until needed. If whale, seal, or fish were not available, chunks of lard were mixed with oatmeal, frozen into blocks, and then chopped into dog-size pieces. Dogs remained more important in Tuk and along the coast than in Inuvik, but were easier to maintain as well, since it was possible to hunt seals on the sea ice in the winter and beluga whale short distances from the harbour entrance during the summer.

Northern dogs were work animals, seldom friends or pets. They were staked out on long gang chains with six-foot (2 metres) cross chains every 12 to 14 feet (4 metres) so they couldn't reach each other to fight. Pregnant female dogs were usually left loose around the house or camp to raise their puppies. They were friendlier than most chained dogs, but still were not really pets. Children played with puppies, but when they became a nuisance around the house or camp or were big enough to begin to work, they joined the chain gang of sled dogs.

In the early 1960s, a working dog team was still essential in isolated settlements such as Sachs Harbour, on the western tip of Banks Island.
© NWT Archives / Robert C. Knights / N-1993-002-0150

Polar bear hunting was usually done with dog teams, but this mostly ended in the western Arctic in 1967 when the federal government mandated much reduced hunting quotas. Fewer bears had been harvested in the west compared to the eastern Arctic prior to

1967 and the quotas would reflect this harvesting history, leaving the west with an almost zero number of bears. When sales of fur outside the North collapsed, the limited quota wasn't the only factor in the loss of opportunity to earn a living from polar bear hunting. The use of dogs for seal hunting would continue out on the ice along the coast, depending on the state of the ice during the winter and spring. Seal hunting was more than hunting animals for their fur and dog food, since seal was also food for the table. While the fur trade remained viable, trapping muskrat, beaver, fox, wolf, wolverine, and weasel (usually called ermine in its winter coat) was a different issue, usually requiring travel to traditional camps, where a large trapping area made the time and cost worthwhile. In the early 1960s, dogs were still used in these camps, since the cost to buy a snowmobile and the expense and logistical problems of flying a snowmobile or even gas alone to distant camps discouraged many trappers from thoughts of switching from their dogs. When the fur trade collapsed, it reduced the need for sled dogs and increased interest in snowmobiles for use around the settlements.

When the viability of trapping fur animals declined at first in response to a sharp drop in fur prices, shortly followed by a complete collapse of the industry, many Indigenous families were left without any income beyond the monthly family allowance cheques. Lobbying and protests by animal rights activists had convinced the fashion industry to first reduce and then totally ban the use of natural fur. In the North, this long-time way of life suddenly ended and unfortunately, this fact did not immediately spur government efforts to identify a replacement industry.

In the past, Indigenous people's lifestyles were entirely intertwined with all the other natural elements and practices that surrounded them. But now, as one part of life changed, that shift touched all other aspects of their lifestyle. The changing role of sled dogs was just one example of many interconnected shifts that were happening. The past harmony within people's environment, when all the parts created patterns for living, was being lost. These patterns in turn had supported the ability to survive and flourish for generations. The question now became, when harmony was disrupted, was the domino effect of change going to be beyond people's ability to successfully adapt?

BESIDES INDIGENOUS PEOPLE, THE WHITE PASSENGERS WHO CAME TO wait for planes in our apartment were another source of many interesting conversations and learning experiences both for David and for me. These passengers included government employees with many titles and responsibilities: medical and legal people, wildlife experts, research scientists, mining and natural resources exploration businesspeople, film and TV crews, and occasionally visiting tourists. I often wondered why the few tourists who challenged themselves to visit the High Arctic came in the summer. I understood those who came to fish needed open water to fish for species not available elsewhere or for the more common fish that grew to extraordinary sizes, but it seemed that those who came to experience "life in the Arctic" came in the three months of summer when the North was most like southern Canada.

Summer was the time when most northern people dressed like less-than-affluent southerners. The colourful traditional clothing was gone, replaced by very functional and ordinary wear, best suited for the work of summer. Sweatshirts, jeans, long-sleeved T-shirts, coveralls, and gumboots were favoured. Just as we made sure we gained full value from our use of potable water, all clothing was well used before it finally became rags or was discarded. Another issue for the visitor was that towns and settlements were isolated, much like tiny islands in a huge sea of wilderness. Travel between locations was restricted to boat or air transport: there were no scenic drives. Summer was also a time when mosquitoes and blackflies plagued animals and humans alike, particularly if you wandered out onto the water-filled tundra. Sled dog lines thawed and turned to mud or dirt, and the dogs coated themselves in the mud to discourage biting insects. As well, many dog teams received minimal care over the summer, so visiting a dog line was not the attraction it would have been during the working months of winter.

Experiencing the almost twenty-four-hour daylight was unique, but it couldn't compare to the wondrous visions of the aurora borealis during the dark months. Summer tourists gained some insights into the activities required to prepare for life in the winter months—like drying fish, drying caribou and moose meat, hunting beluga whales and making muktuk, or curing hides for leather—but the many notable and unusual activities of the other nine months were not seen by these fair-weather visitors. With the harshness of winter came special learning, experiences, and beauty. In the future, as radical changes came to tourism, it would become a large and valued part of the northern economy. Much is now planned and done to make the tourist feel they have "experienced the North," regardless of the time of year they visit. Yet I'm convinced that the months of snow and ice offer more exceptional experiences.

David and I enjoyed learning from each group of passengers, with their wide-ranging knowledge and experience. Transporting oil exploration personnel and supplies would become a larger part of our work as the mid-1960s approached. Many miners and prospectors continued to look for the elusive source of Klondike gold or for other minerals. The prospectors were quite secretive about where they wanted to be flown, but most often they would fly into sites in the Richardson Mountains. We did many emergency and health-related flights each year, picking up people who were hurt in accidents or were sick and in need of medical care. Initially we flew them to the hospital in Aklavik, but when that hospital closed at the end of 1960, patients were transported to the new hospital in Inuvik.

Transportation related to maintaining health and legal or court services all around the western Arctic became a profitable part of our charters. Nurses and doctors flew for travelling medical clinics and on tuberculosis screening trips. We carried RCMP personnel to settlements when their own plane wasn't in the area. The mobile court and judges needed to reach settlements to conduct local trials. In a few more years, more charter work involved tourists and fishermen from the South, during the more hospitable summertime.

Not all customers paid for their transportation in the same way. Most of our trips for Indigenous people were paid with cash up front. Private companies were billed on account, but generally were prompt with payment. Governments, with their cumbersome and inefficient accounting procedures, often failed to pay us for six months or more. This strained our new company, along with other similar businesses, since even different government ministries had their different delays or inconsistencies in payment timelines. Needless to say, payment delays did not help the invariable consistency of our need to meet operating costs.

Succeeding in business in the North required help from others, and many people helped us to establish Arctic Wings and also supported us as we tried to make a place for our family in the North. These included the Catholic Church's fathers, brothers, and nuns, who were always there if we needed something done, needed a hand, or just needed support. Their friendly attitude and willingness to help was admirable, considering we weren't Catholic. This was true in Aklavik, in Inuvik, and later in Tuk. Several fathers became close friends and regular visitors to our homes in Inuvik and Tuk. Among these was Father Max Ruyant, who lived in Inuvik and was the head administrator of the Church in the western Arctic. He was a bright, well-read, and interesting man who loaned us supplies if we ran short, gave business advice, and generally did everything he could to help us succeed. Father Adams and Father Franche were both good at everything mechanical; they seemed able to fix anything as well as manufacture parts and operate any piece of equipment.

Whenever Father William Leising flew the Church's Norseman bush plane into our area, we visited with him and listened to his fascinating stories. Father Leising had written a book on the Church's history of flying in the North. He titled the book *Arctic Wings*, and I never knew if our company name had come from his book, if the reverse was true, or if it was just one of those coincidences. Later, after our company was sold to Nordair, Freddie Carpenter, the first northern Indigenous licensed pilot, would buy Aklavik Flying Service Ltd. from Mike Zubko and then name his new company Arctic Wings and Rotors, so the name would live on, including helicopter as well as fixed-wing service.

As a woman, my relationship with the Catholic fathers was very different from George's. Undoubtedly, this time and place was a man's world, and the fathers seemed to hold the then customary and often rigid belief in the many differences between male and female roles and responsibilities. As a woman, I was always treated with respect, but it was not expected that I should share in decision-making in business issues or relationships. I was considered a wife, mother, and message taker, but neither a full business equal to George nor a partner in Arctic Wings. I found this attitude personally very frustrating, but it was typical and accepted at that time, and I could do nothing to change the situation.

In later years, charges of abuse would be made against some of the lay supervisors in the Catholic residential hostel, Grollier Hall. I didn't hear that the fathers themselves were involved, but the alleged abuse was commonly considered a failure of Father Ruyant's because he didn't pay sufficient attention to supervising Church employees. Most of the Catholic priests and brothers I knew, although they were definitely chauvinists, were also warm friends and supporters, and I would find it difficult to believe they were also child abusers. No doubt, I didn't agree with a number of the

Church's beliefs and policies, but I had always believed the fathers I knew were ethical in following their beliefs and doctrines.

The priest I would know the best was Father Robert Le Meur of Tuk. He became a family member to me and to the children when we moved to Tuk at the beginning of our third summer in the North. Father Le Meur loved to discuss current events, history, and any reading materials we could find to share. He suffered from living in a settlement where he had few people to talk with about subjects beyond what were part of everyone's daily struggles. The two of us spent time debating and discussing the price Inuit would pay for both the government's and the Church's efforts to change their customs, way of life, and behaviours, but I can't remember that we came up with many feasible solutions. Along with sharing our views of the North, he and I had interesting discussions about world events and our literary interests. However, Father Le Meur was disappointed when he learned that I didn't speak French and had no knowledge of French literature.

When we first moved to Tuk, Father Le Meur dropped by frequently to have tea at the cookhouse, but it was really an excuse to talk. We never talked about religion: I expect he waited for me to start that conversation and I never did. We debated most other subjects, except for the few we seemed to tacitly agree were off limits. He gave me a chance to think about and discuss subjects beyond my immediate circumstances, and this was a priceless bonus. I would never feel that Father Le Meur thought, because I was a woman, I was or should be subservient to George. I felt the only label he had for me was that of a good and interesting friend.

I could talk and work at the same time, but I didn't have enough time to sit and play chess with Father Le Meur, so he taught David and thus had a regular partner when he visited. Under the father's tutelage, David became a good chess player, even though he was then only five years old. Father Le Meur was like a grandfather to David. He listened to him and encouraged him rather than being critical or dismissive of him as, unfortunately, his father often was. When we moved back to Inuvik, David and I both missed Father Le Meur, and I know he missed both of us.

During all our years in the North, David was invited to visit the Catholic hostel in Inuvik, where he played with the younger boys living there. If we were just visiting from Tuk, I dropped David at the hostel and picked him up again when it was convenient. I made the time to do this because it gave David a chance to play with different boys from all around the western Arctic. Sister Hébert, a member of the Grey Nuns who took charge of the youngest boys, was always pleased to see David. She was a short, stocky woman who wore a full habit, which made it easy to spread wide her flowing cloak and sweep all the little boys along with her as she moved down the hall. When David visited the hostel, he was swept along with all the rest of the little boys as just another of Sister Hébert's charges.

I was aware of strict discipline in the hostel, but I wasn't aware of the harshness described years later by some of the children. If David thought anything was unusual or uncomfortable for him there, he never said anything to me, nor was he ever reluctant to visit and be left there for periods of time. However, the most obvious difference for him was the certainty that his stay was temporary: I would always come back and pick him up. I had no personal experience of what was happening within the hostels beyond being an occasional visitor. The children seemed healthy, well cared for, and well fed in both hostels, but based on my own seven-year experience in a California residential school, the emotional and mental health of children is not really measurable or necessarily apparent. In my years as a ward of the state, I was fortunate that my language, culture, and way of life were not being challenged or seen to be in need of change. However, the regimentation, the loss of individuality, the loss of personal freedom, and the loss of family and affection were overwhelming for me and would influence the rest of my life. I could only think that residential school would have been equally or more overwhelming for these children.

Later, in our last year in the North, when we returned to live in Inuvik, David would go to school at the Catholic section of the federal day school since his friends were there, even though we still showed no inclination to become Catholic. Our choice of schools raised an unexpected issue, as David became really annoyed when we wouldn't let him be confirmed by the Church, along with all his friends in grade two. George and I told him if he wanted to become a Catholic when he was a teenager, we would not stand in his way, but we felt he didn't know enough about other religious choices to make a life-changing commitment at this young age. I was surprised to learn how the concepts of religion and adults' attitudes towards it could confuse and annoy a seven-year-old.

7

TUKTOYAKTUK IS HOME

As spring breakup and our third summer approached, Arctic Wings continued to have a steady workload that kept both planes busy. Along with celebrating our successes, George switched to focusing on how the company could grow. He decided we needed to have an Arctic Wings agent in Tuk to develop the business there, but he decided the time still wasn't right for the company to operate a helicopter or to operate another fixed-wing aircraft from Tuk. Then, as a result of his conversations with people living in Tuk, he decided to sign a catering contract with the government. This committed us to feeding a construction crew, who were scheduled to build a new school in Tuk over the summer of 1962. George's plan involved hiring a cook, who would also serve as our agent there.

George arranged to use a former military building that had earlier been used as a construction cookhouse. It had been moved to Tuk and came fully outfitted with tables and chairs, two oil cooking stoves, refrigerators, and all the necessary cooking and service equipment. The building had been thoroughly cleaned before it was closed down, so thankfully was entirely unlike the Quonset hut we'd lived in before, which had been abandoned in a state of filth and neglect. Once he knew the necessary cookhouse was available for our contract, George then flew to Edmonton to hire a cook for the construction project. He found a female cook, made all the travel arrangements for her, and ordered all the supplies she decided she would need to feed the twenty-five men for the summer. He arranged, with government help, to get the food and supplies on the first barges to Tuk at breakup. The catering contract was to begin in early June, timed to coincide with the arrival of the first barges containing the construction materials for the school as well as the construction crew.

George's successful bid for the catering contract was just one more example of his ability to create profitable plans, jump into action, and begin getting results. Sometimes, however, implementing these ideas came with unexpected challenges, and his best solutions to most problems also depended on my commitment and energy. The catering contract was just such an instance. George had hired the cook, ordered supplies, and arranged for them to be on the first barges to Tuk; then his plans went awry. The cook turned out to be an out-of-control alcoholic, who was institutionalized just before she was to leave for the North.

With a confirmed cooking contract and no cook, George's immediate solution was to suggest I take the job. In his thinking, this only involved me taking the children, moving us all from Inuvik to Tuk, and honouring our contract. He convinced me this was a short-term plan until he could hire another cook. To meet the contract, I would be required to provide three meals and three coffee breaks a day for these two dozen hungry workers. My only catering experience up till then involved providing meals for a small family, so needless to say, the challenge of this proposed job caused me considerably more anxiety and stress than it created for George. I had no idea what food had been ordered—food that I would be expected to know how to cook. This new responsibility felt well beyond my comfort zone, yet I also knew we had a signed contract to meet and our reputation with the government mattered.

Flying into Tuk required exceptional navigation skills, thanks to winter whiteout conditions as well as the additional hazard of pingos—ice hills of varying heights. © *NWT Archives / NWT Department of Public Works and Services / G-1995-001:7400*

Flying to Tuk was like travelling to a different place altogether. Tuk was 95 miles (150 kilometres) northeast of Inuvik and above the treeline. Our trip there was different from most other local trips since the plane flew over flat, treeless tundra and lakes, all looking so much the same, until we approached the settlement of Tuk, where over a thousand ice hills, called pingos, of varying heights dotted the landscape around the settlement. These features were common only to this area of permafrost, with some rising to more than 230 feet (70 metres), making them high enough to be a real hazard to incoming planes. Knowing where they were, in relationship to the town, was vitally important for pilots, particularly in winter flying conditions. At that season, whiteouts were frequent as strong winds picked up snow off the surface of the frozen Beaufort Sea and blew it ashore and into Tuk. These were times when a pilot might believe it prudent to circle out to sea and approach the settlement from that direction. However, in clear weather, the pingos served as an unmoving navigational aid.

This early view of Tuk's narrow harbour entrance illustrates its value as protection for boats facing Arctic storms. It also offered shelter when pack ice blew ashore from the Beaufort Sea. © *NWT Archives / Kirk Family / N-2005-001-0136*

Tuk was an Inuvialuit settlement located on a long peninsula, with the Beaufort Sea on one side and a very large deep-water harbour on the other. In both winter and summer, the wind blew off the ocean, making it often a cold place to live. Even with the wind, the shape of the land made the Tuk harbour quite sheltered from rough water. Tuktoyaktuk, according to stories told by Elders, meant "place resembling a caribou." The stories described a caribou turned to stone in the nearby Beaufort Sea. I expect it could have been a misshaped small pingo, but the story sounded like more fun.

Tuk in the summertime, looking towards the harbour and the DEW Line station in the far distance. In the centre is the Catholic church, Our Lady of Grace. Lumber and a number of other supplies have been unloaded from a Northern Transportation barge. © *NWT Archives / Emily Stillwell / N-2005-006-0063-0*

Tuk had the only truly sheltered harbour close to the entrance to the Mackenzie River, 16 miles (26 kilometres) to the west. In the past, this harbour had been a secure place for whaling ships to weather unpredictable storms or sudden shifting of the pack ice in the Beaufort Sea. It was seen as a stopping or sheltering place rather than a permanent settlement until 1930, when the Hudson's Bay Company closed its post on Herschel Island and centralized its coastal operations in Tuk. This happened along with new boat and barge service along the Mackenzie River that ended at Tuk. During World War II, the military would establish a semi-secret base nearby to establish radio communication, and for a while, that created wage-earning work for some Inuit men. In addition, a Catholic mission and church were set up in the settlement, followed much later by a one-room day school and a small nursing station.

The house styles in Tuk varied widely, reflecting in their styles and locations the random appearance of the many pingos. Some residences were remnants—mostly uninhabited—of the traditional driftwood and sod dwellings (*igluyuaruit*); others were log houses sealed with mud and cement; yet more were buildings that featured rough-hewn plank siding. In addition, some leftover military buildings had been moved into the settlement.

Finally, some newer buildings had been constructed using the more standard materials and styles seen elsewhere. However, despite the lack of physical continuity in the settlement, I would find a welcome sense of community and closeness in the people that I had not experienced elsewhere.

The Tuk DEW Line station community was on a peninsula, separated from Tuk itself and with restricted admittance. © *NWT Archives / Emily Stillwell / N-2005-006-0065-0*

The building of more than sixty DEW Line radar station sites across the Arctic from 1955 had brought greater change to the community. With the Mackenzie River as a route for shipping large equipment, Tuk became a centre for acquiring and training local labour and for the distribution of equipment and supplies to sites across the Arctic. During construction, Inuit workers made permanent homes in Tuk and went to work building the other DEW Line sites. Many gave up trapping for the advantage of a regular wage and the convenience of having their family live in the community. The Tuk DEW Line site itself was about 6 miles (9.6 kilometres) distant and initially was a restricted area, with little interaction between its operations and the settlement.

The end of construction, early in the 1960s, resulted in no ongoing work for most of these now Tuk-based Inuit. By this time a small elementary day school and a nursing station had been built in the settlement, and most of the settled families were reluctant to return to the isolation of their hunting and trapping camps, inevitably some distance away. Living in Tuk allowed their younger children to live at home and attend school, rather than being required to live at one of the two residential hostels in Inuvik. The older children who attended residential school were gone for the ten-month school year, returning home only for the summer school holiday.

Being located on the Beaufort Sea, with a deep-water harbour, Tuk had unusual opportunities close to home to harvest food both for dogs and for the family table. But, as in many northern communities, lifestyles were changing, with no more jobs and not much to do within the settlements. As a result, abuse of alcohol increasingly created health, social, and family problems. When the children and I moved to Tuk, the lack of jobs was only beginning to become a disruptive issue. At that time, social and family ties remained strong, as did a sense of community. I would learn about the special place children had in the settlement. Inuit believed the children belonged to everyone and each child was the community's responsibility. If any child needed help, the nearest person came to their aid. Any hungry child was welcomed and fed in any home. Once it was recognized that we weren't just passing through, my children also became children of the community.

All children, regardless of parentage, were highly valued both by their families and by their communities. Historically, lack of concern over marital status and parentage was very apparent when children of explorers, miners, and traders were born into these families, without marriage or long-term commitments. As well as the Caucasian children of mixed heritage, children had been sired by Black whalers, creating a continuum from people with red hair, freckled faces, and very light skin to people with very dark hair and dark skin. Regardless of their appearance, their heritage, or the marital status of their mother, all babies and children were highly valued.

Mental, physical, or genetic-based handicaps seemed rare among northern people. As confirmed by a settlement nurse in Tuk, this came about because of high infant and childhood mortality rates, since only the strongest babies and children would survive to adulthood and, in turn, reproduce. Government statistics show that life expectancy among Inuit in the Northwest Territories was 37 years in the 1950s (33 years less than the national average). When I was in the North, life expectancy had risen, but was still only 51 years. Medically assisted births were not usual in my time there, nor had they been in earlier times. Per capita birth rates remained traditionally high, since no government health professional was permitted to provide birth control information or teaching. Infant mortality also remained correspondingly high.

The cookhouse building George had arranged to use was commonly called a five-twelve, so named because it was 512 square feet (47.5 square metres) in total size. When I arrived in Tuk, my first stop was to see the government administrator to pick up the keys to the building. At the same time, I wanted to find a rental house where the children and I could live. I quickly learned that all living space available had been booked for the incoming temporary construction workers. This left no choice but to consider whether a section of the five-twelve building could serve as living space. The building needed a good basic cleaning and some rearranging, but it was very usable as a cookhouse. The whole space was bigger than our hangar apartment, but most of it would be needed as a work-space and dining area. I realized our only feasible option for sleeping quarters was to use the small washroom, located at a back corner of the building (8 x 6 feet / 4.5 square metres). My practical solution involved moving the chemical toilet into an unheated small storage building behind the cookhouse and then converting the tiny washroom into our family's living and sleeping quarters.

After I scrubbed the walls and floor of the washroom, I found someone who could weld together two metal-framed cots, making them into a bunk bed that I bolted to the wall. David and Lesley would sleep with their heads at each end of the lower bunk, leaving the top bunk for me. I added a board on the front of the lower bunk to keep the children from falling out. Clothes and toys I stored in boxes under the bottom bunk, while other clothes I hung up on hooks screwed into the walls. This converted washroom served as our tiny private family space for the next four months. Its significant advantage was that I could work and care for the children at the same time.

This warm, pleasant building, once cleaned and set up, became a very efficient and attractive place to feed the crew. Since the catering contract would end before the weather became cold enough to freeze hard, the honey bucket in the storeroom would work fine despite being very inconvenient, for it meant making a chilly trip outside once September's colder weather arrived. A couple of sheets of plywood separated the toilet from the rest of the storage area, and a blanket curtain over the opening created some privacy in our new bathroom. The rest of the area would be essential storage once the barges arrived with our supplies.

Within a couple of days, the crew and the supplies all arrived at once, so it was quite a scramble to unpack things, find what I needed immediately, cook, establish a routine, and plan the next four months' schedule. Each morning, I started work at five so breakfast was ready between six and seven-thirty. Coffee break came at ten, lunch at twelve, coffee again at three, dinner at six, and evening coffee at nine. The cookhouse operated seven days a week, leaving little time to think about not having a better family living space, a quiet place, or any personal privacy during the sixteen or more hours each day when the cookhouse was open.

As I unpacked the supplies, I wondered why the hired cook had ordered so much pure vanilla. Later, when we opened our trading post, unknowingly, I put the bottles of vanilla left over from the summer catering on the shelves for sale. I was amazed at the immediate run on vanilla. When I shared this story with Father Le Meur, he enlightened me about vanilla's use as a substitute for commercial alcohol. Once I understood, my only choice was to pour it out.

In 1960, Indigenous adults in the North were granted the legal right to buy alcohol from the government liquor store. The only liquor store in the northern part of the Mackenzie Delta was in Inuvik. Consequently, quite a few of our charter flights to and from Tuk and other settlements were basically liquor runs to Inuvik. The right to buy alcohol made a significant and unwelcome difference to both family lifestyle and financial well-being. Home brew and various other dangerous chemicals containing alcohol, such as Aqua Velva aftershave, antifreeze, and—as I later discovered—pure vanilla, were commonly substituted for commercially produced alcohol, resulting in blindness, health issues, and death among some drinkers.

A new cook was never hired (I often asked myself whether George ever planned to hire one), so I cooked for the twenty-five men, plus extra people, from the beginning of June until nearly the end of September. In case I ever thought of sitting down and putting my feet up, I was still in charge of booking flights and monitoring the radio traffic for Arctic Wings, managing passengers, and ordering additional supplies. Extensive regular cleaning and washing were other tasks on my lengthy to-do list. All of these duties did not change my role as mother—a mother who wanted to do a good job caring for her children. Eventually I was able to hire a couple of local women to help me, so my workload became more manageable. Hiring help also gave me a welcome opportunity to learn from these women about this very different place where I was now living.

Besides the circumstances already described, operating this cookhouse in the High Arctic brought various challenges, starting with water and waste disposal. I didn't have running water in the true sense, but I had water delivered a couple of times a week to an oil tank that had been set up outside the building, solely for water. This water was gravity fed to the sink so until winter arrived, the building had a form of cold running water. I could thus avoid the heavy task of filling and cleaning out forty-five-gallon barrels. I did have to fill large pots to heat all the water we needed, but it was a real convenience to have water available when you turned a tap. The grey water from cleaning dishes, laundry, tables, chairs, and floors, as well as the water I used to keep all of us clean, was poured into the large kitchen sink and then it all drained, by a hose connection, out of the building, into a larger plastic pipe and down to the edge of the harbour. Our honey bucket was lined with heavy plastic bags, which, when filled, were collected and hauled by the government truck to a dumping site. Our honey bucket wasn't public and was used mostly by the family and employees. Working for the government, even on contract, had unexpected and very welcome benefits. For example, our garbage was collected a couple of times each week, and I was able to store frozen food in the government freezer space.

Once I left Inuvik and Dell's wonderful washer and dryer, doing laundry became a major chore. In the five-twelve, there was an old wringer-style washer that required a lot of time and attention to use.

I heated water, washed the laundry, used the hand-operated wringer to wring out the soapy clothes, and emptied the soapy water. I then filled the tub with heated clean water again, rinsed the load of clothes in the washer, and fed the clothes by hand into the wringer yet again. I often used the soapy water to wash the floor and then used the rinse water to rinse the floor afterwards.

Managing diapers in the summer was so much easier, with open, ice-free water available. However, once freeze-up came, this diaper job became a permanent challenge, requiring scraping them before trying to rinse them in whatever used water I had available at the time. Although I now only had night diapers to care for, my goal was to have Lesley fully toilet trained as soon as possible after freeze-up. She would be two in December, so I hoped to have her out of diapers at night as soon as I could get her back into a bed of her own. Until then, it didn't seem fair to take the chance of her wetting the bed that she and David shared.

Washing, rinsing, drying, and folding diapers, clothes, and linens was a never-ending work-in-progress. I mostly dried clothes on racks, so the wet wash had to wait for a turn on these drying racks. I also strung a clothesline back and forth in our sleeping area, but it only worked until I needed to go to bed. Most drying happened at night once everyone had left the building. I set up the racks near the stoves and draped wet wash over the backs of chairs. In the morning, I rushed around to collect the dry clothes and linens before the men arrived and threw them on my top bunk until I had time to fold the laundry and put everything away.

Another ongoing challenge was baking. Our workers needed bread, buns, cakes, pies, cookies, desserts, and other bakery products, which made baking yet another major daily job. Preparing and baking was only one part of the work, since again, without hot running water, washing bowls, pots, and pans and trying to get dried dough and baked stuff off everything was a real chore. Eventually, when I had regular help each day, baking and making desserts, washing up, cleaning, and caring for the children became much easier.

Summer was the major shipping time for supplies for the settlement and the nearby DEW Line site. Supplies brought in during the summer needed to last until breakup at the beginning of the following summer, so boats and barges arrived almost daily during the busy summer season. Most of the cooks, who also worked as deckhands on the Northern Transportation boats, became a huge help when I asked for advice. Many worked as full-time cooks in southern cities during the boats' off-season, so they understood my challenges. Thanks to them, I was able to learn new skills and professional shortcuts, and especially how they managed when cooking in large quantities and on a tight schedule. For instance, I learned how to get breakfast down to an art, cooking bacon, sausage, and fried potatoes ahead and leaving them in covered pots on the back of the stove, to keep warm until needed. I could make toast and pancakes ahead as well but could only leave them for a shorter time in covered pots as they became soggy. Eventually, with much practice, I became so well organized that all I had to do was cook each man's breakfast eggs, to order.

Fortunately, the construction workers tended to arrive at different stages for breakfast, so I could deal with just a few men at a time. What I lacked in professional know-how, I tried to make up for by meeting individual needs or tastes, particularly with morning eggs. For all meals, I learned to precook everything that could be done ahead of time, so there wasn't so much work crammed into the last moments of getting food from the kitchen area to the tables. Preplanning and organization seemed to be an answer to being an efficient cook. Another very useful skill I learned was how to put leftover food to good use when I cooked too much of something. I often made extra to avoid any complaints about not getting enough to eat, and was pleased to learn that leftovers could be put into soups, spaghetti sauce, stews, and other multi-ingredient foods like casseroles.

Many of the cooks I met stopped by on each of their subsequent trips to Tuk to find out how I was doing. They shared recipes and taught me so much that made my life as a cook easier. Cooking for a family was very different from cooking in large quantities on a firm schedule. It was also very physical, with heavy lifting, long hours, and manual labour, so I felt blessed that these cooks took an interest and were willing to help me. Some of the boat crews would bring me much-cherished current reading materials. It didn't matter whether the magazines were about sports, cars, nature, or world news.

The following summer, boat crews continued to share leftover reading materials. I started to read Ian Fleming's novel *On Her Majesty's Secret Service*, which was serialized in *Playboy* magazines in spring 1963. I asked the boat crews to find the next issues of *Playboy* for me after I had read the first part. Once I was committed to reading the story, it became a challenge to find all the magazines to eventually finish it. At freeze-up, when the boats left for the season, there was quite a break before I eventually tracked down the issue with the final chapter of the James Bond saga from a PWA crew member travelling to Inuvik. Even Father Le Meur read each chapter of the Fleming story after I received it. I wasn't sure what he thought of the magazine, and I never asked.

A National Film Board crew arrived in Tuk to spend ten days filming a beluga whale hunt. They slept in tents but asked if I could feed them. Extra work wasn't really what I needed, so I quoted a high price, thinking they might choose to feed themselves. To my amazement they immediately accepted my price. I hired extra help and scheduled their meals forty-five minutes after the construction crew's. We began to feed other tourists and visitors to the settlement, and more and more, we served coffee or tea, cinnamon buns, slices of pie, cakes, and cookies to local people, who seemed to enjoy having a place to gather and visit. All these folks understood that when it was time to feed the construction crew, everyone had to immediately leave the cookhouse. During the four months, my days would become eighteen-hour marathons. The work became a true physical endurance test, with the added stress of worrying whether everyone would be satisfied with my menu. Nonetheless, we were making lots of money and the days disappeared in a haze of keeping my many balls in the air at once.

Even with the considerable demands on my time, I tried to make as much time for Lesley and David as I could. Lesley was a year and a half and a very beautiful, busy, active, and happy little person. Fortunately, she had a wonderful, sunny personality, she liked everybody, and was remarkably flexible in facing all the changes and all the people she met each day. Many of the construction workers were family men, so both she and David got plenty of attention.

The cookhouse was right next to the water's edge of Tuk harbour, and I had to be sure Lesley didn't wander out the door as people were coming and going. For her to be outside at all, I decided the safest solution was to make a baby harness out of cloth strips and tie her to the building on a length of rope that prevented her from reaching the water's edge. After her first day tied outside, a delegation of Inuit women came to see me. They were unhappy that I had tied up my child; only dogs should be tied. I explained my dilemma: I didn't have time to be outside with her; her brother was too young to be responsible for her; and the water's edge was so close to our building. This delegation proposed a most helpful solution, with great benefits both for me and for Lesley. Different women would stop by each day and take Lesley for a walk. It was no longer necessary to tie her because I knew that, at least once a day, someone would arrive and take her for a supervised walk about the settlement. Many days she would go on three or four walks with different women who wanted their chance to enjoy sharing time with her. This continued until freeze-up and soon there was no longer a doubt that she was truly the community's child. She seemed to enjoy her walks and all the people who were now a part of her bigger family. I did wonder what she might be eating on these adventures, but I knew she was cherished and well cared for.

David was only five, but I worried less about him near the water's edge because, although he was three when we had come north, he had learned to be competent at swimming a form of breaststroke and dog paddling combined, first while we were living in Nova Scotia and then in California. Other than the short wharf where planes unloaded passengers near us and the docks where barges unloaded, there wasn't a sudden drop-off at the water's edge. And the water was so cold that I didn't need to worry about David deciding he wanted to go swimming. He and all his friends were well warned to stay off any docks. None of the children and, as far as I knew, none of the adults in the community knew how to swim.

Each year adults and children were lost in drowning accidents, since travel by small boat was a major way to get from place to place, from spring breakup until freeze-up. No one wore life preservers, but the water was so cold that death from hypothermia was as likely as death from drowning when a boat was away from the shore. The days could be relatively warm in July and August when there wasn't any wind, but the water never got warmer than just above freezing, and the pack ice was never far from the harbour entrance during the brief summer. Thankfully, though, the cold breezes off the ocean kept mosquitoes and blackflies to a minimum, unlike what we had experienced while living in Inuvik. In addition, a mixture of sand and mud underfoot limited how much dirt was tracked into the cookhouse.

David made a place for himself with the boys of his age and soon became part of the community. Children rarely seemed to fight amongst themselves and happily included David in their games and activities. I was never aware of older children bullying younger ones or that David was bullied because he was different from the other boys. There was little money in the community and very few toys, so the children created their own games and play. David was appreciated because he was a new and rich source of games with his knowledge of different places, different games, and different ways of life. In turn, he learned much about Inuit life from playing with the other boys.

When David and I were in California, before coming north, we had stayed with friends on a horse ranch, where David learned from the other children to pretend to be a galloping and whinnying horse. He learned to change leads or make either one of his legs gallop ahead of the other, depending on the direction the pretend horse wanted to turn. It was fun for me to watch as David taught the other boys to gallop, to change leading legs, to whinny and blow out air from their noses as each of them pretended to be a horse, an animal these boys had never seen. He also taught them to hold the reins and pretend to ride. I expect his descriptions of riding on horses must have sounded like the storytelling by Elders to his friends.

This first summer in Tuk was when I first really became conscious that, compared with my upbringing, Inuit family life could be considered fairly unregulated, even disorganized. My life was regulated by mealtimes for the crew, but all around me, people went to bed when they were tired, ate when they were hungry, and fished and hunted when they needed to. In the nearly twenty-four-hour daylight, David's friends would be out kicking a soccer ball at midnight and then he had no one to play with in the morning, because they were still asleep. I tried to regulate David's life, within reason, because he needed to eat when I was cooking for the men, and I needed to be in bed and asleep as soon as I could after the evening coffee break was over and I could close the cookhouse. Once I had prepared for the breakfast meal and hung wet wash to dry, I was ready for bed. Morning, for me, always came so very soon.

David loved reindeer stew and bannock, so often he would eat at a friend's house when he felt hungry and then not want to eat at our mealtime. Sometimes we both had trouble finding a balance between my schedule, driven by my job, and the non-schedule of the other children. He reluctantly adapted mostly to my requirements even when I had to call him in for bed because I desperately needed to sleep. There was so much to do and so much to learn about being efficient in my cooking and baking while always maintaining a pre-set schedule. Time was money to the construction supervisor, so good and plentiful food, hot or cold as appropriate and on the table when the crew arrived, was his standard and had to be mine too. But even though I was working to my outer limits in Tuk, this didn't slow down George's endless ideas for yet more money-making schemes.

8

THE WORK OF SUCCESS

A month or so after I started the heavy work involved in our cooking contract, when I was wondering why a new cook had not yet been hired to bring an end to my cooking career, George stayed in Tuk overnight, to talk about our future. I quickly understood he was planning that my move to Tuk would be permanent. He shared with me his plan to establish another company, separate from Arctic Wings. The monies I had been making and would make, over the rest of the summer, were to be kept separate from Arctic Wings. He wanted to use this money to start a trading post and to buy and sell furs, sell supplies, continue the café, as well as establish a permanent agent for Arctic Wings in Tuk. Much to my astonishment, my expanded role would include all these new jobs: running a trading post, with the challenge of estimating what supplies to buy, along with learning how to operate as a fur trader.

The thought of what this meant shouldn't have been a surprise, for it seemed that George had already begun the steps necessary to establish the legally independent company. To help with cash flow for this new company, I would need to keep the café going in the future, since there was no competition in the community, and it was becoming a true money-maker beyond the revenue that came from feeding the construction crew. This new company was to be called Tuk Traders Ltd. Neither George's mother nor Al would have an interest in this new company. In addition, Tuk Traders would charge Arctic Wings, on paper at least, for providing flight-booking services.

Without question, George was a gifted person who saw opportunities where others didn't. He could be very persuasive when he had an idea to sell. He was a hard worker when he felt challenged to make an idea work, but he also seemed to lose interest once the challenge had been met. He expected me to work hard, but he didn't expect any less of himself. He put his great ingenuity and talents into getting things started and working. The major difficulty for me was recognizing that, although he was a great starter, once he had proved an idea worked, he lost interest and moved on to dream up a new project. He was very poor at the maintenance component of his ideas. He started things, but it was only with my effort and hard work that they became financially viable. However, at that time I still believed we were both committed to building a wonderful future for our family, so I was enthusiastically swept along with his plans and our new life in Tuk.

George also informed me we should move the house we had bought in the government disposal auction from Aklavik to Tuk. Originally, we had planned to set it up in Inuvik as a permanent home for us there. It had been sitting on a sled in Aklavik, waiting to be moved to Inuvik. Instead, he would arrange to load the house on a barge and send it down the river, across the short run in the Beaufort Sea, and into the Tuk harbour. Clearly, George was planning for the family to stay and make a permanent home in Tuk, running our businesses from there, while Al and Alice ran Arctic Wings in Aklavik. George would run the Inuvik office and live in the hangar apartment until the time he could hire another pilot to take over the Inuvik site. Then, he said, he too would move to Tuk, to fly from there and to help run Tuk Traders. He had identified a vacant storage building in Tuk we could buy to convert into a trading post and restaurant. He planned to set up our barged house next to that building.

As George shared these plans with me, his words constituted a forceful explanation of why a new cook had not been hired and why I had been left to make the government contract work successfully. Here was yet another indication of how unpredictable my life would continue to be. But I did give myself credit for my success in catering for the construction crew (and George knew of my success), which in turn boosted my belief in my personal value and abilities. This helped give me the confidence I could also be successful with this new challenge.

It was an ideal time to launch Tuk Traders. Changes in Aklavik and the completion of the DEW Line meant a range of used and useful equipment and many related supplies were available for sale at a fraction of their original cost—sometimes even for only the cost of transportation to Tuk. In the end, we were able to set up and equip the coffee shop, store, and a small generating plant at minimal cost. The timing of the new venture was excellent, because it was summer and barges were running from the south and between settlements, giving us the cheapest way of moving things during the brief window of open water. George used every opportunity available to transport what we needed, including flights when he was returning empty or had a light load and could move equipment by air. It took great effort, time, and lots of ingenuity to move some equipment from where it was located to our Tuk location, all before freeze-up came again. George was gifted when it came to this type of planning. If we had had to pay the real cost of what we needed, it would have been prohibitive, both in its actual cost but also in the time required to ship supplies from southern Canada. Just as we benefited from the availability of equipment, we also benefited from available labour. We could offer worthwhile employment to experienced local men who were looking for work since their earlier construction jobs had come to an end.

All these ideas had a significant impact on my life. I now faced an even greater variety of demands on my time and even greater tests of my abilities. A pressing issue was the critical decision about what supplies and how much of them we would need to equip trappers, run a trading post and a café, and supply our own family needs until the barges ran again next summer. These supplies—sufficient for ten months—had to be ordered, shipped, and received by barge before freeze-up came to Tuk. I now switched to spending countless hours making lists and talking to people about what supplies they used in trapping camps; I even learned to question them about the brand names they preferred, in both food and equipment. I became an instant expert on things like the type of guns commonly used and the amount of ammunition a person needed for a winter of trapping and hunting.

Trying to understand people's food and equipment needs began to paint interesting pictures of the long-time trapper's lifestyle in the bush as well as needs of a family in the settlement. I was amazed at the consistency between one woman's list for basic food supplies and another woman's list. The men were just as consistent about their traps and other essential equipment. From all these attempts to make my lists and later in buying fur, I would learn Inuvialuktun words for some common items and animals. However, the language was so phonetically different from English and since words weren't written anywhere, I didn't have the opportunity to combine seeing the written words with hearing them spoken. I struggled, but David learned many words from the other boys much more easily than I did, and he didn't seem to get his tongue in a knot with the pronunciations. Fortunately for me, almost everyone, except for some Elders, had a working knowledge of English.

I remembered hearing, as a teen in school, that Inuit had fifty different words for snow. One day, when a group of men were sitting around the café, I asked how many words for snow they could think of. It became a game as we started to count. There were words I had expected, like words for soft snow, deep snow, fresh snow, falling snow, and drifting snow, but then we went on to the unexpected: snow seen in a dream, snow that is cursed, snow remembered from the past, snow marked (peed on) by man and by animal. We didn't quite reach fifty words, but the fun and laughter became more important than the number of words we counted.

After determining food and equipment needs, the next challenge was to try to estimate, reasonably accurately, how many people we might supply in the first year of trading and what we might want to sell in a store. Added to that was the need to include the café's food needs along with our own personal food requirements and preferences. Any mistakes would have serious consequences for our business as well as for our customers. All of this estimating was a huge task, especially combined with my other commitments to cooking and child care. As the summer passed, everyone felt the increased pressure brought on by the impending freeze-up. The construction crew too was pressured to finish the school on deadline (for the fall), because there was a bonus system for early and on-time completion. Hours of work lengthened for all of us as the weather began to get colder, and time seem to be running out before the snows and freeze-up came. I tried to be as creative as I could about the food served because tempers became short, and the men wanted to get finished and go home. The wind off the water increased, it snowed occasionally, and the men found it harder to work in the colder conditions, particularly outside.

Another very unwelcome issue came to the fore when the dropping temperatures at night started to interfere with the five-twelve's water system. Water stopped running into the building as the water in the tank and the lines began to freeze. I now had to heat the water tank with a blow pot each morning to keep the water running. A blow pot was similar to a blowtorch but was wider at the top, to give more breadth to the range of heat produced. It was used to heat an aircraft engine in the extreme cold so the warmed engine oil would circulate when the engine was started. Besides the water tank and freshwater line starting to freeze, the grey-water line had ice forming along its length. That required me to take off the short piece of hose that ran from the sink in the cookhouse to the outside pipe that carried grey water to the harbour, replacing it with an unfrozen line. Draining the one I had taken off left me with a replacement hose for the following morning. It was going to be a close race as to whether we were going to have to start melting ice in barrels before the catering contract was done and the men left.

The thought of moving into my own house, which was to happen once the catering contract was over, became a very exciting prospect. The house had three small bedrooms, a living room, kitchen, eating area, and bathroom. George had had a permanent sled built under the house in Aklavik and the pilings it sat on had been cut away. It had been skidded to the water's edge earlier and now was loaded on a barge to begin its lengthy voyage down the Mackenzie, out to the Beaufort Sea, and east into Tuk harbour. We borrowed a big Cat bulldozer and operator from the DEW Line station, levelled the site, and skidded the house from the barge up the bank, and onto our prepared site. The house was then levelled, still on its sled, and the sled was left in place to create air circulation under the house. Once entry steps were built, the oil tank set up and filled, the generator shed built, and electricity connected, the house was ready for us to occupy, as soon as I could leave the five-twelve and my non-stop catering responsibilities.

I was thrilled with the new space, the privacy, and all the things having a house of our own would offer my family. Earlier we had bought furniture at government auctions and suddenly I was going to have a home again. I looked forward to not having to share it with Arctic Wings passengers or indeed with anyone else, unless they were invited to come in. Passengers could wait in the restaurant, and

I no longer had to bake cookies and make coffee for them. I finally would have a home that was warm, clean, and offered everybody in the family both space and privacy.

Once the construction crew left, my catering contract job came to a welcome end. As I shut the door of the five-twelve, I felt great relief that my commitment to the contract was over and I was free of so many demands on my time and life. Yet that relief was tempered by a fear-filled realization that I was now on my own. I turned the key in the lock and with that click of the bolt, my relationship with the government ended. No longer did the government administrator have any interest in my success or in providing help with water and oil delivery, or picking up my garbage and honey bags. I no longer had the use of such perks as the government freezer and other storage space. With relief of being finished came the uneasy feeling that somehow a security blanket had been lost. After all, my future success in private enterprise and in competition with the Hudson's Bay was a non-issue for the government agent. As I walked back to the house, doubt flooded in. Could I manage what was ahead? Would I be able to meet others' expectations and, most importantly, would the children be happy?

As I approached our newly set-up house, the excitement of what the house would mean to the family helped push some of my doubts into the background. In reality, there was no time to doubt, to pause, or to recover from the exhausting months of work. I immediately started on the very demanding task of learning the many aspects of operating the new trading post and café. Yet again, I plunged headfirst into a job for which I had neither training nor experience. I reminded myself that, with a lot of hard work, I had made a success of the catering job, which reinforced my belief and confidence I could master these new responsibilities.

A Northern Transportation cook, who would normally have left at the end of the summer, had a girlfriend in Tuk and wanted to stay, so he was hired as cook and to run the café. This transformed my job: I became store manager, fur buyer, decision-maker, and book-keeper for trappers' transactions. And I still had the job of booking flights for Arctic Wings, overseeing the café, and caring for the children. I had struggled to learn and keep up with everything that needed to be done over the summer, but now I had to learn a whole new set of skills. Starting with an empty building and creating a café and store would be a challenge, but learning how to be a trader and fur buyer was truly foreign to any of my life experiences. A real plus for me now was to have more control of my time, since I was no longer driven, seven days a week, by crew mealtimes. I quickly realized what a huge amount of work was on my plate. However, I celebrated as we moved into the house and settled the family. My immediate challenge was the construction of the interior shelves in the store before unpacking mountains of supplies, filling the shelves, and sorting and finding storage for things not immediately needed. I also had to establish heated storage areas for certain supplies that should not freeze. Overseeing the work needed to set up the café was yet another priority.

While I was experiencing all these changes and challenges, I began to have trouble keeping food down. I immediately recognized morning sickness and the signs of another pregnancy. I was upset over the thought of another baby and felt I already had less time for the children than I wanted. Thinking of the impact on our lives of another baby also came at a time when I was hearing tales about George's life in Inuvik that left me once again questioning his commitment to me, to our relationship, and to our family. I knew George believed I was essential to running the businesses, but he seemed even less personally involved with me and with the children, and he was spending less and less time in Tuk. As winter set in, I heard more comments about George when people returned from Inuvik. Not everyone in the community considered fidelity an important issue, so sharing what they heard about George's involvement with other women wasn't necessarily seen as being hurtful to me; they were just sharing interesting gossip. This emphasized one significant cultural difference between where I lived now and the behaviour I knew and expected from "outside."

When I asked George about the stories I was hearing, he denied everything, saying that others were jealous of our success and some people were just intent on causing trouble. I wanted to believe him, but it was hard to ignore what I was feeling, and past experience simply couldn't be discounted. His previous behaviour made it much harder to believe his denials. Trust and honesty had always been fundamental to how I wanted to live my life, particularly both trust and honesty within the family. If I accepted that I couldn't trust George or if I didn't believe what he was saying, then I was left with the question of how I could continue to commit to our marriage. An even more troubling question was, what was I going to do about my lack of trust? I saw no reason for people sharing stories that were untrue, but my unplanned pregnancy was pushing me towards wanting to stop questioning George's commitment to me and our family.

My joy over moving into the house was significantly dampened by both my unwanted pregnancy and questions about George's fidelity and truthfulness. I had two wonderful, healthy, and bright children—a boy and a girl. I didn't see how another baby would do anything to improve my life or improve my relationship with or trust in George. In fact, George's response, when he heard I believed I was pregnant, illustrated the deterioration of our relationship. He freely voiced his frustration over what it would mean to his plans for Tuk Traders and to our future to have me tied to the care of another infant. Both of us considered this an unwanted pregnancy, but any distress I felt over our marriage and any personal unhappiness I felt over being pregnant had to be balanced with other feelings. Although I believed every woman should be free to make her own decision or choice, I was not prepared, myself, to abort a healthy fetus. I saw no acceptable alternative other than to focus my thoughts on how to make the arrival of a new baby fit into whatever our future in Tuk would be.

To add to my difficulties during this uncertain time, David's best friend was killed while playing cowboys and Indians with David and his friends. This boy, whose English name was Larry, was shot and killed by his younger brother, who had picked up a loaded twenty-two rifle from his house to join in the game the older boys were playing with their stick guns. He pointed the gun, pulled the trigger, and instantly killed his brother. The whole community went into mourning over the death of one of their children. The boy's death was seen as a tragedy and an accident, but nobody was blamed. David was very confused by what had happened, possibly afraid, and very sad. He became quiet and withdrawn and I would find him off by himself, but I was unable to get him to tell me what he was thinking and feeling. I expect he didn't really understand what death was and couldn't find the words to talk about it or about how someone could be alive and then dead, particularly a child of his own age.

I talked with Father Le Meur, and with his advice, I decided David should be encouraged to be involved in all aspects of the community's grieving process. We both thought it would help David understand what had happened, and its meaning, if he shared in everyone's grief and pain, and later was also part of how the community healed together. He spent a lot of quiet time with his friend's parents and brother; he participated in the grave digging as all the community's men and boys came together to contribute to chipping away the permafrost, an essential step in creating a grave; he attended the funeral service and procession and took part when the men filled in the grave. With other children, he also gathered as many stones as they could find and pry loose from the frozen ground to pile on the grave. He had Father Le Meur's help and support as he joined with the rest of the children, struggling to understand and accept their loss. It was also an important time for

Lesley, David, and me, as we spent quiet time sitting on the chester-field and holding each other. Years later, I would realize how much this time of sharing grief would help to create a lifelong special rela-tionship between the three of us.

Life soon returned to its usual busy ways and David returned to play with the other boys, but periodically I would see him, sitting quietly by himself, lost in his own thoughts. David was never openly expressive of his feelings, so I was left wondering what he was thinking and what else I might do to help him. Sitting close together and good night kisses seemed to take on new meaning for all of us. Lesley was too young to really understand what was going on, but she knew David was sad, so she hugged him a lot.

During the interviews dealing with the shooting accident, I became much better acquainted with Jim Raddi, the RCMP special constable in Tuk. I had been a friend of his wife, Marjorie, and their daughters, Marlene and Evelyn, since first coming to Tuk. Jim was part of local policing, supported by visits of regular RCMP members to the community. Marjorie was an excellent baker, and she had worked for me when I was feeding the construction crew. Marlene, who was a few years older than David, and Evelyn, who was about his age, were regular visitors to the cookhouse. When the girls came to work with Marjorie, they helped care for Lesley and played with David. Jim and Marjorie were examples of Inuit who were more easily moving from their people's past ways into the newer ways and culture of white Canadians. Was that a good thing? I didn't know, but Jim's job gave their family the advantage of being able to count on a regular wage.

Years later, when we lived temporarily in Bellingham, Washington, a teenage Marlene came to live with us for about a year. Her mother left the North and her first husband, Jim, for life in Seattle with a new white husband, whom she had met while he was working in Tuk. Marlene and Evelyn came with their mother and soon after, Marjorie would lose custody of Marlene over issues within the family. We were asked, by the local child protection authority, to take custody of Marlene on a temporary basis while decisions were made about sending her back north.

Bureaucratic red tape between Canada and the United States delayed any decisions, and after Marlene had lived with us for a year, Marjorie left her second husband and was then able to regain custody, and Marlene was returned to her mother in Seattle. My children found this difficult since Marlene had become part of our family, but we needed to be happy for her. While Marlene lived with us, David would learn of racial prejudice—prejudice he had never experienced in the North. Marlene was a beautiful girl with dark hair and dark skin. She faced prejudice at school and in the community, both in Washington State and later when we moved back to Canada, before she was returned to her mother. David tried to defend her at school and wherever he could, but he was greatly confused by others' attitudes and actions towards her. To David, she was a loving big sister, but others saw only a dark-skinned girl who was something other than white.

When David had lived in Tuk, he had been the only white child old enough to be out in the community, and later he was the only white child attending school. However, he was living in a community of generous, caring people. When it was time for school, he started with much broader learning experiences, advanced reading and language skills, and was much better prepared to learn than his classmates. He was often asked to act as the teacher's assistant and help others learn. He was noticeably different from his schoolmates in so many ways, and he understood that his mother and many aspects of our lifestyle were different too, but he was never teased, bullied, or made less welcome in the school or in the community because of those differences. He had never associated being different with being better or worse; he just accepted that people were different. Now, because of others' intolerance, I had conversations with Marlene and David about some people's ignorance and their unwillingness to accept and value the differences they found in others.

———

WHILE WE WERE STILL IN TUK, DAVID WAS OFFERED A PUPPY BY Father Le Meur, giving him something to love and be responsible for. We talked about the dog I had when I was young called Rusty, so David decided to call his beige and red-brown puppy Rusty too. Like all the dogs in the community, Rusty lived outdoors. We got a big truck tire and made him a bed inside it, under the edge of the house, away from the wind and snow. He wore a harness and was chained to the tire. I know people in southern Canada would criticize us for tying him, but erecting fencing in the permafrost was impossible, and tying him kept him at home and protected from wandering into dog lines, where he was likely to be killed. We lived in a place where sled dogs were work animals. Some were treated harshly, and many were not friendly to either people or other dogs.

Rusty and David shared love and great fun together. When Rusty was big enough, we had a small sled and harness made for him and, with the help of an older boy, Rusty learned to pull David as he stood up or sat on the back of the sled. For David, it was like having a bicycle to ride. However, unlike riding a bike, I didn't need to worry about cars or David falling off and breaking something. The only real danger I worried about was David suffering frostbite on parts of his face. In our last spring in Tuk, unfortunately someone took notice of Rusty, who was by then a big, strong, friendly dog. Sometime during one night, while we were asleep, Rusty was unchained and stolen. I felt very sad for David's loss of his friend, but I also felt sorry for Rusty, who had lived a good and gentle life with David. Rusty would now be fated to become a working dog, part of a dog team, and would live on a dog chain line, where gentleness was very unlikely. David and his friends checked every dog line in Tuk and then any teams that came into Tuk, but they never found Rusty.

As the flying hours shortened in late 1962, George decided not to hire another pilot until the spring. He also decided he would continue to split his time between Tuk and Inuvik and overnight in Tuk whenever he could, in order to help me. In reality, this would not happen often, although he assured me he wanted to spend more time with me and the children. He seemed to come and go in our lives, usually being around only long enough to find something else for me to do.

In fairness to him, with the prospects of another winter of flying ahead, George needed to cope with many challenges. Keeping track of where you were when flying over this vast land was one of them. Not getting lost required becoming an excellent observer of subtle differences in the landscape and remembering any unique land or water clues, particularly when flying into the more obscure and difficult-to-find research areas or prospecting, hunting, fishing, and trapping camps. It was so easy to get lost in this great expanse, since each area could look so similar from the air. In the winter, one could easily get caught in whiteouts, when what was up and what was down was no longer very clear. A pilot risked becoming disoriented by the whiteness and shapelessness of everything when it was covered with snow.

One of George's favourite trips lacked the safety component of a visible Mackenzie River. This journey took him to Sachs Harbour, located on the western tip of Banks Island. At any time of the year, it was a most challenging flight, whether in winter's limited daylight hours—with the cold, wind, sudden blowing snow, and storms—or in the summer, with the long distance over open water and the possibility of moving pack ice or small icebergs complicating a landing on floats. George enjoyed the flying challenge of this jour-ney, along with the opportunity to visit the Inuk trapper and trader Fred Carpenter. Fred was always happy to spend time with George, sharing his stories of the island's history and his family's life there. In 1930, Fred had built a permanent cabin at the harbour. Other trappers and their families joined him and a settlement began. Fred eventually established his own small trading post. No doubt the settlement at Sachs Harbour and the presence of people living on Banks Island were important to the Canadian government and its sovereignty issues over the waterways in the Beaufort Sea and the Arctic Ocean. Establishment of an RCMP post and weather station would further focus on Canada's interests and claims.

A sense of isolation is clearly seen in this view of the tiny settlement of Sachs Harbour. On the left is Fred Carpenter's house and trading post, with the RCMP post and weather station visible on the right. © *NWT Archives / Robert C. Knights / N-1993-002-0138*

Banks Island was rich in arctic fox, polar bear, and muskox, and the isolation created a close and traditional lifestyle for the people living there. In many ways, time seemed to have stopped or at least slowed down on the island. However, as always, change came with a downside for people's lives, as the settlement's children were forced to leave home to attend residential school in Inuvik. Fred believed in the need for his children to be educated and several of his children would gain advanced degrees in the South. But his family would pay a high personal price for this commitment to educating their children, as those same children were away from home ten months of the year, being taught that white ways—including language, culture, clothes, and food—were best and were what they should aspire to for themselves.

9

TRADER TO PENNY HOARDER

The decision that I should live permanently in Tuk, oversee the café, and run the trading post, along with acting as an agent for Arctic Wings, left me so busy that I became isolated from the few other white people in the community, except for Father Le Meur. My social life centred mostly on the trading post and café, and sometimes I felt lonely and missed socializing with women who shared with me experiences of life outside the North. It was a reminder of how much I had valued my coffee times with Dell and how much I missed that friendship.

The man hired to run the café turned out to be a rather useless person who restricted his efforts to operating the café and spending time with his Inuit girlfriend, not necessarily in that order. I was left to solve most other maintenance issues, like warming up sluggish outside oil lines in the bitter cold. To do this, I had to use an aircraft blow pot, an oversize blowtorch that made lots of scary noises and was awkward to lift. The generator we used to augment the irregular town electrical service often needed to be encouraged to start in the very cold weather, which was, of course, when it was most needed. As I cranked and cranked, it seemed to be saying, "You have to be kidding." I would crank, crank, swear, and crank some more until it would finally kick over and start, with the welcome sounds first of sputtering and then chug-a-lugging, followed by a steady, smooth idling sound indicating a willingness to run.

After freeze-up, setting up our water supply involved getting large blocks of ice weighing 35 to 50 pounds (15 to 20 kilograms), cut to fit into a drum, from a nearby freshwater lake and hauling them by tractor or dogsled to the house. Forty-five-gallon drums supported an elevated platform where the ice was stored nearby. Keeping the ice elevated was essential to prevent any loose dogs from lifting a leg and peeing on what was actually our clean potable water supply.

Much work and many hands were needed to supply everyone with safe clean water. The job involved cleaning the covering of snow from the ice and sawing it into blocks, which were then hauled to town as needed through the winter months. © *NWT Archives / Emily Stillwell / N-2005-006-0077-0*

Ice blocks had to be stored off the ground to avoid contamination, until they were brought indoors to melt. © *NWT Archives / Robert C. Knights / N-1993-002-0085*

I was able to hire men to bring ice from the lake and load it on the platform, but the blocks still needed to be regularly hauled into the house and café. After freeze-up, melted ice blocks were our only source of water. Once the water was used, it was then hauled back out as grey water or in our honey bags. I was told honey bags were so named because in the clear plastic bags, the urine looked like liquid honey. Although I used the term, I wasn't even trying to appreciate the comparison.

Northern life would have been extraordinarily difficult without the forty-five-gallon drum (capacity about 200 litres). When these drums came north, they contained various kinds of gas or oil. Once emptied, they were cleaned and then put to use for a huge assortment of functions. In the long run, I believe northerners valued these drums far more than their original contents.

Since water was a key element in our lives, clean forty-five-gallon water barrels were essential. Cleaning the barrels was quite a feat, especially when I was pregnant. The barrels stood at about my waist height and needed to be scrubbed out with bleach water about once a week. The ice usually contained a bit of plant life, as well as algae and bacteria embedded in it when the lake froze over. Residue collected in the bottom of the barrels, so it had to be dumped out when the barrel was almost empty. Left too long, without cleaning and near the heat of the stove, the barrels would develop a growth of something unpleasant. Barrel cleaning usually coincided with wash-day, since I often used up my entire supply of melted water doing the wash. I tipped the barrel and bent into it far enough to reach the inside bottom with a rag. As I had learned in the Quonset hut, years before when pregnant, I needed to use a cloth wrapped around a broom to reach the bottom.

Now that we were supplying trappers, I had to quickly learn about fur and the methods of harvesting, skinning, drying, curing, and grading the furs the trappers brought to me. The morality of harvesting animals for their fur was being debated in southern Canada, but in the North, hunting and trapping fur animals was an unquestioned necessity for survival. Food, clothing, bedding, leather, art and spiritual works, toys, games, household items, and other practical equipment such as dog harnesses or parts of the sleds all came from these animals, while selling some of the furs gave families money to buy whatever necessities they could not produce from the land.

Charlie Gruben and Eddie Gruben, two leaders in the community, became my main sources of learning and help. They taught me the nuances of fur quality and the different ways to treat pelts. Given the wide variety of furs I would be dealing with, I hired them to help me do the earliest fur grading. At the same time, they taught me the skills I needed to grade the furs myself. I found that other trappers did not argue with the Grubens' grading standard and the subsequent prices we paid. I was told a different story about arguments with the Hudson's Bay Company manager. I soon heard that problem pelts were now being taken to the Bay manager because trappers knew they wouldn't get past Eddie's or Charlie's scrutiny.

Arctic fox pelts drying on a clothesline. When I started grading fur, it took me a while to learn how to examine each one carefully enough to identify its quality and pinpoint any flaws. © *NWT Archives / Robert C. Knights / N-1993-002-0265*

At times, as I graded muskrat, I would have between a hundred and five hundred greasy-feeling muskrat pelts on the kitchen floor as I sorted them into grading piles. The muskrat fur was pulled off the drowned muskrat in a whole piece, leaving the fur inside and the skin outside. I learned to grade the quality of muskrat skin as well as the level of care taken pulling the pelt off the animal, stretching it, and drying it. Value in the actual fur of the muskrat did not vary much, so in grading these pelts, I was looking for size of the pelt as well as skins without cuts or tears. I could hardly wait to finish grading these pelts, after which I could stuff the skins into burlap bags and stitch the bags closed. Once grading and bagging was finished, I immediately washed down the floor and cupboard fronts with hot soapy water before the children were allowed to play there again.

Other furs were more pleasant to deal with and easier to grade because they were presented opened and flat, with the fur side out. Here I was more concerned with the quality of the fur itself. If not cleaned well, seal hides could feel greasy on their skin side too, but they were cut down the belly and could be valued from the fur side. I did most of the fur buying in the house, where we had privacy to wheel and deal and settle accounts. The fur market and fur prices were very volatile, so I needed to constantly keep up with the latest market prices. When trappers who had sold furs to the Bay came into the café for coffee, I checked with them about the prices they had been given. The most important thing was for me to get the pelts graded right, keep the price paid competitive, and remain aware of current outside market prices.

In those days, my price research could only be done by mail or news radioed me from George. I bought all types of fur, including polar bear, muskrat, white fox, red fox, wolverine, ermine, seal, and occasionally wolf. If I paid too much, we could lose money, but at the same time, I had to be competitive with the prices paid by the Hudson's Bay Company to even have the chance to buy the furs. The endless balancing act—the price I paid for the fur compared with the price eventually paid to Tuk Traders—was volatile, to say the least. My timing in becoming a fur trader was certainly less than ideal, as the fur market was losing all of its past stability. I was lucky to have the Grubens' help as I learned from them the subtleties of different furs, the differences in how the pelts were handled, and the importance of grading each fur pelt with great care.

Another hunter I came to know was Jim Wolki. He and his family lived on their schooner and trapped and hunted along the coast. He was our main source of polar bear hides just before the prohibition on harvesting them went into effect. Jim's family still chose to live in traditional ways and only came to the settlement to sell fur or buy supplies. As a result, some of their children were required to attend school and live in the Catholic residential hostel in Inuvik during the school year, so they paid a high price for their decision to remain independent and self-sufficient. Jim talked with me about his family's disruption, particularly when his children were sent to the residential school. He questioned the need for his children to learn about another people's world when they really needed to learn to survive in the world they lived in. He was unwilling to accept that, in the future, his children's world was going to be different from what he had always known. Jim had spent years sailing his schooner along the coast from Herschel Island and Single Point west of Tuk to the various "stopping places" east along the coastline, to Stanton and Anderson River and north to Holman and on to sites on Banks Island. He and his family faced the changing ice pack, freezing rain, snow, wind, and unpredictable storms, all to be able to survive and be self-sufficient.

I felt a true sadness when talking to Jim, knowing that change was going to be unstoppable. I worried for his family, but I felt blessed to have the opportunity to learn about the lifestyle he was trying to maintain and protect. I bought any polar bear and seal hides he brought in, and I was able to buy a beautiful pair of polar bear mitts, which were made for me by his wife, Bessie. These would keep my hands amazingly warm for the rest of my years in the North. By the next winter, Jim would face the government's permanent prohibition on harvesting polar bear, and later the total collapse of the fur industry.

Over the many years of harvesting furs, as proven by research studies, the reproductive rates of the different types of fur-bearing animals seemed to adjust to the numbers harvested, and thus the natural balance was maintained. However, this didn't apply to the polar bear, whose numbers continued to drop, resulting in the total ban on harvesting and, ultimately, protected status. Once the fur market collapsed, muskrats and other fur-bearing animals were slow to adjust their reproductive rate, which resulted in these animals overpopulating many areas. This overabundance was followed by a die-off from disease until a natural balance was re-established.

Polar bear mitts made for me by Bessie Wolki demonstrate the artistry and skill of Inuit women in creating beautiful and functional northern clothing. The colourful yarn at the top is the harness.

Even when I gained more experience and confidence in grading fur, whenever I faced some uncertainty, I still called on Charlie or Eddie for their help. As a result, I gained a reputation for being fair in my grading and in the prices I paid. Over the winter, we began to significantly cut into the Bay's fur buying. Paying for the pelts was only one part of the package though, since as a trader, I advanced supplies for the trappers to take out to trapping areas and for families remaining in Tuk, made arrangements for flights to and from their camps, flew supplies in and furs out as necessary, and received payment when the trappers returned. To be most profitable, I needed to complete the cycle—furnishing supplies, scheduling flights, and buying furs. We had an advantage over the Bay, since we could offer the complete package by advancing the supplies, charging the cost of flights, and receiving payment for all when the pelts were sold.

The Hudson's Bay could not include transportation costs unless they advanced money or had an account with the charter companies, which they rarely did. The trapper might be able to convince an operator to take them on credit, until they returned with furs and sold them. Arctic Wings offered some credit to the better trappers before Tuk Traders began, but now the debit for supplies, equipment, and flights was a debit to Tuk Traders and we ran an account with Arctic Wings. We also had the advantage of "back loading" furs on our planes whenever a plane was returning to Inuvik without a full load. This saved us money in getting furs to Inuvik for quick shipment outside, a vital advantage given the perpetual volatility of fur prices. We also took advantage of PWA flights, since little freight was shipped out of Inuvik to Edmonton.

No written or legal contract required trappers to sell their furs to us, as long as they paid what was owing when the furs were sold. It may have sounded like a pretty loose financial arrangement, but this was a small community, where everybody knew everyone else's business. Also, a trapper needed to be concerned about getting to his fishing and hunting camps in the summer as well as being able to get supplied and flown to trapping camps the following year, so very few trappers failed to pay. Nobody gave credit to a trapper with a reputation for unreliable payment.

WHEN WE MOVED INTO THE HOUSE, VIOLET AND ROY KIKUAK, AN older couple, became our new neighbours. Roy was in poor health and had difficulty walking. Violet took care of him as well as everything else in their lives, including managing a fishnet in front of her house, when the harbour was ice free. They still had a couple of sled dogs, so she rowed out daily, in a small boat, to check her net to have fish for themselves as well as to feed the dogs. One day I asked Violet if she would sell me a whitefish for our dinner. She was pleased with the thought of the dollar I offered her, as their source of money was very limited. She told me to send David to see her whenever I wanted a fish.

A few days later, I sent David, with the requisite dollar, and watched out the window as Violet, a rotund yet spry sixty-five- to seventy-year-old, dressed in a Mother Hubbard parka and gumboots, waddled down to the water's edge and climbed into her small boat. She pushed off with her paddle and began to pull herself down her net line, stopping to pull up sections of net. She would untangle a fish, look at it, and throw it in the boat behind her. She repeated this until she found the fish she wanted; she then rowed ashore and cleaned the fish. Her hands seemed to fly with her circular ulu knife as she cleaned and scaled the fish with precise movements that had to come from many years' practice. Soon she was trying to help David figure out how he was going to carry the cleaned fish home. The fish was so big that David had to struggle to keep it from dragging along the ground, so I rushed out to help him. Our fish dinner was special, so good, as only very fresh fish taken from very cold water can taste.

The next time I saw Violet, I told her how much we had enjoyed the fish and asked her why she had rejected a number of fish before she found the one she wanted. She told me, with great pride, that she would never sell me a fish that had drowned in the net. She fed those to the dogs. I had now learned something else, and as long as the harbour was ice free, giving Violet access to her fishnet, we continued to enjoy a regular supply of fresh fish.

Cutting and drying muktuk and extracting whale oil was an enterprise that involved the whole community. © *NWT Archives / Native Communications Society / N-2018-010:02964*

When the Beaufort Sea was ice free, it was impressive to watch as beluga whales were harpooned or shot and brought ashore. The community women, with their extraordinary skill with ulu knives, quickly cut the whale meat into usable pieces until there was just a skeleton left. I tried to appreciate the taste of whale meat or muktuk, but I concluded that this food was an acquired taste, probably from birth. When dipped in rancid seal oil, muktuk became even more of a challenge for me to eat. It wasn't just my taste buds that were in total opposition, but also my nose. My lack of interest in eating muktuk became something others teased me about, but fortunately no one seemed to think less of me. My reluctance was just something to laugh over. I had never enjoyed any raw meat or fish, including never developing a taste for sushi or raw oysters, when I lived on the outside.

I also didn't enjoy eating either seal or muskrat: I found them too greasy and never relished the flavours or texture. Now we were living so far north, I asked George to pick up some ptarmigan and arctic hare from the women I knew out in camps, whenever he could. I also ordered reindeer meat from Reindeer Station for our family. I had always loved my grandmother's steak and kidney pies, so one day I asked one of the herders if I could get reindeer kidney. He seemed a bit startled and said that the kidneys were a very special favourite of the herders, and they usually didn't sell them, but he would make an exception for me. After that I very occasionally talked the herders out of a few kidneys so we could enjoy a tasty reindeer steak and kidney pie.

Periodically, when some of the herders came into the café, I had the chance to talk to them about their lives following their herds, so I could begin to understand both the good and not-so-good part of this lifestyle. Prior to World War II, the federal government had attempted to address the lack of employment opportunities in the North. One solution involved copying Alaska's idea of reindeer herding, thought to be a way for some Inuit families to be self-employed. A location north of what was later to become the town of Inuvik, on the east branch of the Mackenzie River, was selected for the government's experiment in Canadian reindeer herding. Reindeer Station —a small settlement with herder houses, a manager's house, corrals, an ice house, and drying racks—was established near where the treeline ended and the vast lichen-covered tundra began. This location also had the the major benefit of being close to the natural migration route for herds of caribou.

In 1929, the Canadian government contracted American "reindeer king" Carl J. Lomen to herd three thousand reindeer from Alaska to Reindeer Station. After the fact, the question arose as to whether these animals were reindeer or caribou, since a good percentage of them appeared to be caribou. This raised the further question as to why the Canadian government would buy caribou when they had so many of their own. It was suggested these purchased reindeer (or caribou) were selected because they had already been trained to be herded.

Following or herding reindeer was a challenge particularly in the summer, when canoes had to be hauled so the herders could cross rivers with the herd. © *NWT Archives / NWT Department of Information / G-1979-023:1769*

Lapland herders were brought to the Northwest Territories to teach the prospective Inuit herders about this new lifestyle. A large component of this training involved helping them understand and accept what herding would mean to their life: they and their families were expected to follow their grazing herds in the extraordinary cold of winter and across the water-filled tundra, which swarmed with mosquitoes in the summer. Genetically the reindeer and the caribou were very similar, so continued interbreeding was part of the plan, and it was anticipated that these crossbreeds would become tamer, becoming more reindeer-like and therefore more easily herded.

In 1964, the last Inuit-owned herd at Reindeer Station was returned to the government. The attempt to turn trappers and hunters into herders had failed. Herding was described to me, by one of the herders, as really boring because they needed to follow their reindeer around all year and from year to year. He went on to tell me how free caribou went anywhere they wanted, took care of themselves, and you could shoot one when you needed food. At times, during the caribou migration, keeping the wandering reindeer herd and the wild caribou separate was very difficult for the herders. Family life also became more complicated because of the need for families to continually follow the reindeer herd, resulting in the need for children to leave their families and go to residential schools. Herders lost interest in the lifestyle, and the herds were returned to the government to become the responsibility of the Canadian Wildlife Service. Eventually those that remained were turned over to a private contractor to see if they could make reindeer herding viable. This attempt also failed, so in the end the reindeer project was abandoned altogether. The animals were left to run wild as caribou again, and Reindeer Station was mostly abandoned.

Just before Christmas in 1962, Lesley turned two. She was a walking, talking, busy little person who had left babyhood behind her so very early. Soon after we moved into the house, she was beyond the need for her night diaper and I rejoiced over being diaper free again, but I also knew, in the late spring, I would need to start all over again with the new baby's diapers. Diapers would always be a real challenge for me in a world without running water and flush toilets in which to rinse them. I now put my diaper scraper away until the arrival of the next baby, and our useable washing water went towards washing floors instead of rinsing diapers.

Disposable diapers had not been invented back then and as I look back, I realize the amount of time, effort, and water I could have saved if only they had been available. Needing a steady supply of clean cloth diapers created a whole labour-intensive routine, starting with scraping them and identifying the water I could use to rinse them. Next began the washing machine routine: hauling ice into the house, melting it, heating it on the stove, washing the diapers in our small wringer washer, wringing them out, emptying the wash water, and hauling it outside. Then came the rinse, again with warm water in the washer, wringing the diapers again, and emptying and hauling the rinse water out to the harbour to dump. Finally, I hung the wet diapers to dry on lines strung around the ceiling or on racks, and once dry, they were folded, ready to begin the whole cycle yet again.

For a bit more than a baby's first year and a half, I would spend an inordinate amount of time trying to keep my baby in clean diapers. But there were other ways. Some Inuit women didn't use diapers on their young ones in the daytime. They kept babies under their own Mother Hubbards bare-bottomed until they were restless, then immediately took them out to do their business on a pot. If the temperature was warm enough, toddlers ran around without wearing much below the waist. The women who did use diapers or rags for their babies usually weren't as compulsive as I was about getting them snowy white.

As in early settler days, bath time was an undertaking that usually included the whole family. Heated water was poured into a small tub by the stove and each family member took a turn. Hot water was added intermittently to keep it warm enough for each person. When everybody was clean, the next decision was how to put the bathwater to good use. Water was never hauled out of the house until all possible uses for it had been exhausted.

———————

ON ONE OF HIS OUTSIDE TRIPS, GEORGE DECIDED TO BUY A PENNY gumball machine along with bags and bags of brightly coloured gumballs. He thought it would be fun for people who had never seen such a machine. Additionally, it would help us to keep pennies available in the store to make change. Even before the government retired the penny in early 2013, most people in southern Canada saw little value in these coins, rarely even bothering to pick up a penny if they saw one on the ground. However, in Tuk in the early 1960s, most families still got their food from the land, and their spending money was often limited to monthly family allowance cheques. As a result, pennies truly mattered, and they became even more important with the arrival of our new gumball machine.

Once the machine was ready, people lined up, waiting for their turn to put a penny in and watch what colour gumball appeared at the bottom. People would discuss which colour they thought would drop, clapped when they were right, or laughed if it turned out to be a different colour. Once our machine had been set up for a short while, people arrived from other settlements and the first thing they wanted to do was to rush to our trading post, pennies in hand, to try our machine. Word of our gumball machine quickly spread around the western Arctic, and it wasn't long until almost all the pennies available in the region ended up in our store in Tuk. When the Hudson's Bay post ran out of pennies for change, they started to give candy or sticks of gum as change, but people objected and wanted pennies to use in our machine. As a result of the Hudson's Bay running out of pennies, people started to buy more food from us, so they would receive penny change.

Oddly, the Bay manager never took the initiative to ask to buy some of our pennies. Since it was after freeze-up, we heard he began flying pennies into Tuk from Inuvik. Then the bank in Inuvik ran out of pennies and had to start flying in more pennies from

Edmonton. As you would expect, bringing in pennies by air cost much more than their face value. In time, the bank in Inuvik learned where all the pennies were and its manager asked George if he would bring them back. Since I didn't have the time to count and roll the pennies, I had been storing them temporarily in large coffee cans under the counter. Rolling pennies was a project I had planned to do when I had nothing else to do—an entirely unlikely event.

The bank manager pleaded with us to return the pennies to Inuvik, saying they were happy to have them arrive in their coffee cans; they would count and roll the pennies at the bank and credit our account. So, whenever we had room, on return flights from Tuk to Inuvik, we began to fly the cans of pennies back to the bank. The next summer, when the barges were running, the bank stocked up on pennies, but we also continued to return our full coffee cans, so the "great penny shortage in the western Arctic" came to an end. The Hudson's Bay Company store in Inuvik had a gumball machine by the following summer. We guessed they wanted to keep the other settlements' Hudson's Bay posts supplied with pennies without the excessive cost of shipping them by air from Edmonton.

10

GROWING FAMILY OF NORTHERNERS

Extreme cold made its mark on our lives in so many ways: it even changed the course of childhood illnesses. Most notable was the fact that, in the Far North, the cold apparently killed residual germs. As a result, northern children didn't seem to build up gradual immunities from regular exposure to various germs. So when a disease outbreak did happen, it could be life-threatening to anyone born since the last round of that particular illness. I was convinced that when my children contracted infectious diseases such as mumps and chicken pox, they were more severely sick than they would have been had we been living outside.

One winter, when Arctic Wings' flying time was officially limited to "twilight only," or less than two hours a day, Tuk experienced a measles outbreak. On a dark snowy night, Special Constable Jim Raddi came to the house to let me know of an emergency that couldn't wait for the twilight hours the next day. The nurse needed to send a child, sick with the measles and having difficulty breathing, to the hospital in Inuvik as soon as possible. I radioed George in Inuvik and, although the nighttime temperature was around forty degrees below zero, he immediately used the engine tent and blow pot to warm the oil in his plane and took off as soon as he could, to fly to Tuk, pick up the child, and fly back to Inuvik.

It was such a very black night in Tuk, with wind and blowing snow. I knew George would have difficulty avoiding the pingos near the settlement, unless he could see the lights from Tuk and then plan his landing approach based on his knowledge of the pingos and the shoreline of the Beaufort Sea. I woke David to watch his sister, and then I went to start our generator and turn on all the lights in our buildings. Jim went to the nursing station and school and got help turning on all their lights. Besides avoiding the pingos, another challenge for George would be determining the point when, descending through the snow-filled sky, he could touch his skis down on the snow-covered ground.

In the winter, we were always prepared for just such emergency landings: we kept a supply of oil-pot lights at the ready. These were made from coffee cans stuffed with rolled cardboard, ready for the addition of old engine oil. Putting out these lighted pots at the beginning of the landing strip would help show George specifically where he needed to start his landing. The lights would also help him with the depth perception needed to figure out where the snow-covered ground began. Jim helped me warm the oil to fill the pots. We then went out to the landing area and planted a number of pots along both sides at the start of the strip.

As soon as we heard the plane, Jim and I each ran down our side on the first part of the strip, using a blowtorch to light the line of pots. George came in low and slow and landed safely. He picked up the child, her mother, and another of the woman's children who appeared to be developing measles. The child who was so sick would survive, but sadly, the other child who went along with his mother would become even sicker and eventually die, even though he was in the hospital at the time. This measles epidemic left the community with more children to bury and mourn.

OUR FIRST CHRISTMAS IN TUK ARRIVED. FATHER LE MEUR JOINED US for Christmas dinner of canned ham, which I decorated with cloves and a pineapple glaze, accompanied by canned potatoes and canned peas. Not a traditional Christmas dinner, for most people, but it was good, and it was a celebration. Life was very busy, so everything, including Christmas, was done in a hurry. I had the café bake an extra pie for our meal, and Dell sent a fruitcake that was a delicious reminder of other Christmas celebrations.

Before Christmas, George flew in a little tree for us that he had cut in Inuvik. Since Tuk was about 37 miles (60 kilometres) north of the treeline, trees were not part of Christmas celebrations in the community. I decorated our tree with ribbons and popcorn strung on thread. It was the only tree in town, so David brought all his friends to see it. Soon the grown-ups wanted to see it as well, so the tree became a reason for a community Christmas celebration at our house, enhanced by my endless supply of tea and cookies. Our little decorated tree was much admired, and after Christmas, David wasn't willing to part with it. In the end, I convinced him it had become a fire hazard since it had lost most of its needles. The children's presents, by southern standards, were not extravagant—mostly books. But compared to the gifts received by the other children in the settlement, David's and Lesley's gifts were impressive, since they included small toys from Vern and Dell and gifts received in the mail from Bud and Pat, my California friends.

George arrived during the day on Christmas Eve and on Boxing Day, he flew back to Inuvik, saying that he had to catch up on work there. The children had the rare opportunity to spend time with their father before he left. Lesley, dressed in her tiny little Mother Hubbard parka with a pink floral fabric cover, took her father to visit her many friends in the community.

Lesley, wearing her Mother Hubbard, is dressed to go visiting with her father.

Lesley's style of parka—the Mother Hubbard—was created many years before in response to missionaries' reaction to the unisex appearance of Inuit clothing. The missionaries convinced the northern people that women shouldn't look like men. They should wear dresses. The answer to this church instruction—enabling women to keep warm in the bitter cold and make sure their dresses were seen—was found in the creativity of the Inuit women in making the dress to fit over fur clothing. So the Mother Hubbard parka became the standard wear for women in the High Arctic. Muskrat skins were sown together to create a long parka, well past the knees, again with fur turned inside next to the body. A cloth "dress" with a hood was made to cover the muskrat skins. Our family celebration ended very quickly, but George's time with us and the community celebration of our tree made it a memorable Christmas.

As the new year began, Tuk Traders was doing well financially, as was Arctic Wings. George was only in and out of Tuk, so I took care of much of the business and family needs while he and Al were managing Arctic Wings in Inuvik and Aklavik. The Hudson's Bay Company manager had become increasingly unhappy with the negative impact of our competition. I expect he was receiving a lot of pressure from head office over the drop in fur purchases and the reduction in store sales. I didn't really think about the possible personal animosity we might be creating until an unexpected incident occurred. David had gone into the Hudson's Bay post with several friends to collect our mail. With encouragement from his friends, he stole a package of gum to share with the other boys. Stealing small things was not an uncommon practice among young Inuit boys, and when they were in our store, I often had to remind them that they couldn't take things, either from the store or from our house. In the store, I kept the most desirable candies and gum out of their reach. Boys and girls seemed to be treated quite differently in the community. Parents considered boys as their future and they were mostly free of expectations, much discipline, or other corrections to their behaviour, although the boys themselves didn't seem to want to do anything that would disappoint or shame their parents.

When David told me he had taken the package of gum, I told him that it was wrong of him to take something that was not his. I explained what it meant to our store and to us when others took things without paying for them and told him he needed to take money from his piggy bank, return to the Bay, apologize to the manager, and give him the money to pay for the gum. I was busy in the store and mistakenly sent David by himself to the Bay post, expecting he could solve the problem he had created when he took the gum.

The manager apparently decided to take out his frustrations, with us and with our successes, on our five-year-old son. David came home in tears: the manager had called him a thief, told David that he was no good, and told him he was barred from ever coming into the post again. I was upset for David, knowing George and I were the real targets of the manager's anger. However, this was going to be an ongoing issue I needed to resolve, since the post was where our mail was delivered after it arrived on the biweekly PWA flight. I usually sent David to pick up the mail, and I planned to continue to make the mail pickup David's responsibility. Seeing his upset, I hugged David and told him that I would have handled the situation differently in our store, but he was still wrong in taking the gum and the manager wanted to make sure he understood it was wrong. To my knowledge, David never stole anything again. I apologized to David though, for sending him alone, and I told him I should have gone with him, so we could have dealt with the manager together.

Later in the day, I made it a point to meet privately with the Bay manager and suggested to him that his response, to a five-year-old who had come to him to apologize and pay for the gum he had taken, was truly inappropriate. I also told him that I would still send David for our mail, although I would tell him he wasn't to go anywhere else within the post, and he was to leave as soon as he had our mail. I made it clear that when David was there, picking up the mail, I expected him to be treated with respect. Afterwards, much to my surprise, on David's next trip to pick up our mail, the manager took him aside and apologized for what he had said, thanked him for coming to pay for the gum, and told him he was welcome in the post anytime. Although a competitor, he was obviously in reality a fair man.

On one flight to the seal hunting camp on Herschel Island, George decided to take David along. Flying, for David, was like travelling by car for children living outside. They flew west over the Beaufort Sea, but the weather soured with blowing snow on their way and after they landed, a storm blew into the seal camp itself, bringing the pack ice ashore. George radioed that they were fine, but they would be staying at the camp until the weather improved and the ice moved out to sea again. The storm continued to build, and by the time they were able to fly again, David had missed nearly a week of school, but he had great fun and a very worthwhile learning experience.

George claimed the only available sleeping bag, leaving David to roll up in seal hides to sleep. Although he rolled up on the fur side, he arrived home both greasy and smelly. It took a hot bath (for him) and repeated washing of his parka, mukluks, and clothing to rid them of the smell. Repeated washing failed to remove the stains, so he needed a new cover for his parka. Regardless of the challenging cleanup, he had the rare experience of seeing life as it had been traditionally lived for generations in a seal hunting camp. He came home with many stories and enjoyed sharing these with his classmates. I wondered what he had eaten and when I asked him, he said the food was okay but did not elaborate much. I didn't think it was reindeer stew and bannock.

I frequently needed to be doing too many things all at the same time and finally came to the realization that I couldn't do it all. My best solution was to hire Eddie Gruben's daughter to help me in the store and in the house, initially part time. Rosemary was in her late teens and a bright, quick learner. Before long, I relied on her work both in the store and when she took care of the children. Sharing the load was such a blessing when I was beyond overloaded, and Rosemary was delighted to help, since working for me made her one of very few Inuit women in the settlement with a job and an income.

IN THE SPRING, WE DECIDED TO FLY OUR CESSNA 180 TO EDMONTON, to order supplies for the trading post and, more importantly, to arrange to get them on the earliest barges after breakup. It was also time for the required maintenance and inspection on the plane George had used throughout the winter. I felt confident that Rosemary, with one winter's experience, could manage the store since fur buying was temporarily over and trappers had returned to Tuk. At first, we planned to take only David but then decided Lesley was old enough to go with us. We created a flat padded area in the back of the plane, and both children slept most of the 12 to 14 hours it took to fly to Edmonton. George and I arrived tired from the long hours in the air. Both children were well rested and ready for their new adventures, although we were not.

For Lesley this marked her very first trip out of the North, and it was the first time David had been outside in almost three years. Lesley was so excited when she saw the city and all the lights. Everywhere she turned, she was seeing new things. This urban environment was so totally foreign to anything she had ever seen or experienced. David got almost as excited as she did. It was obvious that he had forgotten what he had seen and experienced prior to going north, or he was seeing things now through different eyes. The simplest things that other children took for granted were major new experiences, particularly for Lesley. For instance, she had only seen farm animals in books where each animal took the whole page, so she was amazed that cows, chickens, sheep, and horses were not all the same size.

This unidentified Inuit girl and boy, about the same age as Lesley and David on their Edmonton trip, show how our children dressed when flying. © *NWT Archives / Robert C. Knights / N-1993-002-0135*

Our dress reflected our life in the Arctic and our belief that people should never fly in the North without appropriate clothing, which prepared us for travel in these vast, cold, and often inhospitable lands. David wore his traditional northern parka made from sewn muskrat skins, with fur inside and a navy-blue heavy cotton-drill cover. His parka had wolverine fur around the face, cuffs, and along the hem, which prevented snow and cold from getting underneath.

On his feet, he wore his best beaded mukluks. He had embroidered duffel mitts tied with a colourful yarn harness that went around his neck and across his chest so he could take them off, but the mitts were always there, at hand, and available to quickly put back on. The outfits George and I wore were very similar to David's. Lesley's Mother Hubbard had the less functional but very decorative white fox fur lining around her hood and wrists, along with a colourful yarn harness for her mitts. Lesley had never worn anything on her feet but mukluks or gumboots, and she now discovered that other children wore shoes. When we went into stores, she was

Lesley sitting by the window in our Cessna 180, dressed for the uncertainty of flying in the Arctic. For Lesley and her brother, flying in Arctic Wings' Cessna 180 was like going for a car ride to children in southern Canada.

anxious to find the shoe section so she could admire girls' shoes. The first time she saw a pair of little black patent leather shoes on display, Lesley asked if she could hold one. She took it, gazed at it, and then rubbed the leather on her cheek before reluctantly giving it up. Shoes had no place in her life in the North, but I had to resist the temptation to buy them anyway.

Everywhere we went in Edmonton, our clothing marked us as travellers from the High Arctic. The children were noticed not only for their dress, but also due to their infectious enthusiasm for everything they saw or experienced. As people saw their excitement, many decided to contribute to it by giving them extra attention or special treats. I was far enough into my pregnancy that I was feeling well, and we all enjoyed eating the many foods we did not have in the North. The kids loved ice cream cones, fresh fruit, and fresh milk. Since everything the children saw or experienced was an exciting adventure, their response became contagious for their parents, making this business trip truly magical. All of us were a bit sad to see our time in the city end, as we climbed back into our plane and took off to return north.

Shortly after we were back, a group of Ottawa politicians and staffers came to Tuk to talk about business and economic development in our part of the North. We made our small home available for a reception where community leaders could mingle with the Ottawa guests. After the visiting party finished their walkabout tour of Tuk and had a visit with local people in our little community hall, they came to our house for the reception. Government staffers brought all the food and drink for the reception, and they helped me serve and clean up. Basically, all we had to do was provide the space and agree to requests for photos of our children in their northern clothing. We were chosen to be hosts because we represented free enterprise in Tuk. We were recognized as people who ran a chartered air service, a restaurant, and a trading post. George was featured as a bush pilot, and I was notable as a fur trader. We never heard what the group had learned or what policies they proposed as a result of their trip, so we would never know if our efforts had any worthwhile long-term impact.

The only problem we had during the reception, other than a large crowd squeezed together in our relatively small house, was the care and control of the honey bucket. As the bucket filled up, I had to decide whether to carry the clear honey bag of yellow fluid, with its floating toilet paper, through the crowd and out to the ice or whether I should take the whole bucket, which would hide the contents as well as give me a handle to carry it. I tied the top of the bag and decided I should try to be subtle and take the whole bucket. This may seem like an easy decision, except I had to be sure that some unknowing southerners didn't use the toilet, without the inner bucket and its liner in place, during the time it would take me to rush down to the ice and back. The practical solution was to assign David the job of guarding the bathroom door and turning people away, until I had time to weave my way through the crowd, exit the door, empty the honey bucket, get back, and reassemble it.

When I returned with the bucket, I relined it with a plastic bag, poured in the requisite chemical, and left the bathroom. As I came out, I noticed several guests sniffing the air, with apparent confusion. I expected, by the time they had finished their northern fact-finding tour, that one of their olfactory memories would be the all-encompassing smell of Mistovan. In the years since I left the North, whenever I use or smell the cleaning solution Pine-Sol, I remember once again that invasive and unique odour.

In mid-May, just before spring breakup and the seasonal challenges we faced, I accepted Dell's very welcome offer and flew back to Inuvik with David and Lesley to live with her family until the new baby's arrival. Life was easier and it was a luxury to live with running water and flush toilets. The children were pleased to have plenty of people to entertain them and frequent chances to play in the bathtub. I wasn't concerned about leaving Rosemary to run the store because fur buying was over for the moment, and it would not be long before I returned to Tuk. My due date was the third week in May, and I hoped this baby would arrive on schedule, but I wasn't feeling any pressure of business until the barges began to arrive in Tuk once again. As my pregnancy continued, I began to look forward to the baby's arrival. I wanted this baby: I didn't really care whether it was a boy or a girl.

My pregnancy had been a good one after the first months and even then, my morning sickness was less severe than during my first two pregnancies. I had lost weight early but then had a limited but steady weight gain, no kidney problems at all, and my lifestyle ensured I was physically fit. I now had my first opportunity to meet the newly minted doctor, Ed Gramlich, who would deliver my baby, and I was happy to be told that there didn't appear to be any issues with either the baby or me.

The new hospital had opened in Inuvik at the beginning of 1961, two weeks after Lesley was born. She had been the last white baby and the second-last baby born at the old Aklavik hospital (All Saints) before it closed.

In 1963, Duncan was born in the modern, well-equipped government hospital in Inuvik. His first bed would be the sterile medical bassinet found in most southern hospitals.© *NWT Archives / Jean Boulva Photograph Collection / N-2018-002:0013*

The Inuvik Regional Hospital was expansive and modern compared to the one in Aklavik, and was primarily staffed by young doctors who had agreed to work in the hospital on short-term assignments. They usually came north right after finishing their training and before they established their own medical practice or joined one elsewhere. (Dr. Gramlich would go on to co-found the Grandin Medical Clinic in St. Albert, Alberta, in 1966.) Other temporary doctors were those like Norman Schweda, who were foreign trained and had worked in the North to qualify for their Canadian licence.

Typically, women who lived in the outlying settlements did not see a doctor either during pregnancy or for delivery. Prenatal care to monitor a pregnancy was not really an option for many women. A nursing station nurse or a travelling nurse had to identify suspected problems with a pregnancy. However, few nurses or nursing stations were available, depending on the settlement's size. In smaller settlements, where a nurse visited only periodically, if she had concerns about a pregnancy, she would send the woman to be seen by a doctor in Inuvik and later the woman might return to give birth at the hospital. The reality was that most northern babies were born at home, without professional medical care. When a woman came to the hospital to give birth, the doctors usually were expected to respond to whatever problems they encountered at the time of birth, unless the woman lived in Inuvik, where there was the opportunity for regular doctor visits—although women might be attended by a different doctor before their baby was delivered. I always believed it was best to give birth in a hospital, for protection of the baby and myself, so once again I had travelled to the settlement with the hospital as my due date approached.

In May of 1963, people in the Mackenzie Delta were concerned about flooding at breakup. The weather was warming more quickly than usual, and the spring had brought a lot of rain in the South. It appeared that the ice wouldn't have time to candle properly, causing residents to worry about the ice being forced to move in huge blocks, creating ice jams and subsequent flooding. Because of this situation, the Royal Canadian Air Force sent a plane and a helicopter to Inuvik with a team to monitor the ice and to be available to airlift people out of low-lying areas on the delta if sudden flooding developed. There was a special concern about Aklavik, since so many people had refused to leave and it had a history of flooding.

The officer in charge of the air force unit quickly earned himself a reputation as a total jerk: he seemed to be on a personal power trip and was very ready to tell the town's people how lucky they were that he was there to save them. In the short time he had been in Inuvik, his arrogance and lack of respect had alienated most of the inhabitants.

The night before the baby was born, George and some townspeople decided to share some drinks. With their judgment sufficiently impaired, they decided they needed to do something about the overbearing ass of an officer. They drove to the airport, where George started up the air force helicopter, lifted it off the ground just enough to move it, and then hid it behind one of the hangars. This was supposed to be a joke, intended to speak about the town's feelings about the air force officer and his attitude. The less-than-sober group had decided it would be a lark. Afterwards, George came back to Vern and Dell's house and went to sleep. He and his co-conspirators apparently forgot that George, along with the helicopter's pilot, were the only people in town with the knowledge required to move the helicopter.

I started into labour but I couldn't wake George, so about five in the morning, I decided I needed to go to the hospital. We did not have a vehicle at Dell's, so I picked up my bag, wrote a note to Dell, and left the sleeping house to walk to the hospital. I walked the half-mile or so with some stops to practise breathing as contractions came. The walk apparently had been good for me or possibly my body had become used to giving birth, because my baby boy was born, at ten in the morning, without any of the problems I had experienced with my other two deliveries.

A few hours after I left for the hospital, the police arrived at the house, woke everybody, and asked George about the helicopter. The air force people had arrived at the airport and the helicopter had easily been found, but the officer in charge was very angry and did not find the stunt at all amusing. It was obviously going to require a lot of crew time to check for any possible damage to the helicopter, and that would be followed by extensive paperwork to explain to the Air Force Command why some townspeople would want to move their helicopter. The angry officer was determined that all involved would be charged with the most serious offences possible. The townspeople found the whole situation a big joke and enjoyed the opportunity to laugh at him, but the officer in charge wasn't laughing, and George would become his major target.

Initially, George was arrested and charged, by the officer, with a felony theft. He would face additional charges of whatever the officer could possibly apply to the situation. George was jailed but later released and given a summons to appear. It was very scary to realize that, if convicted of a felony, George could possibly lose his pilot's licence, lose his insurance endorsement, and thus put an end to his flying career. Conviction would have a huge impact on our lives and Arctic Wings.

Later, and I suspect with the intervention of the Air Force Command, the charge was reduced to a misdemeanour and George pleaded guilty. He was fined and placed on a short probation period. I think it helped that George had served in both the air force and the navy, and there was no damage to the helicopter. Many townspeople spoke up for him, and doubtless the air force, in its investigation, heard about the degree to which the officer's arrogance had created alienation in the town. However, the officer's poor attitude in no way excused the behaviour and stupidity of George and his co-conspirators.

After his release from police custody, George arrived at the hospital, took one look at our baby boy, and said he wanted to call him Duncan, after his long-time friend in Vancouver. I liked both his friend and the name, so I added a middle name of Glenn and our baby was named on his first day of life. George, for the third time, had managed to miss his child's birth, this time because he was in jail.

11

TRUSTED OUTSIDER—BUT NOT QUITE AN INSIDER

I was anxious to get back to Tuk, to be with all three children and to spend time together as we welcomed Duncan into our family's life. Also I knew that I'd have to catch up on essential jobs that hadn't been done during my almost three weeks away. Living in our house in Tuk, with its amazing amount of privacy, was still special to me, even though the lack of running water and waste disposal made daily tasks an ongoing challenge. No doubt, the children would miss their playtime in the bath. We would all miss Dell's family, and I would once again face the diaper challenge. I would be dippy-doing diapers in the harbour water now the ice was clearing, and that task would continue endlessly until freeze-up came again. Then I would return to my trusty scraping tool, seeking slightly used water for diaper rinsing. The ordinary work of maintaining a family would consume both my time and my energy, but Tuk was home, and I missed the people there.

Five days after Duncan was born, George picked me up at the hospital. We collected the other two children, said goodbye to Dell and her family, and thanked them for their wonderful friendship as well as remarkably consistent help. Then we loaded our family of five into our plane to fly back to Tuk. As he was warming up the engine, George broke the news to me that we were going to have house guests about ten or fifteen minutes after our arrival in Tuk. He explained that he had met Madge Baker and her daughter Noni, who was about my age, earlier in the day, when he was at the airport picking up supplies from the PWA flight. After chatting with them, he had invited them to come to Tuk to visit and stay with us. They would be leaving Inuvik, on the regularly scheduled PWA Otter flight to Tuk, in about half an hour. He said that Madge was the widow of Russ Baker, who had been a well-known bush pilot in the western Arctic and was famous as the founder of Pacific Western Airlines. He had died of a heart attack several years before, at the age of forty-eight.

I was speechless. I couldn't believe George would invite people to be house guests on the day I got out of the hospital, and only five days after giving birth. Besides having to deal with baby issues and establish some routine in our lives again, I was tired and looking forward to some privacy and time with the children. Also, based on past experiences, I had some idea what condition I would find the house in when we arrived, thanks to George's overnighting there a few times while I had been away. I had no idea what I would feed us, let alone feed guests. I realized, once again, how little George understood anything beyond himself and how much he seemed to believe that my main role, in our marriage and in our lives, was to embrace and support his ideas and wishes. Yet again, my feelings or needs were only considered when they matched up with *his* wishes and plans.

Once I got over the shock of unexpected guests, my problem-solving ability kicked into gear and my thoughts raced from issue to issue—like where people would sleep, whether the sheets on the beds were clean, what we would eat, and how I would get food thawed and the house organized. As soon as we landed in Tuk and the plane stopped, I jumped out, put Duncan on my seat, lifted

Lesley and David out, retrieved Duncan, waved to all who had come to see who was arriving in Tuk, and ran for the house with Duncan in my arms, instructing David to bring Lesley. As soon as I was inside, I put down the baby and turned on the cookstove to warm up the house and heat water for dishes. I looked at the dirty dishes and food leftovers sitting on the counter awaiting my return and tried to think how to start bringing order to the chaos.

David brought Lesley in, and I got him to help me tidy up some of the mess. Meanwhile, George stayed at the plane and waited for the Otter's arrival. It seemed like only moments, but within fifteen minutes, I heard George arrive at the door with our guests. By this time Duncan was crying. I picked him up and, catching my breath to produce a smile, rushed to the door to welcome our guests. I hadn't taken off either my parka or the children's in my haste to create some order around me, so we arrived at the door looking like we were about to leave rather than ready to welcome our guests.

A beautifully dressed Madge Baker and Noni walked through the door and were introduced. Whereas my clothing was ordinary and utilitarian, theirs was stylish, well fitting, and obviously expensive. Madge took the crying Duncan from my arms, escorted me to the chesterfield, told me to sit down, and then handed Duncan back to me. She then helped Lesley out of her parka and put water on for tea, seemingly all in one moment. Madge then started issuing orders. To me it was to stay sitting and take care of Duncan, while everyone else was given tasks to do. She sent George off to empty the honey bucket. She gave Noni a broom to sweep the place while we waited for the water to boil. Within an hour, we had tea and Madge had gotten everybody to contribute to bringing some order to the house. She had asked about dinner and now had reindeer meat thawing. Noni helped Madge as she began creating our dinner and mixing bread dough to set it to rise. Before I could say anything, she seemed to understand exactly what was necessary to get the household operating again. She sent George to arrange water delivery.

Then she boiled and cooled water to mix powdered milk for the children. Sometime in her past, Madge had learned to be a masterful multi-tasker, and she hadn't lost her touch.

For the next three days, I was cared for like a daughter, with time to enjoy my new son. Duncan Glenn was the biggest of my babies. He was a very happy infant who appeared healthy. Like his older brother, he liked to sleep and eat. He immediately became a person to me. I felt the same wonder and amazement over his birth as I had for his siblings, and my feelings for him were just as strong as they had been for my other two babies. He was no longer just an unplanned pregnancy; he was Duncan, my third and my last very special child.

Instead of creating additional work and strain, Madge and Noni's visit was a great help and fun for everyone. Sleeping arrangements were tight, but we drank tea and talked for hours about Madge's life in the North some thirty or more years earlier and made interesting comparisons to my current life. Madge apologized for taking advantage of the offer to spend time with us in Tuk. She explained that when she walked down the steps from the scheduled flight from Edmonton, she noticed someone leaning on the wing of a small plane. When she looked closer, she said she got such a shock that she felt like she might fall to her knees. Leaving Noni to try to keep up with her, she immediately rushed over to the man (George) and asked his name.

Madge said George bore an uncanny resemblance to her late husband, Russ Baker. He not only looked like him, but she said he talked and walked like him as well. She was amazed that George was also a bush pilot and when she asked, she learned he had been born in Vancouver at the same time she and Russ were living there. She said the reason she felt she needed to accept George's invitation to come to Tuk was because she needed to know more about him and his family. Madge told me she was convinced that George was the illegitimate son of Russ Baker. She didn't believe he could be so much like Russ without being his son. Madge described Russ as a womanizer: she had been aware of some of his affairs and had learned to accept that when he was younger, he had not always been faithful to her. I didn't know Madge well enough yet to share with her that George might be more like Russ than she knew.

Madge told us about Russ's life and in particular that Russ was widely recognized for his extraordinary flying ability. He had started bush flying in British Columbia and then moved to the Northwest Territories. He had started PWA and by 1958, when he died, it had become the third-largest Canadian airline. After Russ died, Madge became the major stockholder, but had nothing to do with running the business. In future years, PWA would merge with several companies including Nordair, the company that would buy Arctic Wings in 1967. PWA would be sold in 1986 and by 2000, all would merge to become part of Air Canada.

What I knew about Alice, George's mother, made me believe it was possible that she might have been involved with Russ Baker. Alice lived her life with enthusiasm and by her own rules. George's father had been dead many years before George and I met, so I didn't know if George was like him or not. I never thought George really looked like his mother and had assumed he must look like his father's family. It was hard for me to share much with Madge about George's heritage, since I had never met any of his family except for his mother and I hadn't seen any pictures. Thus I felt unable confirm or deny that George might be Russ's son. I expected the only one who would know the answer was his mother, Alice, and I felt if anyone asked her about Russ Baker, it would need to be George. During her visit, Madge became even more certain that George's father had to be Russ. When I asked him if it could be true, his only comment was to say he thought it was a possibility. I never heard whether or not he discussed the issue with his mother.

George's relationship with his mother seemed strained, and my own relationship with her had always been distant. I had tried to understand but finally accepted that this was just the way she wanted it to be. We were part of the same family, but other than booking flights from Aklavik, she wasn't really involved with Arctic Wings. We didn't even share an interest in my children. She usually forgot, or perhaps chose to ignore, their birthdays or other special occasions, and I rarely saw or heard from her. I had heard nothing from her since Duncan's birth. Her and Al's social life and friends were in Aklavik, they were heavy drinkers, and she rarely left there. Three years before, when we were in Aklavik for Lesley's birth, she had not come to the hospital to meet her new granddaughter.

When Madge decided that George was Russ's son, she then believed that George was Noni's and her other daughter Joy's older brother, making George's children also her grandchildren. She seemed particularly entranced with baby Duncan, whose birth she felt had brought us all together. When the time came for our guests to return to Inuvik, I was indeed sorry to see them go, and the house suddenly seemed very empty. It had been a wonderful few days and a great chance for me to regroup and enjoy the conversation and laughter. Some years later, we saw pictures of a younger Russ Baker when visiting Madge's home in Vancouver. The pictures did reflect an amazing resemblance to both George and Duncan. Duncan was the only one of our children who looked like George from the time he was a baby. We would continue to have a close relationship with Madge over many years. I would lose touch with her after George and I went our separate ways, but George continued his relationship with Madge until she died.

Shortly after Madge left, I took Duncan to a meeting at the local community hall to introduce him to everyone. The community's children were included when the adults gathered, so meetings were always busy, noisy events. Children of all ages came to meetings and activities, fell asleep on benches if they were tired, and otherwise played in groups while the adults talked or did any necessary business. When I arrived with Duncan, there was much excitement, as it was the community's first opportunity to welcome him. He was immediately whisked out of my arms and passed from one admiring woman on to another. At one point I lost track of where he was. I followed the path he had taken and saw a woman with both arms inside her Mother Hubbard parka. When I rushed over to her, she told me she was feeding her baby and Duncan seemed hungry, so she was feeding him too. This may seem shocking to people from outside, but it was so natural to people who loved and valued children. However, I did gracefully retrieve Duncan, since tuberculosis was still an issue in that part of the North, and I wasn't sure of the ways it could be transmitted. However, Duncan had been truly welcomed, and he now joined his brother and sister as a child belonging to the community.

Duncan was a good, happy, and flexible baby. He spent a lot of time being carted about in a padded wooden produce box so he could be with me, whether I was in the store, the café, or the house. I threw a heavy blanket over the box as I carried him from building to building. David could dress himself for the outdoors, but Lesley still needed help, so whenever we went outside or even travelled between buildings, I spent some time putting on parkas and mitts as well as covering Duncan's box.

Inuit babies rode on their mother's back under her Mother Hubbard parka in a pouch created by tying a strip of cloth around the mother's waist, keeping the baby in place. As they grew older, babies shared the hood of the mother's Mother Hubbard, allowing the baby to see out. This freed the baby's mother to move about and have both arms and hands free to work. This form of transportation kept the baby safe and warm between the mother's body and the fur inside her parka and was much more efficient than Duncan's box. Years later I would see several commercial variations of this harness, leaving the mother or father with hands free while the baby was secure.

Two babies are safe and warm under their mothers' Mother Hubbard parkas, kept in place by a strap tied around each mother's waist. © *NWT Archives / Robert C. Knights / N-1993-002-0352*

BEFORE LONG, SPRING BREAKUP CAME ONCE AGAIN TO THE MACKENZIE River, and the shoreline ice in the Beaufort Sea near Tuk began its annual melt as well. This promised the inevitable arrival of the summer season, with the excitement of Northern Transportation barges bringing in supplies after a nine-month hiatus. As the season advanced, it became increasingly hazardous to be out on the unpredictable sea ice. However, a few hunters were still venturing out in pursuit of seal meat and hides, despite the growing danger. When a sudden storm blew up, the hunters and dog teams on the ice rushed back to land, but two men, along with their dog team, didn't make it back before the ice split apart along the shoreline. This created a wide, open channel between the pair and the safety of land.

The storm brought strong outflow winds so the pack ice, along with the hunters and their dogs, quickly began moving farther from land and safety. Had it not been for the high winds, canoes could have picked them up while they were still closer to shore, although they would have had to leave their sled and equipment on the ice. The winds kept up during the night and the ice continued to move away from Tuk and to break apart even more. New channels of open water were created and then closed again as ice floe edges crashed into each other. By daylight the two men were no longer visible from shore.

The only way to find them was by an air search, so I was asked to call George in Inuvik and see if he could fly out over the ice to locate the men. Although the river itself was ice free, the lakes and small rivers were still melting. Our Cessna was still on wheels, waiting for the melt to finish. Before he could leave Inuvik, George would need to switch over to floats, since the sea ice was too unpredictable to land on. He felt his best option would be to try to find an open water channel near the men, if he was going to attempt to land and pick them up.

As soon as he had the floats on, George flew over Tuk and out to sea to see if he could find the stranded hunters. He found them and radioed to tell me there was a water channel near them where he felt he could land. However, the men would have to hike about a mile across the ice to the open water, so he would circle until they reached the water. He was concerned that if they took too long getting to the water's edge, the ice would move again, narrowing or eliminating the channel. The men made their move and George landed successfully and brought the plane to the ice edge. The hunters were very thankful to see him, but when he urged them to get in quickly, they insisted they had to take their five dogs too. They knew the dogs would inevitably starve or become polar bear food if they were left on the ice. One man remained on the ice surface and threw each dog in turn to his companion, who had jumped onto the plane floats. Once the second hunter had caught each dog, he passed the animal to George in the plane.

These dogs were used to being chained apart so they couldn't reach each other to fight. Now they were all crowded together in a small space, and even before George took off, dogfights broke out. The hunter in the rear seat tried to control the dogs but soon got bitten in the chaos, and the wars continued as the plane headed to Tuk. The bulkhead at the rear of the storage area became dislodged and the dogs pushed farther back, towards the tail of the plane. Monitoring the flight's progress on the radio, I could hear how anxious George was about landing. Fortunately, the water near the shoreline in Tuk's inner harbour was clear of ice. George landed safely but when he neared the shore and started to power down the engine, the weight of the dogs who had pushed so far back towards the tail made the front of the floats come up, and the back of the floats started to sink. It became vital for George to get the weight out of the tail to reduce power enough to safely come ashore. He told the men he would taxi close to the shore keeping the power up, while they threw the dogs into the water, leaving them to swim ashore. This would rebalance the weight on the plane's floats so he could reduce power and safely beach the aircraft.

As the dogs started flying out of the plane into the water, all the people onshore waiting to welcome the men back to the community grabbed the children and started to run to nearby buildings. These working dogs were less than friendly and possibly even aggressive, so no one wanted to be in their way. But luckily the cold-water swim seemed to have cooled much of their aggressiveness, and the dogs were soon brought under control. Then it was time to celebrate, with George as the centre of much attention. He kept saying what he had done was nothing, but I had been talking to him on the radio while he was trying to rescue the men, and I knew the challenges and uncertainties he had faced. I felt proud that his abilities and his courage had led to a good outcome for the men and their community. It was the type of tough situation where George's talents and bravery came to the fore.

Soon life returned to normal, yet with all that, I was to have an unusual opportunity to feel I too had earned respect within the community. One day most of the male leadership of Tuk gathered in the store and asked if they could talk to me. They sent everybody else out of the store, got coffee, and sat down to raise a very unexpected subject. Eddie Gruben's wife had just returned from the hospital in Inuvik, having given birth to her eleventh child. The current resident nurse in Tuk considered this pregnancy high-risk so had arranged for her to give birth in hospital. While Eddie was there, the doctor had told him his wife shouldn't have any more babies. He asked the doctor how he could prevent more babies, and the doctor explained that regulations prohibited him from giving out birth control information. For years, the influence of the Catholic Church on the government's Indigenous health care policies had remained consistent, and these policies restricted sharing any information that went beyond the Church's teachings.

Eddie and the other men wanted to know about these apparently secret methods to prevent babies. They said they came to ask me because they knew that I didn't have a baby every year and they wanted to know how I managed it. My initial reaction to their questions was both confusion and embarrassment. But, more than that, I had to stop to think what I really knew about birth control, particularly when I considered the missteps that had created Duncan. The silence loomed large, while I tried to think how I would or could answer their questions. These men were bringing up a valid concern and asking valid questions, but my personal sense of privacy and embarrassment made me ask, *Why me?* In hindsight, I realize that I was one of only a very few people who could answer their questions without restrictions.

But first, I needed time to learn more myself, to put my thoughts together, and to organize what I could say. I told the group I needed to find more answers for them, and we could meet in a few days when I had more complete information to share. My first instinct was to find someone more knowledgeable than I was to talk to the men. I started by approaching the nursing station nurse to find out whether she could help. I quickly discovered that she too was restricted by government regulations and policies when it came to giving out birth control information.

So began the first of several occasions when I acted as a sex educator. I started my search for general information about birth control methods and then went on to research what different forms of contraception were available in the North. I learned the extent to which government regulations, as well as expense, limited a northern family's choices in contraception. Although she could not speak to Inuit directly on this topic, the nurse was a great help in furnishing correct and current information. Early on, I discovered that a hysterectomy was one of the few approved methods of real birth control in the North. However, these operations were done only when a doctor decided that a current pregnancy, the outcome of a birth, or disease would create an imminent danger to a woman's life. Apparently, Eddie's wife would not have been eligible, even if she had known to request a hysterectomy, since limiting more pregnancies for her was only a recommendation, not considered a life-threatening issue.

I heard from the nurse that the use and research on birth control pills was very new and still inconclusive about side effects and the possible impact of long-term use. Any woman who was currently taking birth control pills could have the prescription refilled at the hospital. However, Indigenous women could not be given a new prescription for these pills. This meant that only a white woman who came north already on prescribed pills could continue to get them from the hospital's pharmacy—then the only source of prescription drugs in the western Arctic. Condoms could be bought at the hospital pharmacy, but no other forms of birth control were approved for use. The Catholic Church continued to prescribe only abstinence, interrupted ejaculation, or the rhythm method of timing intercourse to avoid ovulation and thus pregnancy. But it was very obvious that these methods were not effectively limiting pregnancies among families in Tuk.

Sexually transmitted diseases, such as gonorrhea and syphilis, were becoming more prevalent in the North, so the best available advice seemed to be the use of condoms or, in the case of couples, possibly using a combination of condoms plus the Church's approved methods for limiting pregnancy. For couples with limited dollars available, regular use of condoms would be too expensive, so to reduce the number of condoms used during a month, some combination of methods seemed likely to be the most cost-effective choice. The nurse suggested that the cost of condoms might encourage washing and reuse, so I needed to caution the men about the risk associated with doing that. Beyond the issue of birth control, even though condoms offered protection against STDs, they were not available through the health department, nor would they be paid for by the government.

The nurse and I developed an outline of what I would need to discuss with the men. She quietly arranged for me to get a few condoms. I planned to begin with ensuring the men had a good understanding of fertility and a woman's ovulation cycle. After that I would explain the principles behind the Church's rhythm method although interrupted ejaculation seemed not to need explanation. I would talk about sexually transmitted diseases and the proper use of condoms. The more I learned, the more I questioned my ability to take on the role of sex educator or if I could do it as well as I wanted to. The nurse was a tremendous help with information, but again, I had to accept that regulations limited her involvement beyond unofficially helping me to become the best messenger possible.

Before undertaking my new role, I talked with Father Le Meur about what had happened and what I was planning. Thankfully, he was a realist, he knew the issues, and he was equally concerned over the health of several older women for whom future pregnancies represented a significant risk. As a representative of the Church, he could not support the discussion of other methods of birth control beyond those approved by the Church, but as a member of the community, he agreed that the information should be made available. He said he was prepared to work with any couples troubled over conflicts with the "teachings of the Church" and the information the men might learn from me. He didn't believe that keeping information from people was a good answer to moral decision-making. He believed in individual decisions and choice. I assured him I would tell the men that if they were troubled by what they might learn from me, he would talk with them.

My sex education meetings began and resulted in Tuk Traders making condoms available for sale in the store. Although I was initially embarrassed, I enjoyed the informal teaching experience and the honest discussions that followed. A significant side benefit of my attempts at sex education was the further trust I was able to build with the men in the community. From then on, the store became a place where people met to ask questions and discuss all sorts of issues in the life of the community. This opportunity to share and become involved in real-life issues brought richness to my thinking and understanding and I no longer felt so isolated, nor did I feel like a total outsider.

I am intrigued when I hear myself using the terms "outside" and "outsider" as I write this story. To the people of the North, every place that was not part of the North was "outside," and anyone who came from any other part of Canada or elsewhere was then considered an "outsider." Inuit considered all government employees to be outsiders, even though many of them had lived in the North for years. I expect this had something to do with many outsiders feeling the North was a place they worked and lived, but it was not "home." Strangely, I never heard anyone refer to themselves as "insiders" or that living in the North was living "inside." The terms "outside" and "outsiders" were unquestioned but, at any rate, I was no longer feeling like a complete outsider. Of course, neither was I considered a native. I fit into some indefinable and odd category of a trustworthy white person, somewhat like Father Le Meur. I felt any similarity put me in good company.

Within the community during my time in the North, I accepted I was female and different and did not try to be anything other than who and what I was. I wanted to understand people's lives as completely as one can who doesn't "walk in their mukluks." I would share many northerners' life experiences and challenges, and I would be aware of many traditions and hear Elders' stories, but still internalize it all from my own life experiences and from my own background. Another way in which I was different from many other outsiders was that I felt no need to try to change others' thinking or behaviours. Unlike the government workers and religion-affiliated whites, my only agenda was to learn, to seek understanding, and to feel I belonged in this place I called home. I hoped by understanding the others around me, I might better understand myself.

When thinking about my role in the community, again my thoughts went to the government's mandate for change and its decision to deny the validity of another people's heredity, lifestyle, and language. The government's single-minded and unquestioned purpose was to manage the North's people and assimilate them into southern Canadian ways, all without northern people's involvement or consent. My reaction to this involved both confusion and sadness. I clearly understood the need for changes in the North. I saw the need for better health care, literacy and education, and opportunities for employment, which would come with business and economic development. However, I continued to question government decision-making without collaboration and the methods proposed to create change. These were designed to destroy so much in the name of creating a "New North."

I understood and valued my chance to decide how much the North would become a part of me. Yet around me people were so quickly losing their opportunities to choose, to make their own decisions about who they wanted to be and how they would live. I wondered whether Father Le Meur's close identity with the community's people, their lives, and their activities would give him a special opportunity to influence what was to happen in Tuk. I myself felt so powerless but still wondered if there was a role for me in guiding Tuk's future.

GRADUALLY MY LIFE AS A MOTHER OF THREE SETTLED DOWN, WITH MY daily focus just trying to get all my tasks done, but George's mind was never idle. His next big idea was a movie theatre for Tuk. We rented Stan Peffer's old, abandoned store building (he owned the new Mackenzie Hotel in Inuvik) and, as soon as the weather was warm enough, we made log benches for seating and I started to show movies. We bought a 16mm movie projector that the DEW Line workers no longer used, flew in movies from Inuvik, made popcorn to sell, and were now in the theatre business—providing it wasn't too cold outside. Our rough-and-ready theatre, which seated fifty people, had minimal insulation and heat, so had to be shut down when the weather became really cold. Westerns were most definitely the very favourite shows, with the result that local children had their first view of the animals David had been teaching them to imitate. Seeing cowboys and Indians portrayed in movies made David's stories of horseback riding become real. Occasionally we would receive a movie about the North and everyone rated it immediately as a great comedy, laughing uproariously about how our northern way of life was portrayed on the screen.

One day George arrived with the newly released Jerry Lewis comedy *The Nutty Professor*, a sci-fi take on *Dr. Jekyll and Mr. Hyde*. That movie to this day stands out in my memory. It was intended as a comedy but quickly became something else to the people of Tuk.

On the first night, the audience came in and the movie started and went along as usual until the first transformation between Dr. Jekyll and Mr. Hyde began, along with the intense and dramatic music that accompanied each of the transformations. The theatre became deadly quiet, other than the film's music. I watched as people's body language became stressed and then suddenly someone jumped to their feet and fled out of the building, starting a stampede that lasted until the theatre was empty and all the audience stood quietly outside in the evening sun. It was such a sudden and universal response, you might have thought someone had yelled "Fire!" in the theatre. Soon the quiet was replaced by everyone seeming to talk at the same time, followed by great laughter. At first I wasn't sure if it was nervous laughter or if the silliness of the film was being enjoyed by all. When the music quieted down, a couple of people peeked in the door, and when a few decided to return, the rest of the audience filed back in and sat down.

As soon as the music started to build again, preparing for the next transformation, it was the signal for a similarly anxious exodus. People stood around outside and listened, talked and laughed until the music began to quiet down, and once again the crowd waited for someone brave enough to be the first to go back inside. Each time the music announced a transformation, the audience fled. Soon a few braver souls, usually older children who spent time in the residential hostel in Inuvik, would peek in the door and tell everybody what was happening during the transformation. It was summer, so there was almost twenty-four-hour daylight, and everyone seemed to be happy standing in the sunlight and just hearing a description of what was happening in the film, waiting until they felt comfortable to return to the darkened building.

After the first night and the audience's dramatic reaction, I wasn't sure if I should show the movie again. However, on the second night, the theatre was packed, and when I asked everyone if they wanted me to show *The Nutty Professor* again or rerun a

different movie that hadn't been returned yet, I was quickly told that
The Nutty Professor was the movie they had come to see. I showed it
each night to a full house until I had to return it. Although the
theatre was at capacity, most of the audience continued to run out
into the sunlight when scary music announced the transformation.
However, by the fourth day, some braver souls stayed inside to watch
the whole movie, although a few of these moved to sit closer to the
doorway. The movie was the greatest hit of any we showed, and
people who had been out of the settlement during the week we had
the film were keen that we should bring it back.

It cost us so little to rent the movies that we were able to charge a
dime for adults and children could attend for free, making the films
affordable for everyone. They became a regular part of settlement
life during that summer. The movies would make the rounds of the
hostels and other venues in Inuvik, Norman Wells, Fort Smith, and
Yellowknife, so they were well used by the time they had completed
their northern circuit. I didn't really have any control over the films
that were sent, but most were well received. Eventually I taught one
of the men to run the projector, so I didn't have to spend every
evening working as a projectionist, with Duncan asleep in his box
while the other two children were fast asleep on benches.

12

THE RISK IS ALWAYS THERE

As the summer season came to an end, both businesses continued to flourish, keeping George, Al, and me busy. One day, Al went out to pick up some prospectors from their camp, located on a lake in the Richardson Mountains near the Arctic Red River. The prospectors were closing camp for the season, and their samples and all their gear went into the Howard. Al then tried to take off on the small lake, with an overload at a high elevation. This was a recipe for disaster and a serious miscalculation, not expected of such an experienced pilot. He almost made it but ran out of lake before he could lift off, become airborne, and clear the shoreline. The plane flipped over and burst into flames. One of the passengers was killed. Al and the other passenger scrambled out of the plane and survived with only minor injuries.

Soon after, the Department of Transport accident investigation clearly found pilot error as the cause. Although the DOT set, monitored, and enforced aviation rules and regulations and investigated accidents, it was really the insurance companies that decided whether they were willing to insure a pilot or an air charter company. After the accident, our insurance company was still willing to insure Arctic Wings, but since the accident was due to pilot error, our insurance costs would be significantly higher if Al continued to fly for us. As well, the Howard was a total write-off and Arctic Wings would need to buy another plane to keep up with our many charter bookings.

Personal issues between Al, George, and his mother had become increasingly obvious and stressful, and the accident findings simply compounded these tensions. As I might have predicted, they quickly decided to go their separate ways. Dissolving the business partnership was not a very friendly process, and Alice and Al moved from Aklavik to Hay River shortly after the accident. Al flew for another company for a short while, but his insurance problems followed him: by this time, his heavy drinking was making the situation worse. In time Alice and Al separated, later divorcing, and Al seemed to just disappear entirely from all our lives. The children and I had had little contact with Al and Alice during these years, and they certainly didn't aspire to the role of caring and interested grandparents. Although the decision that Al and Alice should leave Arctic Wings created problems for George because he needed to sort out financial interests, while also trying to find another plane and hire a new pilot, it changed little for our family in Tuk.

As the summer's successful but very busy schedule wound down and freeze-up approached, we both had some time to slow down. George had found a pilot to replace Al and had bought a replacement plane, another used Cessna 180, in Edmonton. George initially decided that the new pilot would fly this Cessna from Edmonton to Inuvik, once the engine maintenance and inspection were complete. But as the usual downtime for flying was approaching, George changed his plans and decided the two of us should fly out to Edmonton and leave the Cessna 180 he had been flying all summer for its semi-annual maintenance and inspection. We would then fly the fully serviced, newly purchased Cessna back to Inuvik. Our new pilot would wait until all the necessary inspections and maintenance work had been completed on the plane we had flown down. This would give us the advantage of a quick turnaround, returning north after we did some shopping.

Our new plane currently in Edmonton had been changed from floats to wheels, and the one we were bringing down would also be changed from floats to wheels. The floats for both planes would be left in Edmonton until late spring, when maintenance on the planes would be due once again. That work and the change back to floats coincided with breakup and its limited flying time, as we waited for the return of open water. On our return north, we would land at the airport in Inuvik. The wheels would be changed to skis once the ice was thick enough to land on the Mackenzie and other frozen rivers and lakes. In fall, most Arctic air and land travel stopped until the ice thickened, because frozen rivers and lakes were the only available flat surfaces to travel on. The rest of the land featured hills, valleys, and trees that effectively made travel difficult or impossible, whether by dog teams, snowshoes, trucks, or especially, planes on skis. When there was open water, bush planes flew on floats, even though this was more costly because of extra weight and changed aerodynamics. However, the extra cost was offset by the safety and flexibility of having so many lakes and rivers to land on.

Flying in the North was never without risk. Accepting those risks, avoiding complacency, recognizing and, when possible, planning for the unpredictable were the continual challenges we faced. The inevitable lack of certainty pilots dealt with when flying in the northern bush demanded attention, courage, and skill. As George and I planned the trip, we talked again about taking the children with us. Duncan, at less than four months old, was too young to even consider taking, and David had started grade one, so we decided to leave all three children in the North for this quick trip and wait until spring to take them out again to Edmonton. We could not know that fate was on our side, making this a very momentous decision.

The trip down to Edmonton was relatively uneventful, but the trip back with the replacement plane certainly was not. The first issue we faced was freezing rain and fog near Hay River, on the edge of Great Slave Lake. Since we were on wheels, very few landing options were available. Ice started to build up on the wings, making weight a serious concern if we wanted to remain airborne. Flying back to Hay River, to land at the airport, was impossible because it was completely socked in with fog. The rapidly increasing ice buildup left us with very little time to solve this escalating problem, before the weight of the ice brought the plane down.

Our best option was to land on what appeared to be a rarely used road below us. We would then move the plane off the roadway and wait for the weather to change. After we landed successfully, we faced a long, cold night, with little sleep possible as we tried to get comfortable in our seats and needed to start the plane periodically to heat the cabin. As daylight came, the weather improved, and when no vehicle had appeared on the roadway, we were able to take off again and continue our journey north, roughly following the Mackenzie River.

The next, uneventful phase of our journey north lasted only until south of Fort Norman, near the abandoned settlement of Old Fort Point, when we noticed smoke in the cockpit. Smoke soon filled the whole cabin area and appeared to be coming from the engine compartment. This certainly met the definition of a sudden and critical emergency. We needed to find a place to land immediately before the smoke turned to flames, either from the oil or, even worse, involving the aviation gas. The first step was to call a mayday, giving our location, while we were still airborne and before we made any attempt to land.

During the mayday call, we continued to search for a relatively flat area where we could possibly land on wheels. We knew we didn't have the time to fly to Norman Wells, where there was a big airstrip with firefighting equipment. A quick and somewhat frantic search failed to produce any good option, indeed any option at all. We were still well within the Arctic treeline so all the land we could see, in every direction, was covered with trees and scrubby brush. The Mackenzie was icing up but still flowing. A river landing was not possible without floats, and even if we'd had floats, it would have been too dangerous to attempt because of the ice cakes on the water surface.

Smoke was making it very difficult to both breathe and see, which emphasized how little time we had left to locate a safe landing place. Getting on the ground, shutting down the engine, and getting away from the smoking plane all needed to happen as quickly as possible. Fortunately, we were so busy looking for a place to land that we didn't have much time to dwell on our life-threatening situation. All I could think about, as everything started to go wrong, was *Who will raise our orphaned children?*

Just as our options were running out, we spotted an island in the river that appeared to have a sandy strip of land, free of trees and brush, next to the water's edge. The island was the only open space we could see where it might be possible to land a plane with wheels. Choosing to land on an island, close to the still flowing river, wasn't a great plan, but all our other options were gone. The smoke was blinding us, we were having even more trouble breathing, and the prospect of an open fire and explosion increased with each passing minute.

We committed to land on the strip of sand, and I radioed our decision to Hay River. George positioned the plane for our descent, cutting back his airspeed as much as he could without stalling the plane, and slowly we approached the small treeless bit of land. As soon as our wheels touched down, it was obvious this might have been a poor choice, but trying to land amongst small trees probably would have been even more chaotic. Water runoff channels cut diagonally across our landing area, mostly filled with snow. A light coating of sand had blown over the snow, which helped to hide these depressions. The strip was nowhere near as flat as it had appeared from the air, since the snow and blowing sand had effectively hidden all these irregularities.

The wheels caught in the first depression, so we bounced high into the air and then slammed down hard. The whole plane shuddered and at the same time a loud screeching, grinding, and sounds of metal tearing filled the cabin. I watched as what seemed to be the undercarriage forcibly broke through the plane's floor by my feet on my side of the cockpit, with pieces of metal shooting up into my seat area on my right side. I was immediately engulfed by excruciating pain. The plane rocked backwards, bringing its nose up, and then its forward momentum drove us onwards and we seemed briefly airborne again. As gravity brought the plane down again and we bounced off the next high spot, the nose tipped down, catching the snow, which stopped the prop: the plane shuddered again and came to a sudden stop. It sat frozen with its nose down and tail up for a few breathless moments when it felt like the plane might flip over onto its back. Then the tail slowly settled back down, and the plane came to rest in a mostly upright position.

George yelled for me to get out. I undid my belt and tried to reach my arm backwards around the twisted metal to reach the door handle. A sudden severe pain shot up my arm to my shoulder. I turned in my seat and tried again to reach the handle, reaching across my chest to push the door with my left hand. Everything seemed to be hurting as I pushed as hard as I could, but the door wouldn't budge. When the undercarriage had ruptured the cabin shell, the door had warped around the doorframe on my side. I then felt George grab the hood of my parka and pull me across his seat. I got my legs under me to help push myself out of the plane. In the next moment, as I pushed off, I seemed to be flying through the air, landing in a painful heap in the snow. George seemed to have found superhuman strength when he believed the plane might explode. I landed at what must have been twenty feet from the cockpit. I had obviously helped by pushing off when he was trying to throw me away from the plane but, in retrospect, it was still quite a throw.

Fortunately, George had turned the engine ignition off when we had first started to touch down and were committed to land. We both now scrambled farther away from the plane to watch at a safer distance. Suddenly, I was breathing wonderfully clean air again. The question was what to do next. We didn't really have anything to use to fight a fire if the gas caught. Our small fire extinguisher was located behind the pilot's seat in the cockpit, buried under cases of produce, so we decided the best we could do was use snow as a fire suppressant. However, we didn't have anything handy like a shovel to throw snow on the engine if it caught fire.

As we watched, with the engine shut down, it cooled, and the smoke began to die back. George decided he wanted to open up the engine cowling to clear it more. We took off our parkas, filled them with snow, and I stood ready to throw snow on the engine if fire erupted. As he opened the compartment, when no open flame was obvious, we decided to stand back and just watch, letting the air cool down the engine even more and get rid of lingering smoke. Had the plane burned, we would have been left with just the clothes we were wearing and no way to communicate, stranded on a small inhospitable island in a very cold and formidable environment. Once everything had burned and snow had covered the burned frame of the plane, two people, alone in the snow, would have been almost impossible to see from the air, and survival and rescue would truly have become problematic.

As we waited for the smoke to clear, I began to be more aware of pain in my elbow, down my right leg, and in my lower back, but I was standing, and I could move. My outer pants had some tears and all my clothes smelled of smoke. I looked at George and it seemed that neither of us was visibly bleeding, so there didn't appear to be any immediate medical emergency. Amazingly, the damage to the frame of the plane was mostly limited to my side of the cabin. When we tried the passenger door, it still wouldn't open, even from the outside. The prop was bent, but fortunately, the plane had not been under power when it hit the snow. Otherwise, the plane showed little damage and, although it sat at an awkward angle, both wings and the tail were undamaged and mostly clear of the snow.

Once it was safe to enter the plane again, the important next step was to radio Hay River to let them know we had landed. After our mayday, they would be waiting to hear from us. If they didn't hear, they would immediately initiate search and rescue procedures. George used his map to identify exactly where we were. We unwound and stretched out the trailing antenna, and I stood and held it clear of the snow behind the plane. George needed the antenna out to ensure his message was heard as far south as Hay River. When he turned on power to use the radio, the sharp jolt of electricity ran down the wire, which made me cry out and drop it. It isn't a good idea to hold an antenna, with power on, when wearing snow-filled wet boots. We had better results when we propped the antenna on a case of oranges from the plane.

George connected with the Hay River radio operator and told him that we were down, the fire was out, and he provided them with our exact location. He went on to tell the operator that the plane was damaged, we would not be able to take off again, we had no serious injuries, but we were stranded on an island in the middle of the Mackenzie River. George then explained that our only option was to wait where we were until we had help to get off the island. He told the operator that we would look for a place where we could possibly create a crude temporary landing strip on the island for a small plane on skis. We were told that the RCMP Beaver had just landed at Hay River, in freezing rain, and was planning to continue north as soon as the weather permitted. They had been advised of our mayday and were standing by to help if possible.

The Beaver was on wheels but could add skis if we could identify a suitable place where it could land on the island. Unless we could find a bit of flat land where we could create a useable though makeshift landing strip, things were going to get a whole lot more complicated for us and especially for anyone trying to reach us. In the early 1960s, no helicopters regularly operated in the North, which meant our only hope for a helicopter rescue would be a military aircraft. The Hay River operator said he would try to find out if there might be a military helicopter available in Alberta. The river ice was already forming, making it no longer safe or possible for a small-boat rescue or to safely land a plane on floats. Nor was the ice, on the fast-flowing river, solid or stable enough to even walk on, so we were truly stranded on the island and could not walk to the mainland until the ice thickened. When that eventually happened, before a plane on skis could land, it would still mean quite a hike for us to reach the nearest settlement, at Fort Norman. We estimated it would be at least another two weeks or more before a small plane could land on the river ice at our location.

The operator went on to tell us the weather was so bad in Hay River that he didn't believe the RCMP could leave until the next day, at the soonest. He advised us to plan for at least one night where we were. We arranged to contact the operator again when we determined if landing on the island was possible. We were definitely between a rock and a hard place—or, more precisely, on a small piece of land surrounded by a wide expanse of deep, fast-flowing river that had only the beginnings of thin ice layers between floating ice cakes. Time was against us, and the prospect of an extended wait on the island, with the increasing cold and shortening flying hours, made finding a possible landing site a very high priority. If we couldn't find a landing site on the island, then finding an available helicopter would become much more important. However, locating a helicopter close by and equipped to fly in our challenging weather made such a rescue an unlikely option.

After the radio call, our first step was to plan how we would spend the night before the light disappeared and the temperature fell. On board, we had a new engine tent, bought for heating the engine during the winter. Unfortunately, we didn't have an aircraft blow pot since ours were in Inuvik, awaiting the plane's conversion to skis. We needed to gather wood and get a fire started soon because it was ten below in the daylight and we knew it would be a lot colder once darkness fell. Fort Norman was above the Arctic Circle but fortunately still below the treeline, giving us access to lots of driftwood. Both of us knew what needed to be done and worked together on our immediate tasks. First we selected a location to make camp and decided how to use the engine tent. We found some limbs to prop up the tent in the lee of a sandbank. We built a fire and once it was going well, we added bigger logs and shoved the fire as close in front of our tent as we safely could.

We then unloaded all the fruit and vegetables we had on board the plane and put them behind the tent. It was obvious we would lose all of this fresh produce, since there wasn't any way we could keep it from freezing, even close to the fire, but we needed to get it all out of the plane to find our survival equipment. Our plight went from bad to worse when we discovered we had no survival box on board. It was to have been transferred from the plane we'd brought down onto this new one. The maintenance people had said they would do it before they loaded the extra plane parts we were taking back with us. A new box was being assembled for the other plane, but it hadn't been completed before we left.

Ultimately, this was a serious error on George's part, since as the pilot of the aircraft, he alone was responsible for ensuring survival supplies were on board. George had moved the hatchet he always carried under his seat himself, but we were without the cooking pot, plates, cups, first aid kit, tea, crackers, chocolate, nuts, raisins, and the small down sleeping bag we usually carried: in other words, we totally lacked the gear essential for our survival. To try to offset this disastrous oversight, I went through everything in the plane looking for something—anything—we could use as a pot in which to heat water. I found nothing that looked like a possible substitute except for the spinnaker on the nose of the plane. George told me our plight wasn't desperate enough to ruin a seventy-dollar aluminum spinnaker, so without a pot, I couldn't heat water. As well, getting the hot water into us without cups would present another challenge. At this point, we fully grasped how poorly we were equipped to survive. Finding a possible landing strip became an even greater priority.

We had a couple heads of cabbage in the produce we were taking back to Inuvik, so later I would carve out the center of one, fill it with water, and try to warm it near the fire. I thought we might use some clothing as potholders and then drink out of the cabbage "pots," but I was never able to get the water even warm before the hollowed-out cabbage began to burn through. So deciding how to get the water to our mouths *from* the burning cabbage became a non-starter. Burning cabbage didn't smell very good either, so I gave up, deciding the idea wasn't workable.

Looking back, our plight would have been so much less difficult if we'd had access to the now abundant, multi-purpose, indeed ubiquitous plastic bag. But this was the early 1960s, so we didn't have the easy option of filling a bag with water from the river and making a hole in the bag to create a small flow, which would be an easy way to drink. Without a bag, a cup of any kind, or a pot (travel mugs were also a feature of the future), we had to go to the river, push away the ice, and scoop up very cold water to drink with our hands. Having to drink icy water from equally cold hands served as a forceful reminder of just how cold our environment was.

Before darkness fell, we started our search for a flat safe area with enough landing space for the RCMP Beaver and, more importantly, sufficient length to take off again. The island was less than a mile long (1.6 kilometres), so our choices were limited. We eventually found a possible location, but even that was a bit marginal in terms of length. It was also on a slight slant because one side sloped towards the river, but George was confident he could land there.

Fortunately, as we walked along this provisional landing strip, we found it was mostly hard under the snow, without any of the channels or ditches we'd encountered when we touched down. To make the strip wide enough and free of obstructions, we would need to dig into the snow and cut out several small bushes as well as roll some pieces of driftwood down to the water's edge. We stomped around until dark, packing down the snow to make sure we hadn't missed any possibly serious problem areas underneath it. We marked out what would be the start and end of our ad hoc landing strip, and George paced out its length one more time to ensure his estimate was accurate. If George was correct, and a small plane could land on this strip, it was going to make a huge difference to our odds of getting off the island. Otherwise, before long, we would face the dire issue of surviving as our world continued to get colder.

13

COURAGE MATTERS

As darkness descended, bringing with it increasing cold, we returned to our camp to plan what more we needed to do before we could settle in for the night. Another vital question was what we might dine on. Our choices were mostly limited to produce and eggs. On return trips, we usually carried as much fresh produce as possible to share with close friends and good neighbours, because this was both scarce and very expensive in the North, and therefore exceptionally welcome. With these very limited choices, we stuck oranges on sticks, warmed them up over the fire, and then sucked on their warm juice. It was so good to have something warm to drink instead of only ice water. We dined on the oranges along with raw cabbage and apples.

After "dinner," we settled in for a long night of stoking the fire and moving every so often to keep both sides of our bodies warm. We always travelled in parkas and warm clothes, and as it got colder, we began to put on as many additional layers as possible. Without a sleeping bag, we would be sitting up, alternately dozing and stoking to keep the fire going all night. We were expecting snow, so the engine tent would help to limit the snow that fell on us. I cut small fir branches for us to sit on. Although we might have considered using the tent to roll up in as a sleeping bag, its most important function was as a windbreak, helping to capture heat from the fire and also providing a place to sit out of the snow. We considered stacking logs to create a more permanent windbreak, but we hoped not to be there long enough to need to do this. Everything depended on our stop-gap strip being long enough to allow landing and takeoff for the Beaver.

The tent did help because, to some degree, it trapped warmth from the fire and limited the flow of wind around us. Above all, we had to focus on keeping our feet and heads warm. After we had done everything possible to make ourselves as comfortable as we could, we settled in for what would be a very long night. I now had time to sit and assess what had happened to my body during the crash. I became very aware of some serious aches and pains. My elbow continued to throb, and I was having trouble getting down and then getting back to my feet once I'd sat down. My lower back and right leg ached, and it felt like a layer of skin had been scraped off my leg and arm. My inner pants and shirt were stuck to my skin in places. George seemed fine although he too complained about being stiff and sore.

For the first time in a very long while, the two of us had a chance to talk. We talked about the danger we'd faced in landing, our risk of dying, and what our deaths would mean to our children. We talked of the challenges we were facing to get off the island, and, yes, we talked of our marriage, infidelity, and lost trust. We spoke of the dream that had brought us to the North and the nightmares that now seemed to interfere with us reaching our goals. How this special time together would influence our future was unknown, but for now we could remember what we meant to each other as we'd started our life and dream together.

It was a very long, very cold night until finally the sky began to lighten, promising the return of daylight and slightly warmer temperatures. If daytime wasn't warmer, at least it was brighter. Breakfast became the next challenge. We had eggs with us that I had buried in the snow to try to keep them from freezing. I had hoped to use the cabbage pot to boil eggs, but since I had abandoned the burnt cabbage idea, I put eggs near the fire on top of the sand and started turning them with sticks in the heat. In a short while the eggs closest to the fire started to explode. Next, I gathered a number of small rocks and made a rock pit at the edge of the fire, buried some of the eggs in the sand inside the pit, added coals on top, and left the eggs to cook for a few hours. Some of them got too hot and disintegrated once again, but others were cooked to varying degrees, could be peeled, and were edible. Our diet had now expanded to cooked eggs and toasted oranges and apples until all the eggs froze. I found it hard to decide when they were cooked, and as they thawed, many leaked into the sand before they cooked.

Shortly after daybreak, we called Hay River to tell them about our possible landing strip and to find out when the RCMP plane might be taking off on its trip north. We were told that the weather was still bad, with freezing rain and fog changing to snow showers at Hay River, creating doubt that they could get away that day. The flying hours were getting shorter as winter approached and our location was about four or five flying hours from Hay River, so the Beaver would have a very limited window to reach our location, particularly with the added concern over weather. George talked to the RCMP pilot and explained in detail the dynamics of our landing strip. Since George seemed to think it was feasible to land there, the RCMP pilot thought it was worth a look when he arrived over us. He told George that the weather was still an issue at Hay River and more snow was in the forecast for our site during the day. As well, there was a prediction of heavy snow all along the southern section of the Mackenzie River. He said a Department of Transport accident investigator was trying to catch up with the RCMP Beaver flight in Hay River before they left, but regardless, he would take off as soon as he could.

I felt overwhelmed by the prospect of another night on the island. By this time the cold invaded my every thought and my total being. I was having increasing physical difficulty moving about because of pain, but moving helped to deal with the invasive cold. Throughout the day, it continued to snow heavily on the island. Visibility was down to nothing, and my thoughts kept wandering to cups of hot coffee or tea, though by now I would have been delighted with just hot water.

We decided to collect more firewood to build up the fire and to make it as visible as possible once the plane was in our area. Then we went to our makeshift landing strip to do more work on it, cutting out some additional small bushes and ensuring it could be seen from the air. We dragged the cut bushes into a pile that we could set on fire if the Beaver had difficulty seeing us. We knew it was likely to begin snowing more heavily and we needed to plan how to clearly mark our possible landing strip when the Beaver arrived overhead. The strip was amazingly short, so to make the surface as compact as possible, we repeatedly side-walked the area, stomping down the snow as it kept falling. The Beaver was going to need to put down at the very beginning of our strip so it could stop before it ran out of runway. No doubt, the pilot and the two of us watching on the ground would be holding our collective breaths. Trying to take off from the island with the added weight of two more passengers would be another reason to hold our breath. Our last task was to bring some clothing from the plane to mark the start and end of the runway for the pilot.

Later, we called Hay River again to find out whether the Beaver had been able to take off. We were told they had taken off accompanied by the DOT accident investigator, who had made the flight. George said the investigator might be a helpful sounding board for the pilot when he had to decide whether he should attempt to land at our site. They expected to be over our island just before dark. After carefully viewing our strip from the air, they planned to fly on north to Norman Wells. There they would unload passengers and everything they wouldn't need, for it was essential to lighten the plane's load and add skis before possibly committing to a landing at our makeshift strip. They planned their return for the next day, during the best light, and depending on the weather at both locations.

We were to watch and make sure they saw us as they flew over. Everyone was hoping the snow would quit or at least lessen enough so they could see us and the strip from the air. The pilot also wanted to confirm exactly where we were in case the weather worsened, or there were further delays trying to get back to us. If he didn't think our strip was workable for the Beaver, they would need to find another way of getting us off the island. The radio operator said that all military helicopters were currently in eastern Canada or Vancouver, British Columbia, so there would be considerable delay in getting one to Alberta and then north to us. However, the military had been notified of our problem and were monitoring the situation. Finally, he wished us luck and told us we were being switched to the radio operator in Norman Wells as our primary contact, but he would be listening to hear how we did.

We prepared yet again to build up our fire and collected green branches to create visible smoke, so we were ready for the Beaver's arrival. We expected the pilot would have some difficulty finding us. Visibility was not very good, but at least the snow was lessening. We took off our parkas and used them to brush the snow off the plane's wings so it would be more visible. We went to the landing strip and laid out more clothing to mark the start and end. Then we went to work on the strip until the light began to fade. The sky darkened, but otherwise we were surrounded by white.

Now that it was certain we would spend a second night on the island, I began to eye the plane's spinnaker again. George insisted I leave it alone. In reality, it was fun to just kid George about the spinnaker, since putting it in the flames would probably create toxic fumes from the paint. This grasping at straws was along the lines of my idea of carving wooden cups from driftwood with only a hatchet as a tool! Meanwhile, George had inspected the damage to the plane and felt he could return with the necessary equipment to salvage it quickly. He would do temporary repairs to the bulkhead and brace the undercarriage on the passenger side, change to skis, put on a new prop, and hope the engine hadn't been seriously damaged when the prop hit the snow.

While checking the damage, George had discovered a serious leak in the oil filter, which he believed had dripped oil onto the manifold and caused our smoking problem. George's opinion was that the oil filter should have been replaced in Edmonton during maintenance, but it had not been, making it possible for us to have a claim against the company responsible for the work. In that event, all the costs of salvaging the plane would be covered. However, we would need support from the crash site investigator and a confirmation from him that the accident was caused by the oil leak. Within minutes of our mayday call, the Department of Transport had been notified and the investigator had then left Edmonton immediately for Hay River. It was fortunate for us that the investigator had caught the RCMP Beaver before it left Hay River, and we hoped that if the Beaver was able to land, he could do his investigation of the crash then.

As it was getting dark, we added more logs to the fire and sat and waited until we heard the drone of the Beaver's engine as it approached, growing ever louder in the silent snow-filled sky. We scanned the sky and saw it making wide circles, but the crew obviously hadn't seen us. George ran to the plane to use the radio to help direct the pilot to our site and I added branches to the fire. He finally saw us and then came in low to have a look at our makeshift runway. George told the pilot of the strip's slight downhill list and the approximate distance he would have in which to stop and then take off again. Everybody could see this landing was our only hope. There was no other way, at that time, for us to get off the island. Without significant survival equipment and food, we would have a very difficult time waiting for the river ice to thicken enough for a plane to safely land on it. A long wait was also involved in locating a helicopter and getting it to our site.

The pilot indicated that he and the DOT investigator would return the next day, weather permitting, during full daylight. He would then make the final decision about landing. Before leaving, he asked if either of us was hurt and if we needed anything else for the night. I kept telling George to say "yes, a sleeping bag, a sleeping bag, a pot, a pot." George shushed me and went back on the air and said, "No, we're fine." After he signed off, I very forcibly told him we were *not* fine. We needed something hot to drink and a chance to sleep. Our life on the island would have been a whole lot more comfortable if we had had our emergency supplies, including a cooking pot and sleeping bag. The thought of managing through the rest of our second day and facing another cold night made it difficult for me to feel positive, and I had long since lost any interest in being a "good sport," knowing we needed something warm to eat, something warm to drink, and the opportunity to sleep.

However, having emergency equipment on board was the pilot's responsibility, and if George admitted we didn't have it, he felt that could confuse his claim against the maintenance company. He was determined that no fault could be pointed in his direction. George flatly told me he was not going to let the accident investigator know we didn't have our emergency supplies and equipment. Besides, he was sure it would only be one more day before we got off the island, and once again I was reminded to be a good sport.

How often, over the years, had George told me to be a good sport? Now that we'd been found, I couldn't say that we were any longer suffering a real emergency; we were just very uncomfortable

—cold, hungry, sleep deprived, but neither of us was burned, bleeding, or had apparent broken bones or breathing difficulties. Yet I was sick of eating toasted oranges and apples and being cold. Another factor reducing my ability to be a good sport was my ongoing pain as I moved about. My positive attitude was also sorely tested when it started to snow heavily again; I worried whether the plane would be able to get back to us the next day. As the drone of the Beaver faded into the night air, our world—the land, the plane, and even the sky—became entirely white as big flakes of falling snow began to cover everything.

We stacked some logs alongside the engine tent to make a better windbreak and settled in for another night by the fire. Again, there was time to talk. If the Beaver wasn't going to land, we would have to build a makeshift shelter and have food and emergency equipment and supplies dropped to us, since we would then have to wait two or three weeks for rescue. We would need to let the people caring for our children know it would be quite a while until we could return.

About midnight the snow began to lessen, giving us hope for better visibility the next day. However, daylight brought more heavy snow. We knew that unless conditions improved, the plane would not be able to get back. As each hour of daylight passed, I wished I had been more insistent that we needed a sleeping bag and a pot. We went to the landing strip to shake out the clothes marking the start and end of the strip, to make sure they were clearly visible. We again side-stepped the new snow in two parallel tracks that were the right width apart for the plane's skis. The landing strip was just a few feet wider, on the brush side, than the usual distance from the centre line of a Beaver to its wingtip. The river was on the other side, so clearance there wasn't a concern if the pilot had reasonable visibility and could line up his aircraft and stay on track. Once again, we made sure the width was consistent along the length of the strip and there was nothing immediately underneath the snow to catch a ski on.

Hours passed. The daylight seemed to be quickly disappearing and still there was no let-up in the snow. If the plane didn't arrive soon, we'd need to spend yet another night on the island. We radioed Norman Wells to find out the status of their weather. We were very happy to hear that the plane had been airborne for a while, flying to our site to see if there might be enough of a break in the snow to consider landing. Once the call was over, George said we should break camp and roll up the engine tent so, if they landed, it would appear we had put all the emergency stuff away. I told George that if the Beaver couldn't land, he had to ask for a sleeping bag. We could claim that the bag was an extra one since there were two of us and we normally carried only one bag. Two other essentials were a pot and some tea. He could find any reason he wanted for needing the pot, such as I had dropped ours in the river when I was getting water. As far as I was concerned, enough was enough. I told him I was cold, in pain, needed something warm to drink, and had completely given up on the idea of being a good sport.

––––––––

LUCKILY FOR US, NATURE DECIDED TO COOPERATE. A SHORT WHILE before the RCMP plane was due to arrive, the snow stopped and visibility improved. I got a few of our things together and moved to the strip to wait for the plane's arrival. Once at our location, the plane circled low over our strip a few times. I could appreciate that the pilot was not too impressed with it and wanted time to consider it before he committed to landing. Finally, he radioed George that he was ready, and he came in as slowly as he possibly could without stalling the plane. He lined up to touch down on his skis at the very start and to continue down the middle of our strip. Once his skis touched, he bumped along for a bit but then came to a safe stop before he ran out of space.

Stuck at our crash site on an island in the Mackenzie River for two nights in the freezing cold, we were overjoyed when this RCMP Beaver arrived to rescue us. © *NWT Archives / Robert C. Knights / N-1993-002-0457*

After a few minutes of relieved greetings, the pilot suggested I warm up in the plane while he, George, and the investigator examined the crash site and our plane. He said they had brought warm soup and coffee in thermos jugs. You could tell everyone was feeling the stress of thinking about our takeoff and clearly wanted to be in the air and on our way to Norman Wells before the weather closed in again. I picked up the clothes we had used on the runway and climbed into the plane. I was very grateful for this brief time alone. All the stresses of the last few days caught up with me as I sat alone in a back seat, huddled over a steaming cup of coffee, and cried.

After the others had checked the downed plane and removed the suspect oil filter, we all strapped ourselves into our seats. I realized, as I was fastening my seat belt, that I was committed to go wherever the Beaver went. All I could do was say a silent prayer and put my belief in the plane and our pilot's obvious skills. After he'd started the engine, we turned and taxied down the strip to its very beginning to gain lift with the wind direction and to get the full benefit of the strip's length. The pilot made some comments about how it was going to be really close. I began sucking in air, preparing to hold my breath, as though the added air in my lungs would help with lift. I thought the others were doing just the same as we began to roll forward. I knew all of us would be willing the plane to start quickly, to gain lift, and at the very soonest, to want to fly.

Fortunately, once we were airborne, we would not have to gain height immediately because the river was in front of us, but it was also a place where we would not want to lose height and catch a ski in the water. Once we were free of the drag of the snow, we needed to quickly gain speed and gain lift. The pilot throttled the engine up to full power and slowly, at first, we started to move. I sat with muscles tight, holding my breath, trying to sense if we were moving fast enough. Our pilot resisted the temptation to pull up too soon, so we rapidly seemed to be approaching the end of our makeshift runway. He gave the plane every chance to fly itself off the ground, ensuring it had gained enough velocity to keep it from losing height and dropping into the river.

Suddenly, we went from taxiing to flying, gaining height and then turning north over the land. Everyone started breathing again; noisy conversation and laughter gave evidence of huge relief. Seated in the warm cabin, I watched out the window as our little island faded from view. As I thought of our last days, I would never again remember being as cold as I was during those three days and two long nights. Indeed, the memory of cold helped blot out my thoughts of the pain that had been so much a part of all I did to survive and get off the island. At any rate, Norman Wells was ahead, and our survival adventure was behind us.

The regularly scheduled PWA return flight from Inuvik to Edmonton was to land in Norman Wells on its trip south at about the same time we would get there. Our pilot radioed ahead, asking them to wait until we arrived. He booked seats for the DOT investigator and George. They wanted to get to Edmonton as quickly as they could, with plans to examine the oil filter, talk to the mechanics, and look at the service records of the company where the plane had been certified. George's other priority was to get the salvaging process underway, so he could get the plane off the island as soon as possible. He had trappers and other people to supply and other flying responsibilities to meet as soon as the ice was ready. We needed to get back to operating two planes to fulfill Arctic Wings' commitments to our customers.

Our short flight to Norman Wells was relaxing and when he landed, the RCMP pilot planned to reload his plane and continue his flight to Inuvik at daylight the next day. Unfortunately, regulations prohibited me from continuing to Inuvik aboard the RCMP plane. Our emergency was over, so the pilot didn't have authorization for me to travel onwards. I would have to wait for a couple of days, until the next scheduled PWA flight.

During the flight to Norman Wells, I had separated out a few of George's clothes, his toothbrush and the like into a small bag, and as soon as we landed, George and the investigator rushed off to catch the plane to Edmonton. The RCMP people were busy getting their plane reloaded and prepared for the next day's flight, so I found myself on my own, thinking about what I would do with myself for two days, until I could fly to Inuvik. Once the flight to Edmonton had taken off, one of the PWA local staff came to claim me as I stood by myself, watching all the activity around me, wondering what I should do next. I was a smelly, sorry-looking sight, forlorn, bedraggled, in a stained and torn parka and pants. I was very cheered by the agent's smiling welcome, given the fears and stresses of the previous few days.

George's plans to salvage the crashed plane went ahead within a couple of weeks. He decided to fly our other Cessna 180, with our new pilot, from Edmonton to the Old Fort Point area. By that time, the river ice was strong enough that they could land on skis. The two pilots made the necessary temporary repairs to salvage the damaged Cessna, put skis on it, and manhandled it with its makeshift patches onto the river ice. Our temporary landing strip suited a Cessna 180 better than it had the Beaver, but even so, George decided the additional length available on river ice, considering the patched undercarriage and new prop, made taking off safer, in case of unexpected problems. Once George was in the air, on his way to Edmonton, our new pilot flew the other Cessna to Inuvik.

So, what damage *had* the crash inflicted on my body? Once I had been shown to a bedroom in the PWA crew quarters, although I was hungry, I was less interested in the 6:00 p.m. dinner than in having a shower and examining my various injuries. Undressing for a shower was my first real chance to assess the damage. On the island, I had been so busy trying to keep warm that I'd made sure none of my body was exposed to the cold that didn't have to be. Now the bad news was all too visible. My right elbow was swollen, my arm was black and blue, and I had scraped the skin off my arm as far as the elbow as well as around my right knee. My knee was very swollen and my leg, near my knee, was also badly bruised. Dried blood had glued sections of my clothing to my hide, so I had to use water and a washcloth to pry the clothing loose. When I got into the shower, I soon found I was gasping in pain as the water reached the large areas of raw skin on my leg and arm. Using as little soap as possible was the only way to avoid the breathtaking pain that water and soap inflicted on raw flesh. When I had finished washing away the sand, grit, and the smell of both cockpit and campfire smoke, I made another assessment as I dried myself and knew I should seek medical attention if I wanted to avoid infection. I had little clothing with me except extra underwear and socks, but the PWA crew had found sweatpants and a sweatshirt that I could borrow, which were somewhere near my size. When I wanted to go outside to find the doctor, they loaned me insulated coveralls that reminded me of George's navy flying suit.

The oil company doctor in Norman Wells had sent a message when I arrived, asking if I was hurt and needed any help, so I decided I had to see him. He said he thought I might have sprained my elbow and just badly bruised my knee, but he was more concerned about my back and said he wasn't able to even guess the extent of any spinal injury I might have suffered. He had limited diagnostic equipment since his job mostly involved stabilizing any injured or sick oil company employees and shipping them out to Edmonton. Unfortunately, he decided my scrapes needed more cleaning, which again proved very painful, but at least he did cover them with antiseptic ointment afterwards. He gave me some pain pills and a couple of sleeping pills and advised me to see a doctor when I reached Inuvik, because it would require x-rays of my elbow, knee, and back to diagnose the true extent of my injuries.

After dinner with the PWA crew, I just didn't have the energy to push myself any more and retreated to my room to sleep. Now that I had the luxury of a warm bed in a warm room, a full stomach, and had taken a pain pill, I thought all I would need to do was close my eyes, yet I found myself lying awake, staring into the darkness. I got up and took a sleeping pill, but still I couldn't relax enough to fall asleep. As I lay there, my thoughts went to all that had happened during the past few days. Regardless of my concerns over our marriage and family issues, I knew George was as great a pilot as Russ Baker was reputed to have been. He had done all the right things to get us down safely, especially once the smoke increased and our choices became so limited. He had come in to land as close to stalling speed as he could. Had we been going any faster, I'm sure our forward motion would have caused the plane to flip over. As things started to go wrong, if George had tried to second-guess himself or tried to add power and regain flight as we were landing, the accident would have been much worse and possibly fatal, particularly if we had ended up in the river. I thought about the courage it took George to commit to landing, to believe in his decision, and then to keep thinking rather than reacting when the reality of our extensive problems became all too obvious.

I thought about the RCMP pilot and the courage it had taken to decide to land on our crude little strip. Afterwards, he'd had the confidence to let the plane fly itself off the strip rather than questioning himself about whether we were moving quickly enough to gain lift or whether there would be enough strip. Had he pulled the nose up too early, trying to get the plane to fly before it was ready, we would have probably caught the plane's undercarriage in the water and found ourselves in the river. To wait for the plane to gain lift and wait for it to fly took courage. I recognized there had to have been significant trust between both pilots when the Beaver pilot decided to believe George that the landing and takeoff from our strip were doable. As well, the RCMP pilot had had to believe in his own skills to be willing to challenge himself to land. As a pilot, it was well within his control and his responsibility for his plane and passenger, not to mention himself, to decide he wouldn't take the chance of landing on the island.

It had been such an amazing four days, and these two skilled pilots were the reason we'd had a happy ending. They had both clearly demonstrated the "make-do or improvise" attitude, along with the skills and courage, that made bush pilots so famous. There was no question: bush pilots like these two deserved to be held in great esteem, not only in the North but throughout Canada.

Finally, sometime in the early morning hours, I fell asleep. I slept right through until lunchtime. When I tried to move, I had difficulty figuring out how to turn over. The next challenge was to try to get out of bed. I had to roll out and land on my hands and knees and then push myself to my feet, first putting my hands on my knees and finally straightening up. The next challenge was to dress myself so I could join the PWA staff for lunch. After lunch, I went back to bed and slept until dinner. When dinner was finished, I visited with some of the staff and townspeople for a short while and then went to bed and slept again. Finally, after I'd spent two days mostly eating and sleeping, along with washing my clothes and stitching up some of the tears in my parka and pants, the PWA plane arrived so I could return to Inuvik. I said thank-you and goodbye to my hosts; then it was off to pick up Duncan and Lesley in Inuvik. There we'd catch the scheduled Otter flight to Tuk and home, where we could all be together with David.

14

TROUBLING TIMES

When I landed in Inuvik, Vern and Dell had brought Lesley and Duncan to meet me at the plane. I had only been gone for two weeks, but it seemed like forever, and I badly wanted to get home and regroup. While I understood how important it was for me to see a doctor, I definitely wasn't prepared to deal with at least a three-day stopover in Inuvik if I missed the Otter flight to Tuk. This was the time of freeze-up and flights to Tuk were limited. Getting home was my single-minded focus, and I thought all my aches and pains would heal given time.

When I arrived home and walked in the door, I felt so relieved as I gathered all my little ones around me. During quiet times on the island and later in Norman Wells, I had thought about what would have happened to the children if both George and I had been killed. The accident had made me realize I needed to have a will that defined a plan for the children. It was vital that I identify someone who wanted to care for them if we couldn't, in the event of our deaths. Within the month, I had made a will and made legal arrangements for the children to be cared for by Bud and Pat, my friends in California, whom I knew would love them as well as take care of them.

Regardless of the death-defying adventures I had experienced in the past days, things had not changed in Tuk, so I was right back to my usual routine of demanding physical work. Returning to work made my back worse rather than better, but in Tuk there was little I could do about it. The pain in my back and numbness and pain in my leg were making mobility and sleep very difficult, but I thought I just needed to be patient and give my injuries more time to heal. Meanwhile, after our new pilot had helped George salvage the plane on the island, our new recruit had flown our older Cessna 180 to Inuvik. George left the salvaged plane to be fixed in Edmonton and returned north immediately to share the flying load with this new employee. Leaving this pilot alone to do all the flying already waiting for Arctic Wings was unrealistic, especially when he was new to bush flying and had limited hours on the Cessna 180.

Our new hire had only logged flying hours in the air force so had no previous bush flying or Arctic experience. Although George too had lacked bush experience as he began his career, when he hired this pilot, I think he underestimated the unique skills he himself had brought to flying in the North. It was immediately evident that our new employee was weak in the many skills essential to becoming a competent bush pilot. To fly in the Arctic, a pilot first of all needed a strong natural sense of direction, and he also had to have the essential skills of map-reading, landscape observation, memory, and identification. A pilot's success depended on the ability to recognize and remember even the smallest variances in the landscape. Self-confidence, believing in your skills, as well as being a quick and effective decision-maker were standard characteristics of any safe and successful bush pilot. Unfortunately, since he lacked many of these essential abilities, before long our new hire began making excuses to avoid flying to remote and other challenging locations. Even his flying time on some of his trips seemed excessive, leaving George to suspect he might have been unsure of where he was.

After a short while, and before George had time to act on the realization that this pilot was unsuitable, our new pilot announced he was quitting. He would subsequently get a job flying in the Yellowknife area and in 1967, he would get lost flying fish to Yellowknife. He would fly lost until he ran out of gas. Once out of gas, he landed on a lake without damaging either the plane or himself. He was quite a distance off course by that time, so many weeks passed before he was found. His descriptions of his survival while waiting to be found left many questions and doubts, as did his failure to accurately radio in his approximate location while he was still flying. As far as I know he never had a job flying in the North again. The ultimate irony of this story is that the southern press enjoyed his tale of survival, failing to understand that they were making him into a hero for his lack of ability as a bush pilot, rather than for his skills.

When George first returned to Inuvik, I asked him to get painkillers from the doctor there so I could stay mobile until my back healed. I was having increasing difficulty doing all the normal movements required in a day's work. Often I had to carry Duncan while bent over and I trained Lesley to do most things for herself, because I couldn't bend easily or pick her up any more. I had to rely even more on paying Rosemary to help me with my usual workload.

At the hospital in Inuvik, doctors came and went frequently, so no one seemed concerned about the regular prescription renewals for pain pills George was getting for me, and neither was anyone keeping track of how long I had been taking them. As time passed, the pills were barely taking the edge off the pain, but they did keep me somewhat mobile. As a result of being in pain, along with the side effects of the medication, I was eating very little. I steadily lost weight, and one day when George was in Tuk, he mentioned that I was dragging my right leg behind me as I walked. Even still, I was convinced that waiting for my many injuries to heal was my best option. Seeing a doctor would be tricky. Winter had closed in and a trip to Inuvik to visit the hospital would mean at least two or three days away from Tuk because of the short flying hours.

George and I both had our own agendas: I wanted to be available for the children and to be in Tuk, while he wasn't about to recommend actions that would have left him without his very competent manager and trader—a trader who was busy getting trappers supplied and arranging for flights to their camps. So we both put off accepting the reality that I was not recovering, and I needed medical help to diagnose and treat my obviously serious health issues.

Our second plane, now repaired, remained in Edmonton since George was now our only pilot, leaving him with a hectic schedule as he tried to do the work of two. Hiring another pilot, especially one with proven experience in bush flying, seemed an impossible challenge, and George decided he would only schedule work for himself until he found another skilled, experienced person. Now he was even busier, and we only saw him when he had a charter in the Tuk area.

Duncan's first Christmas was a very quiet family holiday. I was in so much pain I couldn't do much beyond what was absolutely necessary. Before Christmas, George flew a small tree to Tuk for us. He cut the tree and stuffed it into the plane without warming up the sap, which then caused it to lose most of its needles. Regardless, David and I decorated the branches, so again we had a Christmas tree. We ate a canned ham and canned sweet potatoes. Dell had sent some baking, so Christmas Day and dinner were both good. We lived a pretty minimalist sort of life, so the kids were used to receiving just a few presents. We didn't have many visitors over the holidays as my poor health limited any community celebration of our tree. George only stayed in Tuk for Christmas Eve and Christmas dinner and then returned to Inuvik, so the holiday was short.

By the end of December, moving at all became extremely agonizing and I had to have help to care for the children, clean the house, and operate the trading post as well as to grade fur. I continued to lose weight and had a tough time finding a pain-free way to move or sleep. Fortunately for me, the next general duty physician from Edmonton's University Hospital who came to Inuvik on rotation happened to be an orthopaedic intern. As part of his rotation, he was scheduled to fly to Tuk to do a general medical clinic at the nursing station. The station nurse asked him to visit me at home. She had become increasingly concerned over my very noticeable pain in moving and my loss of weight and general poor health.

As we talked, the doctor quite emphatically advised me that my failure to recover from my injuries was very serious. My declining general health as well as my long-term use of prescribed painkillers only increased his level of concern. As a result, he insisted that I fly out with him to Inuvik for x-rays and tests. He said he thought one or more discs in my back were ruptured and also that vertebrae had been damaged in the crash. This had resulted in nerve damage affecting my leg and foot. He said I had developed possible inflammation from irritating the spinal area. By this time I was too sick to argue, so I arranged for Rosemary to take care of David and Lesley full time and, taking Duncan with me to stay with Dell, flew to Inuvik with the doctor on his return trip.

I was immediately hospitalized and stayed for a month in traction and on antibiotics, anti-inflammatories, and pain control medicines. However, at the end of the month, there was still no noticeable improvement. The doctor didn't have the appropriate diagnostic equipment to determine the extent of my injuries and he was certain that I would need surgery, since rest had not improved either my pain or my mobility. He felt he had done everything possible with the services available in the North. He recommended an appointment with an orthopaedic specialist at University Hospital and made arrangements for me to fly to Edmonton.

My life seemed to be coming apart, and I knew I couldn't return to Tuk until I was better. I lacked the heart to push myself any more. I was having trouble tolerating some of the medication prescribed, I had continued to lose weight, and my general health had only marginally improved. I finally accepted I had no choice, so I reluctantly agreed I would fly out to Edmonton. Before I left, I arranged for Duncan to continue to stay with Dell while I was away. Much to my relief, the Hawleys agreed to make my now seven-month-old baby part of their lives until I could get back. Vern had a responsibility, during the spring, to go out to the Canadian Wildlife Service research cabin to work on his muskrat research contract. He had planned to take his family to the cabin, where Dell would home-school the children for this part of their school year. They were willing to take Duncan with them, and we could pick him up at the cabin when I returned from Edmonton.

Three-year-old Lesley was to stay with the Burnetts in Inuvik, where she could be around other children. David stayed at our house in Tuk, to attend school, and Rosemary would take care of him and the store while I was away. Eddie offered to grade and buy furs for me. It all seemed like a good plan, but I didn't anticipate that Lesley would not handle the separation from both me and her older brother at all well. I received a letter from the Burnetts to let me know of her challenges. She had always been such an outgoing child and I thought she would thrive in the busy, child-oriented Burnett household. After I left, she became quiet, withdrawn, and didn't seem to want to be involved with all the people and activities happening around her. As a result, I wrote to George and asked him to take her back to Tuk, to be with her brother and among the community of people she knew and loved. Once again, the community was there for her and she settled back into being home with her brother, helping Rosemary in the store, and being in the world she knew. Soon she was her usual happy, outgoing, and confident self again.

After a series of tests at University Hospital, I was told that I had cracked vertebrae in my spine and ruptured discs that were pressing on the sciatic nerve, causing nerve pain and damage, all the result of the plane crash. Lack of treatment, along with the overall deterioration of my health, had also caused inflammation around my spine. My treatment involved undergoing a new spinal surgery procedure that would include removal of the ruptured discs, followed by a spinal fusion to both strengthen and immobilize vertebrae in my lower spine. The fusion would require taking bone from my hip to add to my spine to strengthen it and to give it time to fuse the vertebrae. This was considered experimental surgery at the time. Today it has been replaced by treatment that uses rods and screws to strengthen and immobilize vertebrae in the spinal column and which can be adjusted as needed with minor surgery.

The fusion process I faced meant hospital care for a minimum of four months. My specialist physicians hoped that when the pressure and swelling around the spinal cord was gone, some of the nerve damage would repair itself. However, I was warned to expect some permanent damage. I was staggered to learn how long I would have to be in hospital and away from the children. Yet I agreed to the surgery knowing, in my heart, I had no real choice if I wanted to be well again. I wired Inuvik to let George know and asked him to ensure that the children were settled for the four months. It was going to put huge pressures on him to try to fly as well as manage things in Tuk, but he had no other choice.

———

I REMEMBERED VERY LITTLE FOR THE FIRST TWO WEEKS FOLLOWING surgery. The procedures caused major swelling, resulting in heavy sedation. I developed a form of pneumonia, not only because of my general poor health, but also because the lengthy surgery had required prolonged use of anaesthesia. This chest infection was compounded by the need to remain flat on my stomach or on my back following surgery. I was critically ill for a time while my body struggled to rally in the face of these huge challenges.

A strong will to live seemed to make the difference, and slowly I began to recover. Soon I became aware of either looking at the floor or looking at the ceiling. This would be my horizon for four months. I was pancaked between two boards attached to a frame and screwed down so I could be turned over like a rotisserie, in what I would learn was called a Stryker frame (after its inventor, the American orthopaedic surgeon Homer Stryker). I wasn't allowed to move anything but my arms and head at first. It was a frightening experience to realize I had become almost completely dependent on others for almost everything. Eventually I would be able to move my feet in a very limited way, but I wasn't permitted to sit or stand until the last days before I left the hospital.

I was truly limited in what I could do during those months of very long days and nights. In my younger years, I had learned to find comfort in my own mind and thinking, and this ability would serve me well through these trying months. In those days, letter-writing happened only when absolutely necessary, so I received few letters and was completely cut off from the news of Tuk and my friends there, except for some news I got from George about Lesley and David. I would hear news of Duncan, thanks to Dell's regular letters.

The nurses were very good to me, knowing I was alone, without family or friends in Edmonton. When Mother's Day came, they bought chocolates and put the children's names on the box. I would get special little goodies and extra food I liked from the kitchen. If flowers were left behind when other patients went home, the nurses brought them to my room. And if I wanted some junk food or needed personal items, they would shop for me on their off hours and at times, I suspect, using their own money. There wasn't much I could do but read during my waking hours, so the staff collected books and other reading material for me when other patients were through with them, and I borrowed books from the hospital library. The nurses and doctors were a warm, caring group whose professionalism and kindness made me feel that my struggles to recover were important to them.

More than four months after the surgery, I said goodbye to the Stryker frame and was moved into a standard hospital bed. I was told it was time for me to learn to walk again. To me that sounded ludicrous, because I couldn't believe a person could forget how to walk. However, the first day when I stood up, with the help of a physiotherapist, I realized I had indeed "forgotten" what I needed to tell my muscles in order to take a few halting steps and then to walk. Finally, after just one week of physiotherapy, I was turned loose to return to Tuk. We hugged and I bade a tearful goodbye to all the nurses who had been so good to me, got a ride to the airport, and left Edmonton on the regularly scheduled PWA flight. The specialist had made specific arrangements with the airline so I was allowed to stand as much as possible during my very long flight home. Sitting was to be very limited for the next few months.

All I could think of, as we flew north, was picking up Duncan from the Hawleys and taking him back to Tuk to join Lesley and David there. I wanted to have my children home and for us to be a family again. I expected there was a chance Duncan, being so young, would not remember me, and he didn't. He had no idea who I was. When I held him, he turned and wanted Dell to take him back. Dell had become his mother and he didn't want to leave her. Although Duncan's unhappiness at leaving Dell was a bit troubling for me, I knew it was, at least, equally hard for Dell to see him go. He had been loved, well cared for, and would be truly missed by all the Hawley family. Duncan still had the remainder of many mosquito bites all over his face and arms. Dell explained that he had crawled out the screen door at the cabin, but because she could hear him talking to himself, she hadn't realized he was outside. When she came to check on him, he was on the wrong side of the screen door and covered in bites.

George was on hand to fly me and our very unhappy, almost year-old baby boy back to Tuk. Fortunately, both Lesley and David welcomed me back with enthusiasm. Duncan soon returned to being his sunny, happy self and seemed to realize he was in his home; he was with his brother and sister, and I was his caregiver now. But for the rest of her time in the North, Dell would always be a very special person to Duncan.

My workload hadn't changed when I returned to Tuk. Rosemary and Eddie had done a great job of keeping up with the basic chores, but now I needed to plan for next winter and order supplies, which had to arrive during the so short summer ahead. Along with all this busy work, I had to focus on developing new and essential skills— learning new ways to do tasks that required physical effort and muscles. Life in the Arctic always required a lot of strength, but after my surgery, I now needed to be smarter about how I did things. My many responsibilities all involved lifting and carrying: large ice blocks needed to be brought inside and put in forty-five-gallon drums to melt for water; large pots of water had to be lifted onto the stove to be heated for dishes, baths, and clothes washing; water drums had to be washed out to remove the organic matter, then tipped and emptied; and all waste water, including the honey bucket, had to be hauled out of the house to be dumped. In addition, making bread meant mixing, kneading, and bending; clothes had to be washed and hung to dry; dirty diapers meant a trip down to the bay to dippy-do until freeze-up; and the generator had to be cranked to get it started. In the store, unpacking supplies, stocking shelves, and repacking orders went on almost daily. Fortunately, practising what the physiotherapist had taught me about the care and strengthening of my back was successful, so I slowly grew stronger again. In the early days I continued to hire Rosemary to help me, and David helped as much as a seven-year-old could to lift and carry things.

Relieved to be home in Tuk with my youngest children—Lesley and Duncan. This was following the five months I spent in both Inuvik Hospital and University Hospital, Edmonton, recovering from severe spinal injury.

Within weeks of getting back to Tuk, Duncan had his first asthma attack. I didn't know what was wrong with him, but he was obviously having serious trouble breathing. I rushed him to the nursing station, and the nurse said he needed to go to the hospital in Inuvik immediately. Leaving Duncan with the nurse, I hurried home to radio George, to find out if he or any other planes were in our area. Mike Zubko, from Aklavik Flying Service, called back to say he was about to land in Tuk, so I rushed down to the dock, as he landed, to ask if he could fly Duncan and me to the hospital in Inuvik.

He had a full load of passengers and explained to me that his passengers had flown to Tuk for a quick look at the settlement and the Beaufort Sea but were scheduled to leave Inuvik that afternoon on Pacific Western's biweekly flight to Edmonton. He said he could take Duncan, but he didn't have room for me. If he left one of his passengers behind, to take me, that passenger would miss the flight to Edmonton. Listening to our conversation, one of the three passengers asked if they could see Duncan, explaining that he and the other passengers were pathologists, who had been at a conference in Edmonton and decided to take the opportunity to see some of the western Arctic and visit the Inuvik hospital. They now needed to catch the flight to Edmonton to connect to onwards flights to their homes and their practices.

The group of us rushed to the nursing station to see Duncan. After the doctors looked at him and listened to his breathing, they all agreed he needed to get to the hospital right away. They asked if I would let them take Duncan to the hospital without me. Mike said he would let George know Duncan was on his way there and he would call the RCMP in Inuvik to notify them of the emergency. Mike also said he would stay in touch by radio during the flight. I knew, following the arrival of the Edmonton PWA flight, there would be a scheduled PWA Otter flight coming into Tuk, and I could catch a ride to Inuvik on its return trip. It was an amazing coincidence that the passengers on Mike's flight were all doctors, even if their specialty was pathology, but it was still hard to think of Duncan going without me.

The doctors didn't take any time to see Tuk, except what they had seen from the air. I was very grateful to them, but it was still wrenching to hand over my year-old son to strangers, particularly as I stood on the plane's floats and passed him to the closest doctor. I watched as Duncan struggled to find enough air to cry as he fought to breathe. He tried to reach out to me to take him back as I was shutting the cockpit door. I watched the plane taxi out into the harbour and take off. Gradually it disappeared, taking along with it part of my heart.

George met me as soon as I arrived in Inuvik and took me to the hospital, where I was told that Duncan's diagnosis was an asthma attack. After a week in the hospital, Duncan returned home feeling well and was his happy self again, but less than a month later, he had another attack and we made another frantic trip, by air, to the hospital. After the second attack, his asthma was now diagnosed as a chronic condition and, since the cause of the attacks was unknown, we were warned that his attacks would not be predictable or preventable until we learned if there was a pattern or cause for them. We were also told that when Duncan had additional attacks, they would continue to be very serious ones. Without medical intervention, this level of breathing difficulty would be life-threatening. And we were advised that Duncan needed to see a specialist in Edmonton to get allergy or other diagnostic testing, so we could understand what was triggering his attacks. In that way we could determine if there were shots or some other medical intervention that could help control or lessen their severity.

After listening to the doctor, I decided I was no longer prepared to live in Tuk with Duncan, knowing that meant taking the chance of losing him, if we couldn't get him immediate medical help. Up till now we had been lucky, since his emergencies had occurred during the long bright days of summer. However, when short flying days and winter weather arrived, these would pose an altogether unacceptable risk to Duncan's life. I told George he would have to make other plans for someone to run the Tuk operations. The children and I were going to move back to Inuvik to be near the hospital, where Duncan could get medical help whenever he needed it.

In the past, I had been prepared to listen to the idea that I should be a "good sport." This was always a clear message that my priorities must support our businesses or George's needs. I was the one who had to make compromises involving myself and the children. This situation was far beyond the definition of being a good sport, as I was not prepared to risk Duncan's life.

Because George had shown such a sustained lack of concern for Duncan or any real interest in him since his birth, I was surprised when he immediately agreed that we should move back to live in Inuvik. I thought George was finally listening to me and that he was really concerned about Duncan, but I would soon learn that in fact he had his own larger agenda: new plans for the development of much wider business interests in Inuvik. He was tiring of flying and all the issues with finding competent pilots. He felt he could no longer really grow Arctic Wings, and he saw that the fur industry was collapsing much quicker than he'd thought it would. He decided the timing of the family move back to Inuvik would help support his ideas and his pursuit of new objectives. He told me he had originally planned to move more slowly in establishing these changes. Duncan's health and my insistence on living in Inuvik would just force him to move more quickly with his plans, but he was confident his new focus represented a successful strategy for our future.

15

TOO MANY GOODBYES

Characteristically, George had not let my being away in hospital serve as an impediment to progress. He continued to charge ahead with his many ambitious plans. So, it was definitely news to me when I found out that, earlier in the year, George had purchased a commercial lot in the new business section of Inuvik. This lot was to be connected to the utilidor system during the summer. He had also bought an adjacent residential lot on the next street, and that was scheduled to be connected to the utilidor in a later phase. I can't claim all this busy activity was a major surprise: I had come to realize that George was perpetually in search of new challenges or adventures.

Also, during the past winter, George had ordered a large prefab metal-clad building to be shipped on the earliest barges. The commercial lot had been prepared for the building before the barges arrived. Fortunately—or unfortunately, depending on your perspective—unemployed skilled Indigenous workers were readily available so he could put them to work and start assembling the new building as soon as it arrived. George planned that this building would house a Sears catalogue distribution centre and a women's clothing store, along with office space to rent to government agencies. The building shell was to be completed during the summer and the building interior was to be finished in late fall and winter. By that time, flying hours would be limited and George would have much more time to supervise the work.

Originally, George had planned that I would spend one more winter in Tuk, running the businesses there to earn the additional money required to finish the new building. His plans included moving the family back to Inuvik the next summer, when the building was complete and he would need my help to get the stores open, and I would continue to act as building manager. As I heard all this, I was amazed, once again, to find how much of our future life had been decided, while I was away, and completely without my knowledge. However, I couldn't argue that George's ideas lacked potential, creativity, or soundness. I did think he might have shared his plans when I returned from Edmonton, even if it was too late for me to be a party to the decision-making. Duncan's health issues had apparently hastened the sharing of his plans. I wondered if his delay in divulging these plans had been driven by his determination to make it impossible for me to refuse to leave Tuk. I certainly would have been much less willing to leave that wonderful community had Duncan's health issues not made the move necessary.

Recently, George had received inquiries about a contract to expedite and deliver fresh food and supplies to the oil company camps being set up around the western Arctic. Work crews would move into these camps beginning at this year's freeze-up. Now that I would be back in Inuvik by freeze-up, George felt free to add these expediting contracts to my list of new jobs. Monies earned here would help replace the reduced income from Tuk and would be used to complete the new building.

George put people to work immediately to close up the new prefab building, connect it to the utilidor, and finish the storage area at the back. This storage area would be our temporary living quarters until our house could be barged from Tuk, skidded from the riverbank to the residential lot, and set up on permanent pilings. To do this would require enough compacted snow on the roads to pull the house on its sled to our lot. However, George didn't expect to get the house set up until he had the time and equipment to drive the house pilings, since his priority was to finish the new commercial building. The house could not be connected to the utilidor until it was off the sled and on permanent pilings; the plan was to get it all done during the next summer. Impending freeze-up pushed George to take the first steps in the planned move: arranging to barge our house from Tuk to Inuvik.

George had obviously lost interest in our Tuk businesses, so he decided to let the man he had hired years before manage both the store and café over the winter and have Rosemary continue her job in the store. George clearly recognized the impact that the end of the fashion fur market would have on the town, and he was no longer interested in trying to grow Arctic Wings there either. He had abandoned any attempt to hire another pilot and was now limiting the company's flying to what he himself could do. If I wasn't going to be managing the businesses in Tuk any longer, then he wanted to only support a store and restaurant and to end our trading and fur buying altogether. George made it clear to his Tuk manager that he had no authority to give trappers credit for supplies or their flights to camps during the coming trapping season: only George could make those decisions.

At the end of summer, when it was time for us to leave Tuk, George took Duncan to Inuvik to stay with Dell. As we prepared to leave, the other two children and I said our tearful goodbyes to Father Le Meur, Rosemary, Eddie, Violet, and our many friends. For more than two years, we had been part of the warm Tuk community, and now we had to leave good friends and a place where we'd felt sincerely welcomed. Although it had been a challenging life, a feeling of belonging and the love the community had for my children meant so much to me. We boarded the barge, along with our house, and waved goodbye to everyone lining the shore to watch as the tug pushed our house, loaded on the barge, out of the harbour and into the Beaufort Sea to begin our westbound journey to the mouth of the Mackenzie River.

The barge was being pushed ahead of the boat, rather than pulled behind, so its direction was easier to control and turns could be made more easily. As we approached the entrance to the river, I took a two-way radio and went up into the attic at the peak of the house, to watch for sandbars and direct the boat's skipper. The house was so big that it blocked much of the skipper's ability to see in front of him. Yet he had to pick a careful route through the shallower water and the sandbars at the mouth of the river. We cleared this area with no difficulty and began our journey of 95 miles (150 kilometres) south along the river. We were moving against the water's flow and gusts periodically caught the bulk of the house, causing it to try to sail with the wind. The multi-day trip was very slow going, but it was also peaceful and quiet. The sound of the boat's engine seemed to dissipate and spread out across the broad expanse of the river and tundra. We lived in the house, sleeping in our own beds and cooking on a camp stove, as we chugged along the river, with its unlimited view of the horizon and faraway mountains.

Before we reached Reindeer Station, we began to see the scrubby little trees that marked the beginning of the treeline. Also, near Reindeer Station, the river split: we followed the east branch to Inuvik and our trip ended after three days, far too soon for me. I truly enjoyed the brief respite and the beauty surrounding us as we watched from our floating house. Meanwhile, in Inuvik, the rush was on to finish the storeroom area for us to live in. I knew, when we arrived, my life would once again become endlessly busy with many things to be done, consuming long hours of my time.

Our new home in the storage room was small, but it was connected to the utilidor, which meant I would have running water for the first time during my life in the North, except for our very short sublet when we'd lived in Dell and Vern's house. The public bathroom, which had been built as part of the shopping centre, was located just outside the storage room. It included a shower, along with a washer and dryer, and was easily accessible for our use. A small kitchen counter, sink, electric stove, and fridge were in the open storage room, which would later be walled off to become a lunchroom. Temporary walls had been put up in the storage room to create a tiny bedroom, just big enough to contain bunk beds for Lesley and David and a crib for Duncan. Our bed and a table and chairs from the Tuk house were in the open storage room, along with many boxes containing our year's food supplies that couldn't be allowed to freeze. All the rest of our things, for which freezing was not a concern, were left in our much-travelled house, where it sat on the riverbank. Our living space was very small, but it was clean and warm, and I rejoiced over having running water. I would begin to toilet train Duncan in the next few months, but cleaning diapers, getting and disposing of water, and heating our home were no longer the time-consuming chores they'd been in Tuk.

As expected, on my arrival back in Inuvik, my days had already been earmarked to implement George's latest projects. Once more, much was expected of me as we settled into our new life in Inuvik. I was to manage and expedite the distribution of fresh food and supplies for the three (to start with) new oil exploration camps, including ordering fresh food in bulk, as well as repacking the food and distributing it to the camps. Whatever equipment, supplies, and food that could be sent by barge had already arrived at or near the camp sites before freeze-up, but I would be in charge of making sure each camp received regular deliveries of fresh food and supplies, along with smaller replacement parts and equipment, until the barges ran again after spring breakup. My work started immediately as food began arriving on the scheduled PWA flights from Edmonton, since crews were already working at the various camps.

Occasionally large planes, chartered by the oil companies, arrived with larger amounts of equipment and supplies, and these instantly became my major distribution nightmare.

My family enjoyed a special benefit from my new job: while ordering food for the camps, I could also order small amounts of fresh food for us, which was delivered along with the camp orders. Now the children had some apples, oranges, and fresh eggs to eat. Once the orders arrived, food and supplies had to be rapidly sorted and repacked, based on each camp's orders. On the day they arrived, I worked throughout the night sorting the perishables so they could be delivered the following day. We had limited spaces at the appropriate temperature to maintain fresh food, so it had to be sorted and ready to ship to the oil camps during the limited flying hours the next day, whether using Arctic Wings' or another company's planes. In contrast, frozen foods and non-perishables were not an immediate concern now that freeze-up had arrived and distribution didn't need to be so instant.

Many of the cooks working at the oil camps were Chinese, and I was challenged to understand or even spell some of the things they ordered over the radio. Then, when the food arrived, my next challenge was to match my order with what was delivered, such as Chinese meats and vegetables, fresh and dried spices, along with an assortment of fresh noodles and wraps. I got a pamphlet from the Edmonton distributor that detailed Chinese foods so I could identify items when they arrived. Sorting and repacking required a great deal of physical work, mostly bending and lifting, but it was good for me physically, providing I followed what I had learned from the hospital physiotherapist. As a result of all this physical effort, my general health continued to improve, and I became stronger and more flexible.

George still had a heavy flying workload, so most of the sorting, repackaging, and distributing work was left to me. As winter continued, George finished sections of the commercial building, leased limited office space to a government agency, and continued to prepare the rest of the space for additional new businesses.

It was great to be in the same town as Dell once again, but our time together was coming to an end. Vern was finishing his contract with the Canadian Wildlife Service and had accepted a new job outside. The family was scheduled to leave shortly after we arrived back in Inuvik. It was hard for me to think of losing such a special friend so soon after saying goodbye to friends in Tuk. We had felt such a part of that community when we had to leave our life and friends there, and now I would have to say goodbye to Dell and her family. There seemed to be too many goodbyes.

I knew things in Inuvik would not be the same as when we'd lived there before. The pressures for change had become more intense as the number of southern Canadians living in Inuvik increased, bringing with them the expectations to make Inuvik more like the South. Many more cars had been barged north, and more services and private businesses were developing. Social activities, community sports, and celebrations seemed to be keeping people busy. Regardless of the apparent busyness of the community, I soon realized that Inuvik lacked that continuity, cohesiveness, and sense of community I had experienced in Aklavik and in Tuk. Divisions between the lifestyle and status of people were evident, and Inuvik seemed to be a town in the process of becoming something. However, I felt that no one knew what that something would be, or even when and how it would happen.

Inuvik was a strangely unique town surrounded by an Arctic environment where Indigenous people had a long history of living in balance with nature. Before the latter half of the 1950s, Indigenous ways of doing things and life in the broader Arctic had been largely unchanging and predictable for many generations. Now it was becoming increasingly obvious how much of the old ways would be lost in the future, if Inuvik was the model of what was planned for the "New North." It took only a few days for me to become aware of how much Inuvik had changed in the two years I had been away. During those years, I too had changed, in my thinking and understanding of the North as well as who I was as a person.

George's tendency to be abrasive and his practice of being impatient with people he believed to be fools had antagonized many government people, setting me up to be isolated in my life and work even before I arrived. Many of the government people I had known had left, and there didn't seem to be the same sense of closeness I had experienced with my earlier non-government friends. However, those involved in aviation still seemed to maintain their personal connections and their willingness to help and support each other. Once again, I turned to the PWA staff for social activities and for fun and friendship.

The pilot Wray Douglas and a new aircrew arrived in Inuvik soon after I did, as a replacement crew for PWA's single-engine DCH-3 Otter. (The turboprop DCH-6 Twin Otter was still being developed at this time.) After we had settled into our life in the shopping centre, Wray and the Otter crew became good friends to me and the children. I now had a welcoming place to visit and chat. At the PWA hangar, there was always a cup of coffee, laughter, and fun, and even more enjoyable for me was when the crew shared stories and reading materials about recent events in the rest of Canada. The Otter flew scheduled flights to settlements, but it was also available for charter trips. If our perishable foods or other shipments for an oil exploration camp were too large for our Cessna 180, or it was more economical to make one Otter trip rather than two smaller Cessna trips, I would pass the flight to the Otter crew. I began to rely on this friendship and having a place to visit, making my days less lonely. I was really missing Dell as well as my friends in Tuk, but I also had very little time to dwell on what I no longer had.

Now that George and I were living in the same town, I saw he viewed our marriage primarily as one of convenience. He seemed not to be as interested in me, as a woman, and once again, I had become very aware that he had been involved with other women. No longer did I question whether the gossip was true; rather, I was struggling to understand why my love and trust seemed so unimportant to him. George agreed he had made mistakes: he yet again claimed it was because we were living in two different communities, but he assured me of his love and that things would be different now that I was in Inuvik. He asked me to forgive him, but I had serious doubts that I ever could. His repeated blows to my trust had affected my sense of personal worth as well as how I felt about myself as a woman. Even more worrying, and indeed disturbing, was his obvious lack of commitment to his children. He regularly made it clear that he resented the time the children and their care took away from the work he expected me to do for him and the businesses.

Duncan's health continued to be a problem and added more pressure to everything I did. His frequent asthma attacks and his increased hospital stays demanded more of my time. I was advised, by the various short-stay doctors, to take Duncan to Edmonton to have him tested so we could develop an ongoing plan to control his attacks. George kept putting off such a trip because he wanted me to run things in Inuvik while he was flying. He said we would make time during spring breakup to take Duncan to a specialist in Edmonton.

Fortunately, Duncan was a happy, outgoing baby with easy smiles and laughter most of the time. The government hospital had a training program for Indigenous nursing aides and with this large number of aides-in-training, someone was always available to hold Duncan and totally spoil their young patient. Thankfully, when he came home from a hospital stay and he was active again with his brother and sister, he seemed to understand that I didn't have time to hold him or entertain him every moment he was awake.

AS SPRING BREAKUP APPROACHED, MY FOCUS SHIFTED TO ORDERING clothing to sell in the new women's shop along with other building supplies, because they needed to be shipped on the earliest possible barges. George decided I should go out to Edmonton and do the ordering, as he was very motivated to open the women's shop as soon as possible. He wanted me to make the rounds of the wholesalers, ordering and arranging shipment of the clothing I thought we could sell. He himself was committed to fly to the oil exploration camps, continuing to deliver perishables during breakup. The companies had built small landing strips to ensure year-round access to each site. This ongoing delivery work was essential as it provided the funds to pay for our planned orders and shipping.

I thought this trip would be my opportunity to take Duncan to see a specialist, but George told me that wouldn't be possible since he had arranged for me to fly out, free, on the PWA Otter that was going out for servicing. He wanted me to get our planned ordering done quickly so I could fly back within the week, because, during my absence, he would be responsible for expediting orders for the oil company camps as well as his usual flying requirements. At the same time, he was rushing to finish the new shop before ice-free water diverted him to the demands of full-time flying. He arranged for a woman to take care of the children during the day but promised he would be home with them at night until I came back. He also promised we would take Duncan outside to see a specialist at least by freeze-up, when we would plan for the whole family to travel to Edmonton to have a holiday.

The trip on the Otter would be long—a possible ten hours, allowing for comfort and refuelling stops—but Wray was a competent, experienced pilot, and the crew were friends. Undoubtedly, saving money was helpful since we had so much to buy. The PWA people knew we were friends of Madge Baker and having a free trip didn't seem unusual. Regardless of the practical efficiency of George's plan, I remained concerned since he had created yet one more reason to delay Duncan's visit to a specialist. It was now close to a year since his first asthma attack and we hadn't done anything to try to understand what caused these attacks, and what we could do to try to minimize or even prevent them. We were only reacting to his attacks, not looking for solutions for the future.

On our trip south, the Otter's oil pressure suddenly began to drop, after which one of the single engine's sixteen cylinders blew. At that point, we were south of Fort Good Hope and had passed over the abandoned trading post of Little Chicago. When the Otter's oil pressure had first started to drop, we were still too far north of Norman Wells to make it there to land. Then the engine itself suddenly stopped, leaving Wray with the only possible choice—a forced landing on the river. Fortunately, the ice had moved down-river and, most important to us, the Otter had been changed over to floats. The Mackenzie was a wonderfully wide and long landing place for a plane on floats.

The Otter's aerodynamics gave it a good glide path, lots of wing lift, and a forgiving angle of descent that allowed for a slow landing speed, without dropping its nose and falling out of the sky. If Wray could maintain enough forward speed, it wasn't at all difficult to position the plane to safely land on the river, even without engine power. Knowing Wray was experienced, I wasn't particularly worried, although it is amazing how quiet a plane is when it is flying without the usual engine noise and the only sound, in the near silence, is that of the plane cutting through the air as it descends.

Once we were down on the river, the lack of power did matter, as we tried to beach the plane on the riverbank. We had to fight the forces of the fast-flowing river; it was wide and deep and bent on returning us to Inuvik. Not only that, but the wind caught the plane, causing it to sail downstream, rather than head for the riverbank. All four men on board got out, kneeled on the floats, and paddled hard, till we eventually reached the riverbank.

Wray had radioed a mayday when we lost power and faced a

forced landing. Once we grounded on the riverbank, he radioed our location, letting them know that all five of us were fine and the plane was undamaged. He told the operator he would need to talk to the PWA senior mechanic, to give him a list of parts we needed to repair the engine on site. After a later conversation with people at the PWA office, they arranged for a Beaver on floats to fly the necessary parts and tools from Edmonton. Both mechanics on board were qualified to make the repairs once we had the necessary parts. We were likely to be down on the river for up to three days—the time required for the parts to be flown in and then to make the repairs—before we could take off and continue on to Edmonton. Wray asked the office to notify George that we were down and that I was fine, but I would be delayed arriving in Edmonton.

There was little for me to do as the crew began to dismantle part of the engine, assess repairs, and check the parts needed, so when I had these moments to reflect, I couldn't help but contrast our circumstances with another unexpected landing on an island in the middle of the mighty Mackenzie. This time, however, everything was in our favour: it was late spring and nearly summer, and although the temperature was cold at night, there was no longer a threat of snow and freezing. We had long hours of daylight, the plane was undamaged, we had our emergency supplies with us, including a cooking pot, and I was not injured.

Our group of castaways included one pilot, two mechanics, an office staffer, and me. Since I was the only woman on board, I enjoyed everyone's efforts to soothe my anxiety. It was such a treat to have others care about my feelings. While Wray and the mechanics worked on the plane, the young clerk helped me set up camp, survey our available food, and pitch a lean-to tent—again calling into service the engine tent. Together we cut boughs to create a mattress, rolled out the three available sleeping bags, collected firewood, built a fire, and made coffee. Conditions would be just above freezing during the twilight and dark hours, but sunny and pleasant during the day. The days were lengthening, giving us many daylight hours to work on the plane or sit in the sunshine and tell stories. Even with the lengthening daylight, it was still cold enough to discourage mosquitoes and blackflies, a very good thing since we were going to spend three days outside. Another major difference from my first adventure of landing unexpectedly and finding myself living outdoors was that everyone remained happy and full of laughter. Everything that happened became a source of fun and something to laugh over. We were having fun, like kids on a camp-out, probably because we knew that all the problems would be easily resolved and we weren't in any danger. No doubt, we would be uncomfortable, but our lack of comfort became yet one more story to laugh about.

Because there were not enough sleeping bags for all five of us, our solution was to unzip the three we had available, add a piece of canvas we found in the plane and then tape them all together as a single top cover, with a thick mattress of tree boughs to keep us up off the cold ground. This set-up would entail all of us huddling together to sleep. When one person wanted to turn over, everybody had to turn at the same time and in the same direction. Wray, the senior mechanic, and I got the middle positions, while the junior mechanic and the clerk were assigned the two outside places. The bags and canvas taped together were not really wide enough, so the two outside people struggled to stay warm and covered. The clerk had to maintain the fire, getting up several times during the night to add logs to keep it burning at the mouth of the tent. When he rose to mind the fire, it was a signal for everyone to turn over. When he came back from the fire, there was usually a bit of tugging, swearing, and laughing while he tried to claim enough sleeping bag to cover himself once again.

The emergency food supply carried by most bush planes was left in the planes for long periods and was therefore subject to endless freezing and thawing. Any canned meats or fish carried in emergency supplies became some sort of unidentifiable and unpleasant mush, but the usual tea, coffee, sugar, and raisins were all okay. The chocolate often turned a strange grey colour and usually peanuts and crackers became stale, but all were edible.

I found a very small fishnet in the Otter's emergency box and strung it off the plane's pontoons to see if I could catch fish to add to our diet. However, the sounds and vibrations of the work on the plane seemed to scare any fish away. Without a fishing pole, I couldn't cast a line far enough away from the noise and vibration. We had no guns on board, so hunting ptarmigan or arctic hare wasn't viable either. I had never learned the skill of snaring hare, so initially we had to be satisfied with our limited emergency rations. Thankfully, we had a cooking pot and a coffee pot, so we drank a lot of tea and black coffee and waited for the PWA Beaver to arrive with the required parts and, we hoped, something more appealing or filling to eat.

By the time the sun was up the next morning, there was nothing left to do on the plane until the new parts arrived. I had some hope for my small fishnet again, but no luck. I thought a few hooks, weights, and fishing line would have been more useful, and I thought I would suggest that George add them to our planes' emergency supplies. Had I had them when we were downed on the island, perhaps by digging in the sand or in the bark of trees, I could have found some bugs or worms and tried casting from the shore with the line wound on a stick. As we waited for the Beaver's arrival, I filled some time by wandering along the riverbank and was amazed to find several fossils, primarily sea creatures. I never really knew how these fossils ended up so far from the sea, but I expect it was due to the ice age and glacier activity or higher sea levels at some point in the past. It was fun to marvel at them and think of the story they could tell, if only we could communicate.

After noon on our second day, a Northern Transportation boat and barge—travelling past us on its way north with the now open water, just behind the retreating ice—was a very welcome sight. The crew had been advised, by radio, to look out for us and check if we needed anything. By this time, everyone was very hungry, making something to eat our greatest need, so after some yelling back and forth, the crew sent a skiff to help me board the tug. There I choose wieners and buns, easily prepared for immediate consumption. As I boiled the wieners, I quickly made sandwiches for our dinner, with help from the tug's cook. I also asked for some canned milk for coffee cream and was given some more coffee and tea bags, bananas and apples, and freshly baked brownies.

The PWA Beaver was due at our site the next morning, so I left the tug with more than enough food to supply us until then. We were told the Beaver would bring food, and we expected to be on our way soon after its arrival and once the engine had been repaired. We also borrowed a few blankets from the boat crew to supplement our sleeping arrangements. That night, the two who had to sleep at each end of our makeshift bed particularly welcomed the blankets, and we could separate the sleeping bags for the other three of us.

We ate the hot dogs immediately, saved the sandwiches, coffee, bananas, and brownies for dinner, and went to bed that night with full stomachs. The Beaver arrived at our site the next morning with more food and our engine parts. What a different experience this adventure was from my earlier one on the little island! After the mechanics put in a number of hours of work on the engine, we were ready to take off and continue our trip to Edmonton. I was offered a seat in the Beaver to Edmonton if I felt concern over the Otter's engine, but the Otter was more comfortable given the long distance we still had to fly, and I was confident in the mechanics' repairs.

As I sat in the Otter, strapped in, listening carefully to the engine coming up to full power before we began to taxi, my mind was remembering another takeoff. Quickly the plane began to gain speed. To break the drag of the water on the plane's floats, Wray shifted the weight of the plane to one side, taking the plane up on the "step" on one float. He then rocked the Otter the other way until the plane came up on the "step" on the other float. We were soon skimming along on top of the water until our speed broke us free of the water's grasp altogether. The Otter flew itself off the surface and we were airborne again. We followed the river closely until Wray was sure the oil pressure was remaining stable and the engine performing well. The rest of our long trip was uneventful, and soon after takeoff I stopped listening to the engine or worrying whether it might cough, sputter, and shut down once again.

16

THE END OF THE DREAM

The Otter's unexpected mechanical failure left me with three fewer days in Edmonton than planned, so I had to move quickly to do the rounds of the wholesalers and complete my orders to be ready for the flight home. I enjoyed seeing all the new women's styles and colours in sportswear; it had been some time since I had caught up with the latest trends or even thought much about my own clothing. My choices required careful thought, however: I had to consider what styles could be worn and to what events, especially in Inuvik. Clothes had to be washable because dry cleaning wasn't readily available, and uniquely, I had to think of mosquitoes and blackflies, since most women kept their necks and arms covered outdoors in summer. The need to layer clothing for icy winter weather meant selecting good combinations of both styles and colours. I was convinced that the best choices had to be casual and comfortable, so I decided on mostly classic styles. And, of course, I had to consider what would sell well, as we couldn't risk excessive unsold inventory.

The next issue was to buy the most in-demand sizes in as many colours and styles as I could find, so women had the option of choosing their personal look. I selected jeans, trousers in corduroys and heavy cottons, sportswear like sweatshirts, all kinds of sweaters, long-sleeved and short-sleeved blouses, socks, PJs, nightgowns, and thermal long johns. The bright colours were in contrast to the lack of colour in the northern landscape, and much like the variety of coloured houses in Inuvik. The professional staff at the wholesalers made my task easier, as they listened to what I was trying to do and didn't waste my time trying to sell me things that were not suitable for the Arctic. After I'd visited the clothing wholesalers, most of my ordering could be done by presenting lists of what was needed, arranging shipping, and paying for our orders.

When I returned to Inuvik, I was incensed when I found out George had left the children with the sitter overnight and, predictably, that was the night Duncan had had an asthma attack. David knew Duncan should go to the hospital right away and told the sitter to call the RCMP to get their help. I couldn't believe that George had abandoned the children overnight, leaving it to eight-year-old David to make decisions about Duncan's well-being, especially when George had assured me I could rely on him to be there for them. Once again, he had put himself and his business interests ahead of the care and safety of our children. It was obvious that he and I did not share the core belief that nothing was more important than our children. I was reminded again that George thought he was the centre of everything, and the family's priority was to always adapt and be supportive of him, his decisions, and his actions, regardless of the impact on me and the children.

Trying to tell George why I was so angry and why I believed I couldn't trust him to keep the children safe once again fell upon deaf ears. But again, the key question was what could I do about it? I didn't have any extended family for support, either in the North or elsewhere, so a decision to leave presented the overwhelming challenge of where I would go and what I would do. I wasn't even sure what country I would live in. I had friends in California and elsewhere, but they were busy living their own lives, and the jobs available to me ten years previously were questionable now. Lacking answers, confidence, and direction, I felt only a sense of powerlessness that, once again, drove inaction on my part. My only firm decision was to make a commitment to myself not to leave the children in George's care again.

My confusion and my unhappiness over what had happened to the children were soon pushed into the background by my predictably massive workload, although I began to accept my heart wasn't in the dream any longer. One of George's top tasks was getting the house ready for occupancy. It had arrived in Inuvik in September and been skidded onto our lot in December, when snow conditions had made moving it feasible. However, driving permanent pilings into the permafrost had waited until the weather was warm enough, in June. Then the house was finally ready for occupancy, but its connection to the utilidor system was still pending. So, after ten months, in July 1965, the family was finally scheduled to move from living in the building storage area to our house. We were under pressure to make this happen as quickly as possible because storage space was needed for our growing commitment to the expediting business. Also, some of the government tenants in the building were keen to use the lunchroom. Moving back into our house should have been exciting, but it didn't seem to matter to me as much as it once had.

One night, while we were still living in the storeroom, I was sorting and repacking camp supplies in the hallway outside of our living area and the children were asleep in their bedroom. Duncan woke up and managed to figure out how to quietly climb out of his crib. He then moved a chair up to the counter, climbed up to the sink, and spilled a large can of strawberry jam sitting on the counter into the sink. He ate jam with both hands until he either got full or became weary enough to fall asleep again. His upper body was on the counter and the edge of the sink and now he couldn't get his fat little legs and feet back down onto the chair. Amazingly, he was able to make himself comfortable enough to fall asleep. I came in to check on the children and there he was, lying in what, at first glance, looked like a sea of blood. I rushed to grab him and instantly realized I had a sticky, crying toddler in my arms, smelling like strawberry jam. I was so relieved he wasn't hurt that I just hugged him, cleaned the jam off both of us, and put him back to bed without so much as a reprimand.

The move back into the house, which wouldn't be connected to the utilidor until some unknown time in the future, meant we returned to using a honey bucket and living once again without the wonders of accessible running water. The storage area had been small and crowded, but it was new, easily cleaned, warm, and we had had running water. Now I could move the children back into their own bedrooms, giving us more privacy, but the price of the move was to return to the challenges involved in dealing with water use and disposal. And again I would be using an oil stove for cooking and as our only source of heat. Child care was also a problem since, with limited help, I constantly needed to pack the younger two between the building and the house as demands on my time increased with the store opening.

However, family life in the house was easier now, because, during the summer, I could run a hose with water from the commercial building to the house, wash and dry clothes in the washer and dryer in the building, and shower myself and David and bathe the younger children in a small portable tub I kept there. As well, Duncan was now out of diapers and with great joy I tossed my scraper into the trash. I could haul grey water and dispose of it down the building's laundry sink, leaving just the honey bucket to deal with. George had promised to connect the house to the utilidor, but of course that would only happen when he had time and it was convenient for him. I looked forward to a day when I would have running water, a flush toilet, as well as space and privacy for everyone.

Moving back into the house brought up another issue that caused me great concern and stress. A couple of nights each week, my work involved sorting and repacking fresh food and supplies, so I was in the commercial building throughout the night, while the children slept in the house. Most nights, George would be sleeping in the house too, but some nights he was in another settlement, and I still needed to do the expediting work, even if it meant leaving the children alone. Learning that George wouldn't be at home on an expediting night usually happened without warning, and I couldn't always get a sitter to sleep with the children. I could see the house from the building as I worked, but I wasn't happy to have them there alone. On those nights, I would make multiple trips back and forth to check on them and to reassure myself that all was well. I couldn't convince myself the children were as safe as they should be, regardless of how many trips I made back and forth, so the night's work was also stress-filled.

With warm weather, as the days lengthened to twenty-four hours of daylight, I found times between the plague-like invasions of mosquitoes to drive the children to a small pond at Inuvik's gravel pit. I wanted to teach Lesley to swim and give David a chance to renew his swimming skills. With the long hours of sunlight, the shallow pond became reasonably warm. Lesley was four and I was committed to teaching her to be safe near water. We had no bathing suits, so the kids swam in their underwear, and I went in with them in my jeans. We went to the pond, as mosquitoes allowed, for a few weeks until I felt Lesley was reasonably strong at dog-paddling, had developed some comfort in the water, and should be able to stay afloat for a period of time. On our trips to the pond, I had the chance to begin to introduce Duncan to being comfortable in water.

I knew that when the children were near any large body of water, its temperature would never be warm enough for a person to survive hypothermia for very long, but I wanted them all to know how to stay afloat long enough to either reach something or have someone reach them. I truly believed swimming was a basic life skill that all children should learn. However, when a number of my Indigenous friends heard I was driving to the gravel pit and making my children go into the water for fun, they thought I was very strange. They didn't see swimming as an option in a place where the water was breathtakingly cold, and no one even wore life preservers to stay afloat if they fell or were thrown into the cold water.

My children's swimming lessons reminded me of how much I still represented the thinking of the South even after five years of making the North my home. Yet I thought I was different from many other southerners living in the North, since, after five years, I didn't need to convince others to change, to be like me, nor did I believe I knew the best way to live. I was comfortable to call the North home, to learn, to experience, and to be accepted and welcomed even if different, as I welcomed and accepted the differences I found in others. I reminded myself of the physician's oath to "first, do no harm," and I guess that was my most consistent personal guide and the expectation I hoped to find in other people.

George told me in mid-August that any idea of a family holiday or a trip to see a specialist for Duncan at freeze-up had to be postponed once again. He insisted I was essential to managing the expediting while he was away in Edmonton getting the plane serviced. I told George that I could hire someone and teach them to do the work for the few weeks we would be away. But he was adamant the contracts were too important financially to leave the work to someone else.

Duncan had continued to have breathing difficulties and had been hospitalized a number of times during the past months. His doctors had told me that the frequency of his attacks was a significant concern. At the same time as our trip to see a specialist was being postponed once again, I was feeling increasing pressure from

George because I wasn't consistently available to work on company responsibilities. In my mind, Duncan's health issues created a necessary focus for my energy and time. I felt I was being pushed and pulled too many ways. The time had come to leave, regardless of my concerns over whether I could manage to care for the children on my own or where and how we might live. I could no longer continue to minimize Duncan's health concerns or ignore the pressing need to find answers to his asthma attacks.

So I found the courage to tell George that, regardless of business demands, I planned to take the children outside for a while. That is how I came to learn the staggering reality that I would not have access to any of what I believed was "our money": the money I might need to establish a home outside for us. I was told I didn't own anything, since everything I thought we owned together was in George's name only and therefore was in his sole control. I realized then that he had planned for me to be financially dependent upon him. This was clearly his deliberate strategy to control my actions and to limit my decisions and options.

Although I didn't know how we would live or how I could make a living, I knew there should be more to life and that trust in our relationship mattered. The children should be surrounded by more love, laughter, and joy. Obviously, George and I did not share the belief that the safety and well-being of our children was our highest priority. It would be up to me alone to ensure Duncan had the best opportunity to grow into a healthy boy and man. I also now realized that my decision to leave the North was effectively a decision to leave George and all we had worked to build. The dream was over. I had grown to believe the North was my home, not just where I lived, so the thought of everything I was leaving and losing was overwhelming.

It was frightening to think about the implications of such a decision and what it would mean for the future—both for the children and for me. Yet when I thought of the alternative, I realized there was no other responsible choice. I couldn't continue to let George push the children's needs into the background and take chances with their well-being. I was disappointed that I had taken so long to accept that I had no ability to make things different. I had harboured an illusion that I was an equal partner in our marriage and all that we had accomplished. Calling on the courage I knew was hidden inside me somewhere, I packed a few essential things for the children and myself.

Fortunately, I had been saving a little cash, planning for that cancelled fall holiday trip and the opportunity to buy some clothes, toys, and other things for the children. With these few dollars in my pocket, I charged our airline tickets and a motel reservation near University Hospital to the company account, got a referral for Duncan to see a specialist there, and the four of us caught the PWA flight to Edmonton. I knew this step was the best and only decision I could make, but in no way did that lessen my fears. I had no money, no job prospects, and no idea of where we might live. But to do nothing was no longer a responsible choice.

I did not blame the North for the problems in our marriage. Our problems were problems created by the two of us, and the North was just the place where the problems had happened. No doubt, the challenges of managing our businesses and daily lives had been difficult and pressure filled at times, but the serious value and ethical differences between George and me were possibly made apparent sooner because of the lifestyle and business pressures we faced, all compounded by Duncan's health challenges. The North had given my family so much: the caring people, the unique places we lived, the natural beauty surrounding us, and the learning, experiences, and adventures that were ours as a permanent part of our lives and memories.

My immediate priority once we got to Edmonton was to take Duncan to a specialist physician: he confirmed my sense that the asthma was life-threatening. He also told me that Duncan's reaction to cold air was one of several precursors to his asthma attacks. The mosquito bites he'd had as a baby at the wildlife camp had probably triggered the onset of a genetic predisposition for asthma. Duncan would need extensive allergy testing to identify other triggers and he would face a regime of desensitizing shots. I was told he could not return to the extreme cold of the North without exposing him to repeated, dangerous, and possibly fatal attacks. For a short while, as residents of the Northwest Territories, the children and I would have free medical care. I needed to find answers as quickly as possible so we could start Duncan's asthma treatment. We also had dental coverage, so all three children, along with me, visited the dentist—a new experience for the young ones. As someone who had gone for five years and two pregnancies without dental care, I wanted to take full advantage of having coverage for that limited time.

I enrolled David at a school nearby, even though I didn't know how long we would stay at the motel. Without consulting me, on his second day, the school gave him what they termed an intelligence test because he seemed shy and didn't understand some of what they were saying. I was called to the school to be told he had been tested and had been found to be a "slow learner." I immediately asked to see the test they had given him, and it was, as I suspected, a series of questions and pictures of the world a southern child would recognize and understand. Trying to control my temper, I suggested the teacher should have given him a series of math problems to do, or had him read a book appropriate for his age and then ask him what he had read. If the teacher was still in doubt about his ability to think and learn, someone should sit down and play a couple of games of chess with him.

I said that the test he'd been given was totally inappropriate for a child from the High Arctic whose life experiences were so completely different from what the school's test was designed to measure. I also advised them that they did not have my permission to give him this test and if, after they checked his reading and math levels, they still felt a need to test him further, then it must be a Wechsler or Stanford-Binet standardized IQ test. Such a test would have to be administered by a qualified psychologist who was fully briefed on David's unique background. I also emphasized that the results of their first test must not appear on any of David's permanent records.

This frustrating incident gave me first-hand experience of the disadvantages northern children faced when they were measured by southern standards. My personal knowledge (from university studies and my teaching experience in Nova Scotia) fortunately prevented David from being labelled, but not many northern parents had my advantages. It made me sad to think of all the potential that might be lost when the North's children were subjected to this type of ignorant and inappropriate testing and the resulting inaccurate labelling.

George soon followed us to Edmonton and was mostly convincing when he said our marriage and his children were the most important things to him. He said he had made serious mistakes and he wanted the chance to rebuild our marriage. He also said he would ensure our finances were resolved so I had an equal share in all we had worked so hard to build. I convinced myself I could believe him and that he really understood why I was willing to leave him and the North. As a family we moved to the Lower Mainland of British Columbia, where Duncan could live in a milder climate and get the medical care he needed. At the same time, he avoided the risk of asthma inherent in the extreme-cold climate of the North.

In British Columbia we settled on a farm and the children's lives radically changed. Farm animals became a focus of life, and having something to love and care for helped them as they learned about this new world "outside." David was our only child old enough to attend school and was fortunate that his teacher, at the small farm school he attended, was wise enough to realize his classmates should understand why David was different. She invited him to tell the class about his life in the North, and this "show and tell" created interest in the other students. On regular occasions, she would ask him to contrast his northern experiences with a subject they were studying. Although this pointed out David's differences, it also helped the other children to value his experiences and him. It wasn't until later in another school that he experienced bullying, but the North had taught him much about being different and accepting differences in others, allowing him to ignore others' intolerance. By the time Lesley and Duncan attended school, their unique early life was not so readily apparent to their fellow students.

Once we settled in British Columbia, George had lost interest in Arctic Wings and in bush flying, as he was the only pilot and our small company no longer had any obvious growth potential. He planned to commute to the North from B.C. to fly during the busiest periods and to manage our businesses until he could sell all our interests there. After a couple of years commuting, George returned from a trip to announce that he had decided to leave our family, to return to the North and live permanently there with his new family: a family he had started during his trips north and while he was claiming to be committed to our children, to our marriage, and to me. It wasn't easy to face yet again how wrong I had been to trust George.

As he left us, to return north, along with the sorrow I felt over our inability to make our marriage work or hold our family together, I felt anger beyond anything I had ever felt before when I discovered George had taken none of the promised steps to ensure the children and I were financially secure. All our business and any other personal assets were still in his name alone, and because of the lack of family legislation and limited property law in the Northwest

Territories, I would not be able to make a legal claim for any of what I believed belonged to both of us. Neither could George be legally compelled to pay child support, while he remained in the NWT. George had arranged to sell everything we had outside of the territories, so, once more, I found myself homeless, and the children and I faced an uncertain future. Only now I knew I needed to turn my anger towards more effective problem-solving, recognizing the children's and my future was up to me alone.

George would continue to live in the North, where he would own and fly a personal Cessna 180 for most of his life. He would start but predictably fail to maintain a number of businesses; he would marry four more times, have additional children, and would be divorced, living on his own, when he died at age eighty-nine.

Our years of marriage and our dreams of a life in the North, once they ended, left me with three exceptional children and very little else. However, I understood that I still had what truly mattered from the years of marriage: the children. But where had our dream for Arctic Wings and for our marriage gone? I couldn't think of an answer, but I deeply regretted the trust I had given George. I regretted not protecting the financial interests of the children and myself, but I didn't regret my time and life in the North. To this day, I cherish and value the wonderful memories of the people I met and my many amazing learning opportunities, adventures, and experiences there. Together, these gave me a reliably solid foundation to build a future for myself and the children—a rich and meaningful life on the outside.

ENDINGS CAN BE BEGINNINGS

E ven though I had to redesign and rebuild most aspects of our future after George left the family and returned to the North, on reflection, my time there was a much-valued gift. My experiences during my five years in the Arctic helped strengthen my belief in my ability to find answers and learn new and necessary skills. As a result, I successfully accomplished so many things that at first I would have believed were beyond me. In hindsight, I realize that my unique life history had given me a focus on learning and, more importantly, shown me how to put that learning to good use.

Starting over would require sacrifices and changes for both me and the children. The children would never be hungry, but for a time, materially, they had much less and enjoyed fewer opportunities than their friends. The breakdown of our marriage and George's self-serving actions to keep sole ownership of what were in effect joint assets resulted in my being unable to gain any benefit for either myself or my children from what I had helped to build in the North. The Northwest Territories' lack of appropriate legislation to protect the interests and rights of women and children let us down as well.

That was the past and I needed to focus on the future. Obviously, in today's world I would have been less naïve and more aware of the ongoing need to ensure ownership of our property legally reflected our joint interests, ensuring these assets were available to help me provide for our children if needed.

After George left, we faced many challenges, but we also experienced fun, laughter, and joy. For example, one Christmas, the children decided to give me decorated toilet paper cardboard rolls as electric cord holders. Each empty roll was saved, and much collaboration went into the final design and finish. Their creations were beautiful and I was sad as, one by one, they wore out and fell apart.

Our lack of money was highlighted when David asked me if we were poor because we were shopping for his school clothes at the second-hand stores. Another disappointing and, indeed, heart-wrenching moment came when Duncan was studying the toys in the Sears Christmas catalogue. He asked David whether he could ask Santa for a particular toy and David told him no. He kept looking and kept asking and David kept saying no. Finally, in frustration, Duncan asked why other boys could ask for the toys they wanted, and he couldn't. Listening from another room, I heard David tell Duncan that I was Santa, and I couldn't afford to buy the toys he was choosing. If he asked, I would feel very sad because I didn't have the money to buy what he wanted. I was heartbroken and in tears because five-year-old Duncan was already having to learn about life's hard realities. I felt I had let him down and he should have been able to dream and enjoy make-believe for a bit longer, like his friends.

I had little time, energy, or interest to worry about my personal well-being, either physical or mental. My focus was single-mindedly directed towards problem-solving, planning, and the non-stop effort required to make everything work. Focusing elsewhere simply seemed to be less important. Thanks to the excellent doctors and care in Edmonton, I would have many years without any serious issues with my back. Later on, the old injuries would catch up with me. I would require further spinal surgery to reduce bone growth and arthritis issues, but even today, as I celebrate my ninetieth birthday, I am still able to be active.

Luckily, I suffered few negative mental health consequences from the difficult problems I had to face and solve in the North—particularly the possibly fatal "hard landing" George and I had suffered when our plane crash-landed on a tiny island in the Mackenzie River. My resulting months of immobilization, treatment, and back surgery forced me to draw on my ability to use my mind as my primary source of problem-solving and comfort, although with so much time to think, I struggled with unusual bouts of depression. Usually when I faced times of stress, heartbreak, and disaster, I knew how to go on. I coped by seeking answers and implementing solutions, or learning to accept and adapt to situations that were beyond my control. Of course, the diagnosis of post-traumatic stress disorder did not enter public consciousness till many years later, but looking at the many symptoms used to diagnose this, I only remember feeling a huge sense of guilt with marriage breakdown and when I couldn't give my children all the advantages and opportunities I felt they deserved. Although at times I felt pain, sorrow, disappointment, lack of control, and fear, I simply believed it was up to me to sort out how to manage. The knowledge there were three children who depended on me to meet all their needs kept me well focused. This solution-seeking approach would serve me well as I turned my energies towards making a new and good life in the South for the four of us.

Looking back, I'm sure an explanation for some of my possibly unique drive, particularly for a woman in those years, came from the seven years I lived in a residential school. During that time, I faced loss of family, lack of love and nurturing, regimentation, inflexible discipline that was sometimes physical, expectations of work habits, and the need to learn to care for myself. By the age of four, I had been forcibly taught not to whine or cry or to look to others to solve problems for me. I also learned where I might have some control over what happened and where I had to accept I was powerless. Undoubtedly, these experiences contributed to my developing a practical mindset and a strong and reliable determination. These very worthwhile and valuable character traits have touched the rest of my life.

Once I became a single parent, my sights became firmly fixed on the future. I worked at a variety of jobs and focused on advancing my education. I crossed the Canada-U.S. border to attend Western Washington University in Bellingham. There, I successfully finished a bachelor's degree in psychology and sociology. After I had an undergraduate psychology research project published, I was then offered a seat in the graduate program in psychology, which included a job in the university's psych lab. This position was a vast improvement over my previous employment as housekeeper, fruit picker, waitress, and veterinary assistant.

After finishing my master's degree, I was employed as a faculty member at Douglas College and then as a faculty member and administrator at Kwantlen College, in the Fraser Valley. During this time, I became a registered psychologist in the province of British Columbia. I left Kwantlen in 1992 to establish a very satisfying role as a consultant to a broad range of health-related organizations. My focus was primarily on strategic planning, evaluation, policy-making, and value-based governance. As well as developing this meaningful career in post-secondary education and health care governance, I married again—to a man who wanted a true life partner and who was interested in helping me raise caring, competent, and successful children. I did extensive volunteer work, enjoyed laughter and rich friendships, and was blessed by having so many opportunities to put my hard-earned capabilities to work, along with the support and caring of so many people.

In the later part of my life, my focus turned to another area of long-time interest. In partnership, my husband Gord and I committed to breeding the best Labrador Retrievers we could. Together, over more than twenty-five years, we became widely respected breeders, routinely earning both breed and performance titles with our many dogs, including Conformation, Master Obedience Trial, and Grand Master Hunting Retriever Championships in Canada as well as similar titles in the United States. Seeking to support excellence in field work, Gord and I qualified as Hunting Retriever judges in Canada; I also qualified to judge in the USA.

I never returned to the North, but I will always remember the experiences I had, the people I met, the friends I made, and what I learned about life and meaningful living while I was there. Over the years, I have recognized that a person can never really go back, since change cannot be controlled or denied and, in reality, nothing ever remains the same. I cherish memories of the indescribable natural beauty of the North: its special sounds, some so loud and encompassing, some so quiet that everything around me seemed to have stopped; nights when I stood on snowshoes in the middle of the frozen river and looked up at the sky to see nature put on a wondrous light show just for me; the feel of the breathtaking cold in my lungs and on my uncovered skin and then the warmth of the spring sun on my face after so many months of biting cold. That world came with its own smells, like the salty wind from the Beaufort Sea blowing over Tuk; the pungent odour of different animal hides; the smoke from wood campfires burning in the still, cold air; drying fish or muktuk racks, reindeer stew cooking on a stove, and freshly baked bannock or bread from the oven, and, especially notable, the smell of Mistovan in a chemical toilet.

Many of my best memories are of my children's diverse experiences in the North. My two younger children were babies and toddlers there, and David's early life was uniquely rich with learning. Throughout those years, my family was consistently supported by caring people. Each of us was touched by our life experiences everywhere we lived in the North. I do regret, however, that so few photographs of the children exist from those days. Like most people in the North, we never took photographs since film had to be sent out to be developed. I have no pictures at all of David during the more than five years we lived in the Arctic. I have few of Lesley and Duncan and only one of George and me with our Cessna 180 plane. All were taken by visitors and mailed to us when the visitors returned home. I was able to acquire some photos of the western Arctic for this book, which were shared with me by the Northwest Territories Archives. These rare images date from the years covered in my story and illustrate some interesting aspects of Arctic life that were key elements of my history. Many were taken by Emily Stillwell, a nurse, and Robert Knights, an RCMP officer, who both worked in the western Arctic during this time and generously released their photo collections to the archives.

When I look back on my children's life experiences in the North, I have a strong sense that they were blessed to have lived, in those years, in a society of kindness, where they were valued and loved. I didn't have to make them afraid or suspicious of the people around them. Not until we came to live outside would I have concerns for their personal safety around others, requiring me to teach them to be wary of some people. Another unwelcome revelation for them was that children in school sometimes bullied each other and picked on others who were considered different.

In Tuk, we were remarkably fortunate to live in a special place where everyone was valued and belonged to the community. People were different from each other, yet there was respect for and acceptance of those differences. Not only did being accepted not require sameness among people, also there was no pressure for me to fit into the more traditional roles of the community's women. I wasn't seen as a man, but I was accepted as a different woman, doing both the usual woman's roles as well as those of a man. This acceptance helped me gain a greater understanding of how I wanted to live the rest of my life, regardless of whether this view was readily accepted in the South. Before living in the North, I had felt so much pressure to conform to others' expectations of a woman's role. This pressure would once again follow me into my future outside, but now I was different. I enjoyed being a woman and a mother, but I didn't feel either role needed to be all that I did, nor should they define my actions and opportunities. I didn't need to deny my intelligence and skills or limit my opportunities because of pressure to conform to society's gender norms.

The respect with which I was treated in the North was strikingly and depressingly different from the lack of respect shown to the North's people by government representatives. Sadly, those who called the North home lacked my free choice to be different. A day would come, in future years, when the North's people would no longer be willing to let others be the sole decision-makers or spokespersons. Ironically, the mandate requiring education for all northern children would help prepare those now-educated adults to assert their rights for respect and to be included in planning, decision-making, and eventually self-government.

Soon after I left the North, the rate of change accelerated. This came about in response to the growing southern financial and business determination to exploit Arctic resources, and the federal government's desire to move more quickly to create the "New North." These pressures for instant change would create significant social distress and disintegration in local people's lives for decades to come.

As I look back on the close to sixty years since I left the Arctic, my time there happened just as the floodgates of change were opening. During the early 1960s, people, particularly people in Tuk, still believed in their freedom of choice and the strength and value of their traditional ways, making it such a special time to live there. In later years, northern life would become easier for outsiders. A wide range of services, transportation, and food choices, along with recreational, medical, dental, and educational opportunities would become more available. These services would closely reflect what these outsiders experienced in southern Canada and expected to find in the North. By that time, it would no longer be the same North or the same lifestyle I had experienced when the Arctic was my home.

Since change was inevitable, was there a better and gentler way to move the North's people towards some necessary accommodations of southern Canadian ways and values? Could there have been a "made in the North" plan for change? I think so. It may seem easy to criticize past actions and decisions and in retrospect to say what should have happened, but even while I was living in Tuk, I can remember discussing with Father Le Meur the need for the government to slow down and seek better ways to create change. We both saw the need for the North's people to participate in planning, allowing more time, thoughtfulness, and wider discussions, before major decisions were made. Instead, decision-makers of the day—decision-makers almost exclusively from southern Canada—simply believed that a southern Canadian model of change should be applied like a blanket to cover all the North's issues and its people.

A simple but obvious example of a "made in the North" solution to change was women's Mother Hubbard parka. Religious pioneers who travelled to Polynesia and other South Pacific islands introduced the "Mother Hubbard dress" to cover the nakedness of Indigenous women. When religious pioneers travelled to the North, they discovered they couldn't tell the men from the women by their clothing. Our "civilized and religious societies" believed that women were different from men and should look different as well, so the Mother Hubbard dress was introduced to Inuit women too. The difficulty was that dressing in fur was necessary to keep warm during much of the year, and the fur outerwear covered the women's Mother Hubbard dresses. A "made in the North" solution was created by Inuit women by simply putting the dress over their fur clothing to produce the Mother Hubbard parka. The breadth of creativity of Inuit women was also demonstrated by the noticeably different designs of Mother Hubbard parkas in the western and eastern Arctic. Why couldn't more time have been taken to seek collaboration with the North's people to consider "made in the North" ideas before implementing government-mandated changes?

Early missionaries wanted to distinguish Inuit men from women. Demonstrating a "made in the North" solution, Inuit women made the recommended dresses big enough to cover their fur clothing, and the so-called Mother Hubbard parka was then worn by Inuit females of all ages. © *NWT Archives / Robert C. Knights / N-1993-002-0349*

A "made in the North" approach to health care could have used all the types of transportation available to take services to people. For instance, a health care services boat could have been funded to travel up and down the Mackenzie River, from Fort Providence to the Beaufort Sea, to Herschel and Banks islands and to Tuk during the ice-free months, stopping wherever there were people in settlements and camps along the river. To some degree, responsive emergency and critical care health services were available, but little was done about routine, preventative, and the many broader health care needs, such as dental care, vision care, birth control, and other health education services. Health care in the North would improve over time, but change could have been achieved with much less harm.

As I wrote this story, I tried to create an understanding of what it was like for a southern white woman to blend her lifestyle and values with the life she found in the western Arctic. I lived alongside people who lived their lives with grace, even as they struggled in a shifting environment, facing changes that were not by their choice or within their control. My unique roles in the community—as a mother, a cook, a fur trader, a sex education advisor, businesswoman, and friend—gave me the richest of opportunities to learn from Inuit neighbours and to grow into a person of greater understanding and character.

For so many years, southerners spoke for the North's people and decided how they should live, think, behave, and what they should believe. People in the North were expected to consider this situation acceptable, even valuable. Sir John A. Macdonald's words, "take the Indian out of the child," spoke to me of such extraordinary arrogance, when the dominant society believes their ways are the only right, good, just, and God-inspired life, and therefore the way everyone should live. This arrogance was often presented as helping a "lesser" people to become better and fulfilled people, which could only be achieved by accepting the ways of the majority cultures. In Canada, the only acceptable and recognized languages and societies were French or English. The peoples of the North were expected to adopt one of these languages, along with their customs and culture. In this memoir I have described what I saw, my personal experiences, and stories I was told, but that wasn't the same as trying to speak or think for my northern neighbours. Thankfully, the

Northwest Territories Archives is collecting and preserving the voices of the people who were living in these times, encouraging them to speak for themselves and tell their own stories—stories that can enrich understanding of the past and keep history honest.

Many parents whose children were forced to attend residential schools shared with me their feelings about the loss of opportunity to be with and raise their children. At the same time, they commented on their sense of being devalued during their children's rare visits home. Their children had been taught to reject their parents' lifestyle, language, customs, and even food. Although I could identify with the parents' distress, realistically I could only reflect on how I would feel if something similar happened to me and my family. Using the words and perspective of a woman raised in the South with very different life experiences would have me speaking for them, something I don't believe I should do. Although I may have had a better understanding than most of what children felt about their life in residential schools, I will not try to speak for them either. Our experiences and gained perspectives were not the same. Literacy has certainly made it possible for these children to speak eloquently for themselves today. From what I witnessed in those days, the government-sanctioned policy to "take the Indian out of the child" appeared to be working at the time. Enforcing this ignorant, damaging, and disrespectful goal would end up being so costly to Indigenous societies, cultures, families, and individuals across Canada. Although education has given First Nations, Inuit, and Métis peoples the power and tools needed to reclaim much, the government's past actions to destroy what it meant to be Indigenous will remain a stain on Canada's past.

I have tried to express my belief that there should have been a better way to manage change in the North. Change was inevitable, but I believe a number of concepts could have lessened the damage. For example, learning from history could have avoided mistakes made before. Showing respect, valuing differences, consultation and collaboration, looking to blend cultures could all have had a positive influence. Making honest and realistic connections between decisions and the breadth of outcomes, while sharing, listening, and communicating, would have enabled flexibility, creativity, and Indigenous-led solutions with the least harm. In thinking and writing about the past, I accept it is not possible to go back to correct errors, but the past can be a teacher and history can help us recognize when we fail to respect the intrinsic value and humanity of every person or group of people. Unfortunately, the methods of enforcing change in the Arctic would become just another one of those errors, but I fervently hope that errors are well remembered so they are not repeated.

In the North, I knew people who approached their lives with courage, adaptability, spirit, laughter, and joy, but were seen as lesser people by others who believed they needed to be controlled and taught to be like southern Canadians. The strength and resilience I saw in these people made me believe that, in spite of challenges to family and social cohesiveness, disappointment over the devaluation of their way of life and culture, and confusion over how they would fit into the "New North," these special people would adapt, restate their values and beliefs, and eventually, regain more control over their future, as a people, once again. Slowly there has been a renewal of Indigenous cultures, languages, and traditions, more support for participation in political processes, and growing self-government during the past few decades. Interestingly, the community of Tuktoyaktuk has been one of the leaders in re-establishing people's hereditary and cultural traditions.

The cost of climate change is another challenge to life in the North. Will this be a challenge beyond the resilience of the North's land and its people? Time may give us the answer, but if history is a teacher, then environmental and climate change planning and decision-making will be led this time by local decision-makers rather than imposed from outside. I think about the North's elders of my age, and I wonder if they too take moments to remember, to think back, and to cherish our earlier shared times. Regrettably, those of us who remember how it was must also accept that our time is past, but we, for a little longer, can be part of the Arctic's living history by sharing our memories.

I have written this story to create a picture in words of my life in the western Canadian Arctic of the early 1960s. I hope my words portrayed clearly for you what I saw, what I did, what I experienced, and what I thought. In sharing my story, it is also my hope that you too will embrace the times and the people and see how very special they were.

ACKNOWLEDGEMENTS

CREATIVE WRITING or writing for fun was something I rarely had time to consider in past busy years. However, in recent times, my son's and daughter's questions about my life and their earlier years convinced me to write a life timeline for them, which then led to yet more questions. Of special interest were stories of our life in the Arctic. My children have been the reason for so much I have attempted and accomplished in my lifetime, and responding to their interest would become the focus of my more expansive writing, with a planned readership of my children, grandchildren, and great-grandchildren. It was the start of an epic journey, beginning with trying to find the words to give life to the story of my northern times and adventures.

Writing for uncritical family readers seemed like a commitment that was within my skills. However, as friends became aware of my early efforts, I was asked if I would share my Arctic story more broadly. My storytelling attempts were considered a good read and interesting by likely biased friends. Two of these friends stepped forward to encourage me to enlarge the story and publish it. As well they offered much-needed help in making the manuscript better.

I am from a generation that grew up without the aid of comput-ers. My limited knowledge and skills made the process of writing on a computer frustrating, as my mistakes seemed to turn my laptop against me—losing copy, rejecting my formatting instructions, or just deleting my efforts. Organizing text as well as sending it to others was a truly annoying challenge, yet at the same time my computer was such a wondrous tool. Happily, my friend Jeffrey Pernitsky not only helped me find lost copy, he also organized my computer and coached me to avoid similar aggravating and time-consuming mistakes.

My friend Lin Perceval gave me the priceless gift of believing in my story and in my skills as a storyteller. Furthermore, she willingly shared her writing skills, which helped me to further develop and improve the manuscript. Her belief in the value of my story was demonstrated by her offer to take on the task of project management, ensuring the manuscript would be published. Without her as its sponsor, this book would have remained just a story shared with family.

Portraying Arctic life as it was in the 1960s using words only was limiting, yet photos of the time were rare, as film needed to be developed and printed in the South, and few people used or owned a camera. Luckily, in my search for visuals, I found a few important photos in the Northwest Territories Archives in Yellowknife. These rare historical images, taken during the years of my story, illustrate aspects of Arctic life key to understanding how unique the northern lifestyle was. I want to acknowledge what the NWT Archives collection and certain individual photographers' gifts to the archives added to this book. Of particular note were photos taken by Emily Stillwell, a nurse in the Aklavik and Inuvik hospitals, and Robert Knights, an RCMP officer serving in Sachs Harbour and Inuvik. One special find was a picture of my daughter, Lesley, as a newborn in her wicker basket in Aklavik's All Saints Hospital taken by Stillwell. Until my research in the NWT Archives just some months ago, I was completely unaware that this precious photo existed.

On this journey of my story becoming a book, I learned of the complex steps needed to publish and would meet talented people who shared their professional expertise and gave guidance in readying the book for publication and distribution. In addition to Lin's ongoing commitment, I would like to note the much-valued contributions of Naomi Pauls, of Paper Trail Publishing, and Crystal Hunt, of TechnoMagical Creatives LLP.

This storytelling and publishing process has occupied many hours of my time—time usually spent in shared adventures, activities, and household chores with my husband, Gord. His generosity, support, indulgence, and, yes—at times—his willingness to do more than his share needs to be recognized as the gift it was.

If "it takes a village to raise a child," it has also taken a number of talented and committed people to make *Hard Landings* into a book. I owe them much and with great appreciation, I share the reality of what my story has become.

ABOUT THE AUTHOR

BONNIE McGHIE spent her early years in California, where her independent and adventurous spirit, along with difficult family circumstances, fostered a lifelong resilience. Undaunted by the endless challenges of being female, she found employment in the movie business, including promoting (on horseback) the westerns of Wild Bill Elliott.

Her thirst for adventure took her, in 1954, to Juneau, Alaska, where she met a handsome young Canadian planning to become a bush pilot. A dream, and a partnership, was born. In 1960, Bonnie moved to the Canadian Arctic, where she helped run the couple's air service, Arctic Wings; operated their trading post, Tuk Traders; and offered entertainment in Tuktoyaktuk's first movie theatre. She gained personal satisfaction from becoming a respected and valued member of this unique—and often frozen—Inuit community.

Unfortunate circumstances required that, together with her three young children, she leave her husband and the North to start, from scratch, to rebuild her life. With characteristic focus and determination, she overcame her husband's questionable but deliberate decision to retain all the family assets in his name, thus leaving Bonnie and her children penniless.

With the same grit that got her through her Arctic challenges, Bonnie earned a graduate degree in psychology, which led to her becoming a faculty member and then an administrator at a British Columbia provincial college. She served in leadership roles with numerous boards, among them Surrey Memorial Hospital, the BC Health Association, Canuck Place, and the BC Cancer Agency and Foundation. Later she worked as a private consultant to the boards of hospitals and other health-care organizations.

Prior to retiring, she served on the board of governors for the University of the Fraser Valley as it transitioned to a full university.

In retirement, Bonnie and her second husband—who she married in 1972—became respected breeders of Labrador Retrievers and qualified as Hunting Retriever judges in Canada and the USA. Bonnie lives with her husband Gord in Chilliwack, B.C., still seeking adventures, to learn and to share skills gained over her multi-faceted career.

Visit Bonnie online at HardLandings.ca or send her an email: bonnie@hardlandings.ca.

Manufactured by Amazon.ca
Acheson, AB